Arthur W. Pink

Spiritual Growth

Baker Books

A Division of Baker Book House Co
Grand Rapids, Michigan 49516

© 1971 by I. C. Herendeen

Published by Baker Books
a division of Baker Book House Company
P. O. Box 6287, Grand Rapids, MI 49516-6287

Paperback edition: First printing, 1976. Third Printing, February 1996

Printed in the United States of America

All rights reserved. No part of this publication may be reproduced, stored in a retrieval system, or transmitted in any form or by any means—for example, electronic, photocopy, recording—without the prior written permission of the publisher. The only exception is brief quotations in printed reviews.

ISBN 0-8010-6862-2

Index prepared by Ms. Clara E. Brown

CONTENTS

1

Introduction

THE name which is usually given to our subject by Christian writers is that of "Growth in Grace" which is a scriptural expression, being found in II Peter 3:18. But it appears to us that, strictly speaking, growing "in grace" has reference to but a single aspect or branch of our theme: "that your *love* may abound yet more and more" (Phil. 1:9) treats of another aspect, and "your *faith* groweth exceedingly" (II Thess. 1:3), with yet another. It seems then that "spiritual growth" is a more comprehensive and inclusive term and more accurately covers that most important and desirable attainment: "may grow up into him in *all* things, which is the Head, even Christ" (Eph. 4:15). Let it not be thought from this that we have selected our title in a captious spirit or because we are striving after originality. Not so: we have no criticism to make against those who may prefer some other appellation. We have chosen this simply because it seems more fitly and fully to describe the ground which we hope to cover. Our readers understand clearly what is connoted by "physical growth" or "mental growth," nor should "spiritual growth" be any the less intelligible.

This Subject Is a Deeply Important One

First, that we should seek to understand aright the Spirit's teaching on this subject. There seems to be comparatively few who do so, and the consequence is that the Lord is robbed of much of the praise which is His due, while many of His people suffer much needless distress. Because so many Christians walk more by sense than by faith, measuring themselves by their feelings and moods rather than by the Word, their peace of mind is greatly destroyed and their joy of heart much decreased. Not a few saints are seriously the losers through misapprehensions upon this subject. Scriptural knowledge is essential if we are better to understand ourselves and diagnose more accurately our spiritual case. Many exercised souls form an erroneous opinion of themselves because of failure at this very point. Surely it is a matter of great practical moment that we should be able to judge aright of our spiritual progress or retrogression that we may not flatter ourselves on the one hand or unduly depreciate ourselves on the other.

Some are tempted in one direction, some in the other — depending partly on their personal temperament and partly on the kind of teaching they have received. Many are inclined to think more highly of themselves than they ought, and because they have obtained considerably in-

7

creased intellectual knowledge of the truth imagine they have made a proportionate spiritual growth. But others with weaker memories and who acquire a mental grasp of things more slowly, suppose this to signify a lack of spirituality. Unless our thoughts about spiritual growth be formed by the Word of God we are certain to err and jump to a wrong conclusion. As it is with our bodies, so it is with our souls. Some suppose they are healthy while they are suffering from an insidious disease; whereas others imagine themselves to be ill when in fact they are hale and sound. Divine revelation and not human imagination ought to be our guide in determining whether or not we be "babes, young men, or fathers" — and our natural age has nothing to do with it.

It is deeply important that our views should be rightly formed, not only that we may be able to ascertain our own spiritual stature, but also that of our fellow Christians. If I long to be made a help and blessing to them, then obviously I must be capable of deciding whether they are in a healthy or unhealthy condition. Or, if I desire spiritual counsel and assistance, then I will meet with disappointment unless I know to whom to go. How can I regulate my course and suit my converse with the saints I contact if I am at a loss to gauge their religious caliber? God has not left us to our own erring judgment in this matter, but has supplied rules to guide us. To mention but one other reason which indicates the importance of our subject: unless I can ascertain wherein I have been enabled to make spiritual progress and wherein I have failed, how can I know what to pray for; and unless I can perceive the same about my brethren how can I intelligently ask for the supply of what they most need?

Our Subject Is a Very Mysterious One

Physical growth is beyond human comprehension. We know something of what is essential to it, and the thing itself may be discovered, but the operation and process is hidden from us: "As thou knowest not what is the way of the spirit, nor how the bones do grow in the womb of her that is with child, even so thou knowest not the works of God who maketh all" (Eccles. 11:5). How much more so must spiritual growth be incomprehensible. The beginning of our spiritual life is shrouded in mystery (John 3:8), and to a considerable extent this is true also of its development. God's workings in the soul are secret, indiscernible to the eye of carnal reason and imperceptible to our senses. "The things of God knoweth no man" save to whom the Spirit is pleased to reveal them (I Cor. 2:11, 12). If we know so little about ourselves and the operation of our faculties in connection with natural things, how much less competent are we to comprehend ourselves and our graces in connection with that which is supernatural.

The "new creature" is from above, whereof our natural reason has no acquaintance: it is a supernatural product and can only be known by supernatural revelation. In like manner, the spiritual life received at the new birth *thrives* as to its degrees, unperceived by our senses. A child, by weighing and measuring himself, may discover that he has grown, yet he was not conscious of the process while growing. So it is with the new man: it is "renewed day by day" (II Cor. 4:16) yet in such a hidden way that the renewing itself is not felt, though its effects become apparent. Thus there is no good reason to be disheartened because we do not *feel* that any progress is being made or to conclude there is no advance because such feeling is absent. "There are some of the Lord's people in whom the essence and reality of holiness dwell who do not perceive in themselves any spiritual growth. It should therefore be remembered that there is a real growth in grace where it is not perceived. We should judge of it not by what we experience of it in ourselves, but by the Word. It is a subject for *faith* to be exercised on" (S. E. Pierce). If we desire the pure "milk of the Word" and feed thereon, then we must not doubt that we duly "grow thereby" (I Peter 2:3).

To quote again from Pierce: "Spiritual growth is a mystery and is more evident in some than in others. The more the Holy Spirit shines upon the mind and puts forth His lifegiving influences in the heart, so much the more sin is seen, felt and loathed as the greatest of all evils. And this is an evidence of spiritual growth, namely, to hate sin as sin and to abhor it on account of its contrariety to the nature of God. The quick perception and insight which we have of inherent sin, and our feeling of it, so as to look on ourselves as most vile, to renounce ourselves and all that we can do for ourselves, and to look wholly and immediately to Christ for relief and strength are growth in grace, and a most certain evidence of it." How little is the natural man capable of understanding that! Having no experience of the same it sounds to him like a doleful delusion. And how the believer needs to beg God to teach him the truth about this! As we know nothing whatever about the new birth save what God has revealed in His Word, so we can form no correct comprehension about spiritual growth except from the same source.

Our Subject Is Also a Difficult One

This is due in part to Satan's having confused the issue by inventing such plausible imitations that multitudes are deceived thereby, and knowing this the conscientious soul is troubled. Under certain influences and from various motives people are induced suddenly and radically to reform their lives; and their absence from the grosser forms of sin accompanied by a zealous performance of the common duties of religion is often mistaken for genuine conversion and progress in the Christian life. These are the "tares" which so closely resemble the "wheat" that they are often indistinguishable until the harvest. Moreover, there is a work of the law, quite distinct from the saving effects wrought by the gospel, which in its fruits both external and internal cannot be distinguished from a work of grace except by the light of Scripture and the teaching of the Spirit. The terrors of the law have come in power to the conscience of many a one, producing poignant convictions of sin and horrors of the wrath to come, issuing in much activity in the works of righteousness, but resulting in no faith in Christ, and no love for Him.

Again: spiritual progress is difficult to discern because growth in grace is often not nearly so apparent as first conversion. In many cases conversion is a radical experience of which we are personally conscious at the time and of which a vivid memory remains with us. It is marked by revolutionary change in our life. It was when we were relieved of the intolerable burden of guilt and the peace of God which passeth all understanding possessed our souls. It was being brought out of the awful and total spiritual darkness of nature into God's marvellous light, whereas spiritual growth is but the enjoying further degrees of that light. It was that tremendous change from having no grace at all to the beginnings of grace within us, whereas that which follows is the receiving of additions of grace. It was a spiritual resurrection, a being brought from death unto life, but the subsequent experience is only renewings of the life then received. For Joseph suddenly to be translated out of prison to sit upon the throne of Egypt, second only to Pharaoh, would affect him far more powerfully than to have any new kingdoms added to him later, such as Alexander had. At first everything in the spiritual life is new to the Christian; later he learns more perfectly what was then discovered to him, yet the effect made is not so perceptible and entrancing.

Further: the spiritual life or nature communicated at regeneration is not the only thing in the Christian: the principle of sin still remains in the soul after the principle of grace as been imparted. Those two principles are at direct variance with each other, engaged in a ceaseless warfare as long as the saint is left in this world. "For the flesh lusteth against the spirit, and the spirit against the flesh: and these are contrary the one to the other; so that ye cannot do the things that ye would" (Gal. 5:17). That fearful conflict is apt to confuse the issue in the mind of its subject; yea, it is certain to lead the believer to draw a false inference from it unless he clearly apprehends the teaching of Scripture thereon. The discovery of so much opposition within, the thwarting of his aspirations and endeavors, his felt inability to wage the warfare successfully, makes him seriously to doubt whether holiness has been imparted to his heart. The ragings of indwelling sin, the discovery of unsuspected corruptions, the consciousness of unbelief, the defeats experienced, all appear to give the lie direct to any spiritual progress. *That* presents an acute problem to a conscientious soul.

Our Subject Is Both a Complex and Comprehensive One

By this we mean that this is a tree with many branches, which bears a different manner of fruits according to the season. It is a subject into which various elements enter, one that needs to be viewed from many angles. Spiritual growth is both upward and downward, and it is both inward and outward. An increased knowledge of God leads to an increased knowledge of self, and as one results in higher adoration of its Object, the other brings deeper humiliation in its subject. These issue in more and more inward denials of self and abounding more and more outwardly in good works. Yet this spiritual growth needs to be most carefully stated lest we repudiate the completeness of regeneration. In the strictest sense, spiritual growth consists of the Spirit's drawing out what He wrought in the soul when He quickened it. When a babe is born into this world it is complete in parts though not in development: no new members can be added to its body nor any additional faculties to its mind.

There is a growth of the natural child, a development of its members, an expansion of its faculties with a fuller expression and clearer manifestation of the latter, but nothing more. The analogy holds good with a babe in Christ. "Though there are innumerable circumstantial differences in the cases and experience of the called people of God, and though there is a growth suited to them, considered as 'babes, young men and fathers,' yet there is but one *common life* in the various stages and degrees of the *same* life carried on to its perfection by the Holy Spirit until it issues in glory eternal. The work of God the Spirit in regeneration is eternally complete. It admits of no increase nor decrease. It is one and the same in all believers. There will not be the least addition to it in Heaven: not one grace, holy affection, desire or disposition then, which is not in it now. The whole of the Spirit's work therefore from the moment of regeneration to our glorification is to draw out those graces into act and exercise which He hath wrought within us. And though one believer may abound in the fruits of righteousness more than another, yet there is not one of them more regenerated than another" (S. E. Pierce).

The complexity of our subject is due in part to both the Divine and the human elements entering into it, and who is competent to explain or set forth their meeting-point! Yet the analogy supplied from the physical realm again affords us some help. Absolutely considered, all growth is due to the Divine operations, yet relatively there are certain conditions which we must meet or there will be no growth — to name no other, the partaking of suitable food is an essential prerequisite; nevertheless that will not nourish unless God be pleased to bless the same. To insist that there are certain conditions which we must meet, certain means which we must use in our spiritual progress is not to divide the honors with God, but is simply pointing out the *order* He has established and the connection He has appointed between one thing and another. In like manner there are certain hindrances which we must avoid or growth will inevitably be arrested and spiritual progress retarded. Nor does that imply that we are thwarting God, but only disregarding His warnings and paying the penalty of breaking those laws which He has instituted.

The Difficulty of Expounding Our Subject

The very complexity of our subject increases the difficulty before the one attempting to expound it, for as is the case with so many other problems presented to our limited intelligence, it involves the matter of seeking to preserve a due balance between the Divine and the human elements. The operations of Divine grace and the discharge of our responsibility must each be insisted upon, and the concurring of the latter with the former, as well as the superabounding of the former over the latter must be proportionately set forth. In like manner our contemplation of spiritual growth upward must not be allowed to crowd out that of our growth downward, nor must our deeper loathing of self be suffered to hinder an increasing living upon Christ. The more sensible we are of our emptiness the more we must draw upon His fulness. Nor is our task rendered easier when we remember what we write will fall into the hands of very different types of readers who sit under varied kinds of ministry — the one needing emphasis upon a different note from another.

That there is such a thing as spiritual growth is abundantly clear from the Scriptures. In addition to the passages alluded to in the opening paragraph we may quote the following. "They go from strength to strength" (Ps. 84:7). "The path of the just is as a shining light, that shineth more and more unto the perfect day" (Prov. 4:18). "Then shall we know if we follow on to know the Lord" (Hos. 6:3). "But unto you that fear the Lord shall the Sun of righteousness arise with healing in his wings, and ye shall go forth and *grow up* as calves of the stall" (Mal. 4:2). "And of his fulness have all we received, and grace for grace" (John 1:16). "Every branch in me that beareth fruit he purgeth it that it may bring forth more fruit" (John 15:2). "But we all, with open face beholding as in a glass the glory of the Lord, are changed into the same image *from glory to glory* as by the Spirit of the Lord" (II Cor. 3:18). "Increasing in the knowledge of God" (Col. 1:10). "As ye have received of us how ye ought to walk and to please God, so ye abound more and more" (I Thess. 4:1). "He giveth more grace" (James 4:6).

The above list might be extended considerably but sufficient references have been given to show that not only is such a thing as spiritual growth clearly revealed in the Scriptures, but that it is given a prominent place therein. Let the reader duly observe the *variety* of expressions which are employed by the Spirit to set forth this progress or development — thereby preserving us from too circumscribed a conception by showing us the many-sidedness of the same. Some of them relate to what is internal, others to what is external. Some of them describe the Divine operations, others the necessary acts and exercises of the Christian. Some of them make mention of increased light and knowledge, others of increased grace and strength, and yet others of increased conformity to Christ and fruitfulness. It is thus that the Holy Spirit has preserved the balance and it is by our carefully noting the same that we shall be kept from a narrow and one-sided idea of what spiritual growth consists. If due attention be paid to this varied description we shall be kept from painful mistakes, and the better enabled to test or measure ourselves and discover what spiritual stature we have attained unto.

This Is an Intensely Practical Subject

From what has been pointed out in the last few paragraphs it will be seen that this is an intensely *practical subject*. It is no small matter that we should be able to arrive at the clear apprehension of what spiritual growth actually consists of, and thereby be delivered from mistaking it for mere fantasy. If there be conditions which we have to comply with in order to the making of progress, it is most desirable that we should acquaint ourselves with the same and then translate such knowledge into prayer. If God has appointed certain means and aids, the sooner we learn what they are and make diligent use of them the better for us. And if there be other things which act as deterents and are inimical to our welfare, the more we are placed upon our guard the less likely we are to be hindered by them. And if Christian growth has many sides to it this should govern our thinking and acting thereon, that we may strive after a fitly-proportioned and well-rounded Christian character, and grow up into Christ not merely in one or two respects but "in *all* things" that our development may be uniform and symmetrical.

2

Its Root

BEFORE attempting to define and describe what the spiritual growth of a Christian consists of, we should first show what it is that is capable of growth, for spiritual growth necessarily supposes the presence of spiritual life: only a regenerated person can grow. Progress in the Christian life is impossible unless I be a Christian. We must therefore begin by explaining what a Christian is. To many of our readers this may appear to be quite superfluous, but in such a day as this, wherein spiritual counterfeits and delusions abound on every side, when so many are deceived on the all-important matter, and because of such widely-different classes, we deem it necessary to follow this course. We dare not take for granted that all our readers are Christians in the Scriptural sense of that term, and may it please the Lord to use what we are about to write to give light to some who are yet in darkness. Moreover, it may be the means of enabling some real Christians, now confused, to see the way of the Lord more clearly. Nor will it be altogether profitless, we hope, even to those more fully established in the faith.

Three Kinds of "Christians"

Broadly speaking there are three kinds of "Christians": preacher-made, self-made, and God-made ones. In the former are included not only those who were "sprinkled" in infancy and thereby made members of a "church" (though not admitted to all its privileges), but those who have reached the age of accountability and are induced by some high-pressure "evangelist" to "make a profession." This high pressure business is in different forms and in varying degrees, from appeals to the emotions to mass hypnotism whereby crowds are induced to "come forward." Under it countless thousands whose consciences were never searched and who had no sense of their lost condition before God were persuaded to "do the manly thing," "enlist under the banner of Christ," "unite with God's people in their crusade against the devil." Such converts are like mushrooms: they spring up in a night and survive but a short time, having no root. Similar too are the vast majority produced under what is called "personal work," which consists of a species of individual "button-holing," and is conducted along the lines used by commercial travellers seeking to make a "forced sale."

The "self-made" class is made up of those who have been warned against what has just been described above, and fearful of being deluded by such religious hucksters they determined to "settle the matter" directly with God in the privacy of their own room or some secluded

14

spot. They had been given to understand that God loves everybody, that Christ died for the whole human race, and that nothing is required of them but faith in the gospel. By saving faith they suppose that a mere intellectual assent to, or acceptance of, such statements as are found in John 3:16 and Romans 10:13 is all that is intended. It matters not that John 2:23, 24 declares that *"many* believed in his name . . . but Jesus did not commit himself unto them,"* that "many believed on him, but because of the Pharisees they did not confess him lest they be put out of the synagogue, for they loved the praise of men more than the praise of God," which shows how much their "believing" was worth. Imagining that the natural man is capable of "receiving Christ as personal Saviour" they make the attempt, doubt not their success, go on their way rejoicing, and none can shake their assurance that they are now real Christians!

"No man *can* come unto me except the Father which has sent me draw him" (John 6:44). Here is a declaration of Christ which has not received even mental assent by the vast majority in Christendom. It is far too flesh-abasing to meet with acceptance from those who wish to think that the settling of a man's eternal destiny lies entirely within his own power. That *fallen* man is wholly at the disposal of God is thoroughly unpalatable to an unhumbled heart. To come to Christ is a spiritual act and not a natural one, and since the unregenerate are dead in sins they are quite incapable of any spiritual exercises. Coming to Christ is the effect of the soul's being made to feel its desperate need of Him, of the understanding's being enlightened to perceive His suitability for a lost sinner, of the affections being drawn out so as to desire Him. But how can one whose natural mind is "enmity against God" have any desire for His Son?

God-made Christians are a miracle of *grace*, the products of *Divine* workmanship (Eph. 2:10). They are a *Divine* creation, brought into existence by supernatural operations. By the new birth we are capacitated for communion with the Triune Jehovah, for it is the spring of new sensibilities and activities. It is not our old nature made better and excited into spiritual acts, but instead, something is communicated which was not there before. That "something" partakes of the same nature as its Begetter: "that which is born of the Spirit is spirit" (John 3:6), and as He is holy so that which He produces is holy. It is the God of all grace who brings us "from death unto life," and therefore it is a principle of grace which He imparts to the soul, and it disposes unto fruits which are well pleasing unto Him. Regeneration is not a protracted process, but an instantaneous thing, to which nothing can be added nor from it anything taken away (Eccles. 3:14). It is the product of a Divine fiat: God speaks and it is done, and the subject of it becomes immediately a "new creature."

Regeneration is not the outcome of any clerical magic nor does the individual experiencing it supply ought thereto: he is the passive and unconscious recipient of it. Said Truth incarnate: "which were born not of blood [heredity makes no contribution thereto, for God has regener-

ated heathens whose ancestors have for centuries been gross idolators]
nor of the will of the flesh [for prior to this Divine quickening the will
of that person was inveterately opposed to God] nor of the will of [a]
man [the preacher was incapable of regenerating himself, much less
others] but of God" (John 1:13) — by His sovereign and almighty power.
And again Christ declared, "The wind bloweth where it listeth and thou
hearest the sound thereof [its effects are quite manifest] but canst not
tell whence it cometh and whither it goeth [its causation and operation
are entirely above human ken, a mystery no finite intelligence can solve]
so is every one that is born of the Spirit" (John 3:8) — not in certain
exceptional cases, but in *all* who experience the same. Such Divine declarations are as far removed from most of the religious teaching of the
day as light is from darkness.

The word "Christian" means "an *annointed* one," as the Lord Jesus is
"The Annointed" or "The Christ." That was one of the titles accorded
Him in the Old Testament: "The kings of the earth have set themselves
and the rulers have taken counsel together against the Lord and against
his annointed" or "Christ" (Ps. 2:2 and cf. Acts 2:26, 27). He is thus
designated because "God annointed Jesus of Nazareth with the Holy
Spirit" (Acts 10:38), for induction into His office and enduement for
the discharge thereof. That office has three branches, for He was to
act as Prophet, Priest and King. And in the Old Testament we find this
foreshadowed in the annointing of Israel's prophets (I Kings 19:16), their
priests (Lev. 8:30) and their kings (I Sam. 10:1; II Sam. 2:4). Accordingly it was upon entrance into His public ministry the Lord Jesus
was "annointed," for at His baptism "the heavens were opened unto
him" and there was seen "the Spirit of God descending like a dove and
lighting upon him," and the Father's voice was heard saying "This is my
beloved Son in whom I am well pleased" (Matt. 3:16, 17). The Spirit of
God had come upon others before that, but never as He now came upon
the incarnate Son, "for God giveth not the Spirit by measure unto him"
(John 3:34), for being the Holy One there was nothing whatever in
Him to oppose the Spirit or grieve Him, but everything to the contrary.

But it was not for Himself alone that Christ received the Spirit, but
to share with and communicate unto His people. Hence in another of
the Old Testament types we read that "The precious ointment upon the
head, that ran down upon the beard, upon Aaron's beard, that ran down
to the skirts of his garments" (Ps. 132:2). Though all Israel's priests
were annointed, none but the high priest was done so upon the *head*
(Lev. 8:12). This foreshadowed the Saviour being annointed not only as
our great High Priest but also as the Head of His church, and the running down of the sacred ungent to the skirts prefigured the communicating of the Spirit to all the members, even the lowliest, of His mystical Body. "Now he who . . . hath annointed us is God, who hath
sealed us and given us the earnest of the Spirit in our hearts" (II Cor.
1:22). "Of his [Christ's] fulness have we all received" (John 1:16).

When the apostles were "filled with the Holy Spirit and began to
speak with other tongues as the Spirit gave them utterance" on the day

of Pentecost, and some mocked, Peter declared "This is that which was spoken by the prophet Joel" and concluded by affirming that Jesus had been by the right hand of God exalted "and having received of the Father *he* that shed forth *this*" (Acts 2:33). A "Christian" then is an anointed one because he has received the Holy Spirit from Christ "the annointed." And hence it is written "But ye have an unction [or "annointing"] from the Holy One," that is, from Christ; and again, "the annointing which ye have received of him abideth in you" (I John 2: 20, 27), for just as we read of "the Spirit descending and *remaining* on him" (John 1:33) so He abides with us "forever" (John 14:16).

This is the inseparable accompaniment of the new birth. The regenerated soul is not only made the recipient of a new life but the Holy Spirit is communicated to him, and by the Spirit he is then vitally united to Christ, for "he that is joined to the Lord is one Spirit" (I Cor. 6: 17). The Spirit comes to indwell so that his body is made His temple. It is by this annointing or inhabitation the regenerate person is sanctified, or set apart unto God, consecrated to Him, and given a place in that "holy priesthood" which is qualified "to offer up spiritual sacrifices acceptable to God by Jesus Christ" (I Peter 2:5). Thereby the saint is sharply distinguished from the world, for "If any man have not the Spirit of Christ, he is none of his" (Rom. 8:9). The Spirit is the identifying mark or seal: as it was by the Spirit's descent on Christ that John recognized Him (John 1:33) and "him hath God the Father *sealed*" (John 6:27), so believers are "sealed with that Holy Spirit" (Eph. 1:13).

But since the individual concerned in regeneration is entirely passive and at the moment unconscious of what is taking place, the question arises, How is a soul to ascertain whether or not he has been Divinely quickened? At first sight it might appear that no satisfactory answer can be forthcoming, yet a little reflection should show that this must be far from being the case. Such a miracle of grace wrought in a person cannot long be imperceptible to him. If spiritual life be imparted to one dead in sins its presence must soon become manifest. This is indeed the case. The new birth becomes apparent by the effects it produces, namely, spiritual desires and spiritual exercises. As the natural infant clings instinctively to its mother, so the spiritual babe turns unto the One who gave it being. The authority of God is felt in the conscience, the holiness of God is perceived by the enlightened understanding, desires after Him stir within the soul. His wondrous grace is now faintly perceived by the renewed heart. There is a poignant consciousness of that which is opposed to the glory of God, a sense of our sinnership such as was not experienced formerly.

The natural man (all that he is as a fallen creature by the first birth) receiveth not the things of the Spirit of God, for they are foolishness unto him, neither can he know them, because they are spiritually discerned" (I Cor. 2:14). By no efforts of his own, by no university education, by no course of religious instruction can he obtain any spiritual or vital knowledge of spiritual things. They are utterly beyond the range of his faculties. Self-love blinds him: self-pleasing chains him to the things of time and sense. Except a man be born again he cannot see the kingdom of God. He may obtain a notional knowledge of them, but until a miracle of grace takes place in his soul he cannot have any spiritual acquaintance with them. Fishes could sooner live on dry ground or birds exist beneath the waves than an unregenerate person enter into a vital and experimental acquaintance with the things of God.

The first effect of the spiritual life in the soul is that its recipient is convicted of his impurity and guilt. The conscience is quickened and there is a piercing realization of both personal pollution and criminality. The illumined mind sees something of the awful malignity of sin, as being in its very nature contrary to the holiness of God, and in its essence nothing but high-handed rebellion against Him. From that arises an abhorrence of it as a most vile and loathsome thing. The demerit of sin is seen, so that the soul is made to feel it has grievously provoked the Most High, exposing him to Divine wrath. Made aware of the plague of his heart, knowing himself to be justly liable to the awful vengeance of the Almighty, his mouth is stopped, he has not a word to say in self-extenuation, he confesses himself to be guilty before Him; and henceforth that which most deeply concerns him is, What must I do to be saved? in what way may I escape the doom of the Law?

The second effect of the spiritual life in the soul is that its recipient becomes aware of the suitability of Christ to such a vile wretch as he now discovers himself to be. The glorious gospel now has an entirely new meaning for him. He requires no urging to listen to its message: it is heavenly music in his ears, "good news from a far country" (Prov. 25:25). Nay, he now searches the Scriptures for himself to make sure that such a gospel is not too good to be true. As he reads therein of who the Saviour is and what He did, of the Divine incarnation and His death on the cross, he is awed as never before. As he learns that it was for sinners, for the ungodly, for enemies that Christ shed His blood, hope is awakened in his heart and he is kept from being overwhelmed by his burden of guilt and from sinking into abject despair. Desires of an interest in Christ spring up within his soul, and he is resolved to look for salvation in none other. He is convinced that pardon and security are to be found in Christ alone if so be that He will show him favor. He searches now to discover what Christ's requirements are.

A Christian is not only one "annointed" by the Spirit, but he is also one who is *a disciple of Christ* (see Matt. 28:19 margin, and Acts 11: 26), that is, a learner and follower of Christ. His terms of discipleship are made known in Luke 14:26-33. Those terms a regenerate soul is enabled to comply with. Convicted of his lost condition, having learned that Christ is the appointed and self-sufficient Saviour for sinners, he now throws down the weapons of his rebellion, repudiates his idols, relinquishes his love of and friendship with the world, surrenders himself to the Lordship of Christ, takes His yoke upon him, and thereby finds rest unto his soul; trusting in the efficacy of His atoning blood the burden of guilt is removed, and henceforth his dominant desire and endeavor is to please and glorify his Saviour. Thus *regeneration* issues in and evidences itself by *conversion,* and genuine conversion makes one a disciple of Christ, following the example He has left us.

3

Its Necessity

WE commenced the last chapter by pointing out that none can possibly make any progress in the Christian life unless he first be a Christian and then devoted the remainder to defining and describing what a "Christian" is. It is indeed striking to note that this title is used by the Holy Spirit in a *twofold* way: primarily it signifies an "annointed one"; subordinately it denotes "a disciple of Christ." Thereby they have brought together in a truly wonderful manner both the Divine and the human sides. Our "anointing" with the Spirit is God's act, wherein we are entirely passive; but our becoming "disciples of Christ" is a voluntary and conscious act of ours, whereby we freely surrender to Christ's lordship and submit to His sceptre. It is by the latter that we obtain evidence of the former. None will yield to the flesh-repellent terms of Christian "discipleship" save those in whom a Divine work of grace has been wrought, but when that miracle *has* occurred conversion is as certain to follow as a cause will produce its effects. One made a new creature by the Divine miracle of the new birth desires and gladly endeavors to meet the holy requirements of Christ.

Here, then, is the root of spiritual growth: the communication to the soul of spiritual life. Here is what makes possible Christian progress: a person's becoming a Christian, first by the Spirit's anointing and then by his own choice. This twofold signification of the term "Christian" is the principal key which opens to us the subject of Christian progress or spiritual growth, for it ever needs to be contemplated from both the Divine and human sides. It requires to be viewed both from the angle of God's operations and from that of the discharge of our responsibilities. The twofold meaning of the title "Christian" must also be borne in mind under the present aspect of our subject, for on the one hand progress is neither necessary nor possible, while in another very real sense it is both desirable and requisite. God's "anointing" is not susceptible of improvement, being perfect; but our "discipleship" is to become more intelligent and productive of good works. Much confusion has resulted from ignoring this distinction, and we shall devote the remainder of this chapter to the negative side, pointing out those respects in which progress or growth *does not* obtain.

1. *Christian progress does not signify advancing in God's favor.* The believer's growth in grace does not further him one iota in God's esteem. How could it, since God is the Giver of his faith and the One who has "wrought all our works in us" (Isa. 26:12)! God's favorable

regard of His people originated not in anything whatever in them, either actual or foreseen. God's grace is absolutely free, being the spontaneous exercise of His own mere good pleasure. The cause of its exercise lies wholly within Himself. The *purposing* grace of God is that good will which He had unto His people from all eternity: "Who hath saved us and called us with an holy calling, not according to our works, but according to his own purpose and grace which was given us in Christ Jesus before the world began" (II Tim. 1:9). And the *dispensing* grace of God is but the execution of His purpose, ministering to His people: thus we read "God *giveth* more grace," yea, that "he giveth more grace" (James 4:6). It is entirely gratuitous, sovereignly bestowed, without any inducement being found in its object.

Furthermore, everything God does for and bestows on His people is *for Christ's sake*. It is in nowise a question of their deserts, but of Christ's deserts or what He merited for them. As Christ is the only Way by which we can approach the Father, so He is the sole channel through which God's grace flows unto us. Hence we read of the "grace of God, and the gift of grace (namely, justifying righteousness) by one man, Jesus Christ" (Rom. 5:15); and again, "the grace of God which is given you by Jesus Christ" (I Cor. 1:4). The love of God toward us is in "Christ Jesus our Lord" (Rom. 8:39). He forgives us "for Christ's sake" (Eph. 4:32). He supplies all our need "according to his riches in glory by Christ Jesus" (Phil. 4:19). He brings us to heaven in answer to Christ's prayer (John 17:24). Yet though Christ merits everything for us, the original cause was the sovereign grace of God. "Although the merits of Christ are the (procuring) cause of our salvation, yet they are not the cause of our being ordained to salvation. They are the cause of purchasing all things decreed unto us, but they are not the cause which first moved God to decree these things unto us" (Thos. Goodwin).

The Christian is not accepted because of his "graces," for the very graces (as their name connotes) are bestowed upon him by Divine bounty, and are not attained by any efforts of his. And so far from these graces being the reason why God accepts him, they are the *fruits* of his being "chosen in Christ before the foundation of the world" and, decretively, "blessed with all spiritual blessings in the heavenlies in Christ" (Eph. 1:3, 4). Settle it then in your own mind once for all, my reader, that growth in grace does not signify growing in the favor of God. This is essentially a Papish delusion, and though creature-flattering it is a horribly Christ-dishonoring one. Since God's elect are "accepted in the beloved" (Eph. 1:6), it is impossible that any subsequent change wrought in or attained by them could render them more excellent in His esteem or advance them in His love. When the Father announced concerning the incarnate Word "This is my beloved Son [not "*with* whom" but] *in whom* I am well pleased" He was expressing His delight in the whole election of grace, for He was speaking of Christ in His federal character, as the last Adam, as Head of His mystical body.

The Christian can neither increase nor decrease in the favor of God, nor can anything he does or fails to do alter or affect to the slightest degree his perfect standing in Christ. Yet let it not be inferred from this that his conduct is of little importance or that God's dealings with him have no relation to his daily walk. While avoiding the Romish conceit of human merits, we must be on our guard against Antinomian licentiousness. As the moral Governor of this world God takes note of our conduct, and in a variety of ways makes manifest His approbation or disapprobation: "No good thing will he withhold from them that walk uprightly" (Ps. 84:11), yet to His own people God says "your sins have withholden good things from you" (Jer. 5:25). So, too, as the Father He maintains discipline in His family, and when His children are refractory He uses the rod (Ps. 89:3-33). Special manifestations of Divine love are granted to the obedient (John 14:21, 23), but are withheld from the disobedient and the careless.

2. *Christian progress does not denote that the work of regeneration was incomplete.* Great care needs to be taken in stating this truth of spiritual growth lest we repudiate the perfection of the new birth. We must repeat here in substance what was pointed out in the first article. When a normal child is born into this world naturally the babe is an entire entity, complete in all its parts, possessing a full set of bodily members and mental faculties. As the child grows there is a strengthening of its body and mind, a development of its members and an expansion of its faculties, with a fuller use of the one and a clearer manifestation of the other; yet no new member or additional faculty is or can be added to him. It is precisely so spiritually. The spiritual life or nature received at the new birth contains within itself all the "senses" (Heb. 5:14) and graces, and though these may be nourished and strengthened, and increased by exercise yet not by addition, no, not in heaven itself. "I know that whatsoever God doeth it shall be forever: nothing can be put to it nor anything taken from it" (Eccles. 3:14). The "babe" in Christ is just as truly and completely a child of God as the most matured "father" in Christ.

Regeneration is a more radical and revolutionizing change than glorification. The one is a passing from death unto life, the other an entrance into the fulness of life. The one is a bringing into existence of "the new man which after God is created in righteousness and true holiness" (Eph. 4:22), the other is a reaching unto the full stature of the new man. The one is a translation into the kingdom of God's dear Son (Col. 1:13), the other an induction into the higher privileges of that kingdom. The one is the begetting of us unto a living hope (I Peter 1:3), the other is a realization of that hope. At regeneration the soul is made a "new creature" in Christ, so that "old things are passed away, behold, all things are become new" (II Cor. 5:17). The regenerate soul is a partaker of every grace of the Spirit so that he is "complete in Christ" (Col. 2:10), and no growth on earth or glorification in heaven can make him more than complete.

3. *Christian progress does not procure a title for heaven.* The perfect and indefeasible title of every believer is in the merits of Christ. His

vicarious fulfilling of the law, whereby He magnified and made it honorable, secured for all in whose stead He acted the full reward of the law. It is on the all-sufficient ground of Christ's perfect obedience being reckoned to his account that the believer is justified by God and assured that he shall "reign in life" (Rom. 5:17). If he had lived on earth another hundred years and served God perfectly it would add nothing to his title. Heaven is the "purchased possession" (Eph. 1:14), purchased for His people by the whole redemptive work of Christ. His precious blood gives every believing sinner the legal right to "enter the holiest" (Heb. 10:19). Our title to glory is found alone in Christ. Of the redeemed now in heaven it is said, they have "washed their robes and made them white in the blood of the Lamb: *therefore* are they before the throne of God and serve Him day and night in His temple" (Rev. 7:14, 15).

It has not been sufficiently realized that God's pronouncement of justification is very much more than a mere sense of acquittal or non-condemnation. It includes as well the positive *imputation* of righteousness. As James Hervey so beautifully illustrated it: "When yonder orb makes his first appearance in the east, what effects are produced? Not only are the shades of night dispersed, but the light of day is diffused. Thus it is when the Author of salvation is manifested to the soul: He brings at once pardon *and acceptance.*" Not only are our "filthy rags" removed, but the "best robe" is put upon us (Luke 15:22) and no efforts or attainments of ours can add anything to such a Divine adornment. Christ not only delivers us from death, but purchased life for us; He not only put away our sins but merited an inheritance for us. The most mature and advanced Christian has nought to plead before God for his acceptance than the righteousness of Christ: *that,* nothing but that, and nothing added to it, as his perfect title to Glory.

4. *Christian progress does not make us meet for heaven.* Many of those who are more or less clear on the three points considered above are far from being so upon this one, and therefore we must enter into it at greater length. Thousands have been taught to believe that when a person has been justified by God and tasted the blessedness of "the man whose transgression is forgiven, whose sin is covered" that much still remains to be done for the soul before it is ready for the celestial courts. A widespread impression prevails that after his justification the believer must undergo the refining process of sanctification, and that for this he must be left for a time amid the trials and conflicts of a hostile world; yea so strongly held is this view that some are likely to take exception to what follows. Nevertheless, such a theory repudiates the fact that it is the new-creative work of the Spirit which not only capacitates the soul to take in and enjoy spiritual things now (John 3:3, 5), but also fits it experimentally for the eternal fruition of God.

One had thought that those laboring under the mistake mentioned above would be corrected by their own experience and by what they observed in their fellow Christians. They frankly acknowledge that their

own progress is most unsatisfactory to them, and they have no means
of knowing when the process is to be successfully completed. They see
their fellow Christians cut off apparently in very varied stages of this
process. If it be said that this process is completed only at death, then
we would point out that even on their death-beds the most eminent
and mature saints have testified to being most humiliated over their attainments and thoroughly dissatisfied with themselves. Their final triumph was not what grace had made them to be in themselves, but what
Christ was made to be unto them. If such a view as the above were
true, how could any believer cherish a desire to depart and be with
Christ (Phil. 1:23) while the very fact that he was still in the body
would be proof (according to this idea) that the process was not yet
complete to fit him for His presence!

But, it may be asked, Is there not such a thing as "progressive
sanctification"? We answer, it all depends on what is signified by that
expression. In our judgment it is one which needs to be carefully and
precisely defined, otherwise God is likely to be grossly dishonored and
His people seriously injured by being brought into bondage by a most
inadequate and defective view of Sanctification as a whole. There are
several essential and fundamental respects in which sanctification is *not*
"progressive," wherein it admits of no degrees and is incapable of aug-
mentation, and those aspects of sanctification need to be plainly stated
and clearly apprehended *before* the subordinate aspect is considered.
First, every believer was *decretively* sanctified by God the Father before
the foundation of the world (Jude 1). Second, he was *meritoriously*
sanctified by God the Son in the redemptive work which He performed
in the stead of and on the behalf of His people, so that it is written
"by one offering he hath *perfected forever* them that are sanctified"
(Heb. 10:14). Third, he was *vitally* sanctified by God the Spirit when
He quickened him into newness of life, united him to Christ, and made
his body His temple.

If by "progressive sanctification" be meant a clearer understanding
and fuller apprehension of what God has made Christ to be unto the
believer and of his perfect standing and state in Him; if by it be meant
the believer living more and more in the enjoyment and power of that,
with the corresponding influence and effect it will have upon his character and conduct; if by it be meant a growth of faith and an increase
of its fruits, manifested in a holy walk, then we have no objection to the
term. But if by "progressive sanctification" be intended a rendering of
the believer more acceptable unto God, or a making of him more fit
for the heavenly Jerusalem, then we have no hesitation in rejecting it as
a serious error. Not only can there be no increase in the purity and ac-
ceptableness of the believer's sanctity before God, but there can be no
addition to that holiness of which he became the possessor at the new
birth, for the new nature he then received is essentially and impeccably
holy. "The babe in Christ, dying as such, is as capable of as high communion with God as Paul in the state of glory" (S. E. Pierce).

Instead of striving after and praying that God would make us more fit for heaven, how much better to join with the apostle in "giving thanks unto the Father who *hath made us meet* to be partakers of the inheritance of the saints in light" (Col. 1:12), and then seek to walk suitably unto such a privilege and dignity! *That* is for the saints to "*possess their possessions*" (Obad. 17); the other is to be robbed of them by a thinly-disguised Romanism. Before pointing out in what the Christian's meetness for heaven consists, let us note that heaven is here termed an "inheritance." Now an inheritance is not something that we acquire by self-denial and mortification, nor purchased by our own labors or good works; rather it is that to which we lawfully succeed in virtue of our relationship to another. Primarily, it is that to which a child succeeds in virtue to his relationship to his father, or as the son of a king inherits the crown. In this case, the inheritance is ours in virtue of our being *sons of God*.

Peter declares that the Father hath "*begotten* us unto a living hope . . . *to* an inheritance incorruptible and undefiled and that fadeth not away" (I Peter 1:4). Paul also speaks of the Holy Spirit witnessing with our spirit that we are the children of God, and then points out: "and if *children*, then *heirs;* heirs of God and joint-heirs with Christ" (Rom. 8:16, 17). If we inquire more distinctly, what is this "inheritance" of the children of God? the next verse (Col. 1:13) tells us: it is the kingdom of God's dear Son." Those who are joint-heirs with Christ must share His kingdom. Already He has made us "kings and priests unto God" (Rev. 1:5), and the inheritance of kings is a crown, a throne, a kingdom. The blessedness which lies before the redeemed is not merely to be subjects of the King of kings, but to sit with Him on His throne, to reign with Him forever (Rom. 5:17; Rev. 22:4). Such is the wondrous dignity of our inheritance: as to its *extent*, we are "joint-heirs with" Him whom God "hath appointed heir of all things" (Heb. 1:2). Our destiny is bound up with His. O that the faith of Christians would rise above their "feelings," "conflicts," and "experiences," and possess their possessions.

The Christian's title to the inheritance is the righteousness of Christ imputed to him; in what, then, consists his "meetness"? First, since it be meetness for the inheritance, they must be *children of God*, and this they are made at the moment of regeneration. Second, since it is the "inheritance of saints," they must be *saints*, and this too they are the moment they believe in Christ, for they are then sanctified by that very blood in which they have forgiveness of sins (Heb. 13:12). Third, since it is an inheritance "in light," they must be made *children of light*, and this also they become when God called them "out of darkness into his marvellous light" (I Peter 2:9). Nor is that characteristic only of certain specially favored saints; "ye are *all* the children of light" (I Thess. 5:5). Fourth, since the inheritance consists of an everlasting kingdom, in order to enjoy it we must have *eternal life;* and that too every Christian possesses: "he that believeth on the Son of God hath everlasting life" (John 3:36).

"For ye are all the children of God by faith in Christ Jesus" (Gal. 3:

26). Are they children in name but not in nature? What a question! It might as well be supposed they have a title to an inheritance and yet be without meetness for it, which would be saying that our sonship was a fiction and not a reality. Very different is the teaching of God's Word: it declares that we become His children by being born again (John 1: 13). And regeneration does not consist in the gradual improvement or purification of the old nature, but the creation of a new one. Nor is becoming children of God a lengthy process at all, but an instantaneous thing. The all-mighty agent of it is the Holy Spirit, and obviously that which is born of *Him* needs no improving or perfecting. The "new man" is itself "created in righteousness and true holiness" (Eph. 4:22) and certainly *it* cannot stand in need of a "progressive" work to be wrought in him! True, the old nature opposes all the aspirations and activities of this new nature, and therefore as long as the believer remains in the flesh he is called upon "through the Spirit to mortify the deeds of the body," yet in spite of the painful and weary conflict, the new nature remains uncontaminated by the vileness in the midst of which he dwells.

That which qualifies the Christian or makes him meet for heaven is the spiritual life which he received at regeneration, for that is the life or nature of God (John 3:5; II Peter 1:4). That new life or nature fits the Christian for communion with God, for the presence of God — the same day the dying thief received it, he was with Christ in Paradise! It is true that while we are left here its *manifestation* is obscured, like the sunbeam shining through opaque glass. Yet the sunbeam itself is not dim, though it appears so because of the unsuitable medium through which it passes; but let that opaque glass be removed and it will at once appear in its beauty. So it is with the spiritual life of the Christian: there is no defeat whatever in the life itself but its manifestation is sadly obscured by a mortal body; all that is necessary for the appearing of its perfections is deliverance from the corrupt medium through which it now acts. The life of God in the soul renders a person meet for glory: no attainment of ours, no growth in grace we experience, can *fit* us for heaven any more than it can *entitle* us to it.

II

If the regeneration of Christians be complete, if their effectual sanctification be effected, if they are already fitted for heaven, then why does God still leave them here on earth? Why not take them to His own immediate presence as soon as they be born again?

Our first answer is, There is no "if" about it. Scripture distinctly and expressly affirms that even now believers are "complete in Christ" (Col. 2:10), that He has "perfected forever them that are sanctified" (Heb. 10:14), that they are "made meet for the inheritance of the saints in light" (Col. 1:12), and more than "complete," "perfect" and "meet" none will ever be. As to why God — generally, though not always — leaves the babe in Christ in this world for a longer or shorter period: even if no satisfactory reason could be suggested, that would not invalidate to the slightest degree what has been demonstrated, for when any truth is clearly established a hundred objections cannot set it aside. However, while we do not pretend to fathom the mind of God, the following consequences are more or less obvious.

By leaving His people here for a season opportunity is given for: 1. God to manifest His keeping power: not only in a hostile world, but sin still indwelling believers. 2. To demonstrate the sufficiency of His grace: supporting them in their weakness. 3. To maintain a witness for Himself in a scene which lieth in the Wicked One. 4. To exhibit His faithfulness in supplying all their need in the wilderness before they reach Canaan. 5. To display His manifold wisdom unto angels (I Cor. 4:9; Eph. 3:10). 6. To act as "salt" in preserving the race from moral suicide: by the purifying and restraining influence they exert. 7. To make evident the reality of their faith: trusting Him in sharpest trials and darkest dispensations. 8. To give them an occasion to glorify Him in the place where they dishonored Him. 9. To preach the gospel to those of His elect yet in unbelief. 10. To afford proof that they will serve Him amid the most disadvantageous circumstances. 11. To deepen their appreciation of what He has prepared for them. 12. To have fellowship with Christ who endured the cross before He was crowned with glory and honor.

Before showing why Christian progress is necessary let us remind the reader once more of the double signification of the term "Christian," namely, "an anointed one" and "a disciple of Christ," and how this supplies the principal key to the subject before us, intimating its *twofoldness*. His "anointing" with the Spirit of God is an act of God wherein he is entirely passive, but his becoming a "disciple of Christ" is a voluntary act of his own, wherein he surrenders to Christ's Lordship and resolves to be ruled by His sceptre. Only as this is duly borne in mind shall we be preserved from error on either side as we pass from one aspect of our theme to another. As the double meaning of the name "Christian" points to both the Divine operations and human activity, so in the Christian's progress we must keep before us the exercise of God's sovereignty and the discharge of our responsibility. Thus from one angle growth is neither necessary nor possible; from another it is both desirable and requisite. It is from this second angle we are now going to view the Christian, setting forth his obligations therein.

Let us illustrate what has been said above on the twofoldness of this truth by a few simple comments on a well-known verse: "So teach us to number our days that we may apply our hearts unto wisdom" (Ps. 90: 12). First, this implies that in our fallen condition we are wayward at heart, prone to follow a course of folly; and such is our present state by nature. Second, it implies that the Lord's people have had a discovery made to them of their woeful case, and are conscious of their sinful inability to correct the same; which is the experience of all the regenerate. Third, it signifies an owning of this humiliating truth, a crying to God for enablement. They beg to be "*so* taught," as to be actually empowered. In other words, it is a prayer for enabling grace. Fourth, it expresses the end in view: "that *we* may apply our hearts unto wisdom" — perform our duty, discharge our obligations, conduct ourselves as "Wisdom's children." Grace is to be improved, turned to good account, traded with.

We all know what is meant by a person's "applying his *mind*" to his studies, namely, that he gathers his wandering thoughts, focuses his attention on the subject before him, concentrates thereon. Equally evident is a person's "applying his *hand*" to a piece of manual labor, namely, that he get down to business, set himself to the work before him, earnestly endeavor to make a good job of it. In either case there is an implication: in the former, that he has been given a sound mind, in the latter that he possesses a healthy body. And in connection with both cases it is universally acknowledged that the one *ought* to so employ his mind and the other his bodily strength. Equally obvious should be the meaning of and the obligation to "apply our *hearts* unto wisdom": that is, diligently, fervently, earnestly make wisdom our quest and walk in her ways. Since God has given a "new heart" at regeneration, it is to be thus employed. If He has quickened us into newness of life then we ought to grow in grace. If He has made us new creatures in Christ we are to progress as Christians.

Because this will be read by such widely-different classes of readers and we are anxious to help all, we must consider here an objection, for the removal of which we quote the renowned John Owen. "It will be said that if not only the beginning of grace, sanctification, and holiness *from God,* but the carrying of it on and the increase of it also be from Him, and not only so in general, but that all the actings of grace, and every act of it, be an immediate effect of the Holy Spirit, then what need is there that we should take any pains in this thing ourselves, or use our own endeavors to grow in grace and holiness as we are commanded? If God worketh all Himself in us, and without His effectual operation in us we can do nothing, there is no place left for our diligence, duty, or obedience.

"Answer. 1. This objection we must expect to meet withal at every turn. Men will not believe there is a consistency between God's effectual grace and our diligent obedience; that is, they will not *believe* what is plainly, clearly, distinctly, revealed in the Scripture, and which is suited unto the experience of all that truly believe, because they cannot, it may be, comprehend it within the compass of carnal reason. 2. Let the apostle answer this objection for this once: 'His Divine power has given unto us all things that pertain unto life and godliness, through the knowledge of his that hath called us to glory and virtue; whereby are given unto us exceeding great and precious promises that by these we might be partakers of the Divine nature, having escaped the corruption that is in the world through lust' (II Peter 1:3, 4). If all things that pertain unto life and godliness, among which doubtless is the preservation and increase of grace, be given unto us by the power of God; if from Him we receive that Divine nature, by virtue whereof our corruptions are subdued, then I pray what need is there of any endeavors of our own? The whole work of sanctification is wrought in us, it seems, and that by the power of God: we, therefore, may let it alone and leave it unto Him whose it is, whilst we are negligent, secure and at ease. Nay, says the apostle, this is not *the use* which the grace of God is to be put unto. The consideration of it is, or ought to be, the principal motive and encouragement unto all diligence for the increase of holiness in us. For so he adds immediately: 'But also for this cause' [Greek] or because of the gracious operations of the Divine power in us; 'giving all diligence, add to your faith virtue,' etc. (v. 5).

"These objectors and this apostle were very diversely minded in these matters: what they make an insuperable discouragement unto diligence in obedience, that he makes the greatest motive and encouragement thereunto. 3. I say, from this consideration it will unavoidably follow, that we ought continually to wait and depend on God for supplies of His Spirit and grace without which we can do nothing; that God is more the Author by His grace of the good we do than we are ourselves (not I, but the grace of God that was with me): that we ought to be careful that by our negligences and sins we provoke not the Holy Spirit to withhold His aids and assistances, and so to leave us to ourselves, in which condition we can do nothing that is spiritually good: these things, I say, will unavoidably follow on the doctrine before declared; and if any one be offended at them it is not in our power to render them relief."

Coming now more directly to the *needs-be* for spiritual growth or Christian progress. This is not optional but obligatory, for we are expressly bidden to "Grow in grace and in the knowledge of our Lord and Saviour Jesus Christ" (II Peter 3:18) — grow from infancy to the vigor of youth, and from the zeal of youth to the wisdom of maturity. And again, to be "building up yourselves on your most holy faith" (Jude 21). It is not sufficient to be grounded and established in the faith, for we must grow more and more therein. At conversion we take upon us the "yoke" of Christ, and then His word is "learn of me," which is to be a lifelong experience. In becoming Christ's disciples we do but enter His school: not remain in the kindergarten but to progress under His tuition. "A wise man will hear and increase learning" (Prov. 1:5), and seek to make good use of that learning. The believer has not yet reached heaven: he is on the way, journeying thither, fleeing from the city of destruction. That is why the Christian life is so often likened unto a *race,* and the believer unto a runner: "forgetting those things which are behind and reaching forth unto those things which are before, I press toward the mark for the prize" (Phil. 3:13, 14).

1. *Only thus is the triune God glorified.* This is so obvious that it really needs no arguing. It brings no glory to God that His children should be dwarfs. As sunshine and rain are sent for the nourishment and fructification of vegetation so the means of grace are provided that we may increase in our spiritual stature. "As newborn babes, desire the sincere milk of the Word that ye may grow thereby" (I Peter 2:2) —

not only in the intellectual knowledge of it, but in a practical conformity thereunto. This should be our chief concern and be made our principal business: to become better acquainted with God, to have the heart more occupied with and affected by His perfections, to seek after a fuller knowledge of His will, to regulate our conduct thereby, and thus "show forth the praises of him who hath called us out of darkness into his marvelous light" (I Peter 2:9). The more we evidence our sonship, the more we conduct ourselves as becometh the children of God before a perverse generation, the more do we honor Him who has set His love upon us.

That our spiritual growth and progress *is* glorifying unto God appears plainly from the prayers of the apostles, for none were more concerned about His glory than they, and nothing occupied so prominent a place in their intercession as this. As we hope to allude to this again later, one or two quotations here must suffice. For the Ephesians Paul prayed, "that ye might be filled with all the fulness of God" (3:19). For the Philippians, "that your love may abound yet more and more, in knowledge and in all judgment . . . being filled with the fruits of righteousness" (1:9-11). For the Colossians, "that ye might walk worthy of the Lord unto all pleasing, being fruitful in every good work and increasing in the knowledge of God" (1:10, 11). From which we learn that it is our privilege and duty to obtain more spiritual views of the Divine perfections, begetting in us an increasing holy delight in Him, making our walk more acceptable. There should be a growing acquaintance with the excellency of Christ, advancing in our love of Him, and the more lively exercises of our graces.

2. *Only thus do we give proof of our regeneration.* "Herein is my Father glorified, that ye bear much fruit: so shall ye be my disciples" (John 15:8). That does not mean we become the disciples of Christ as a result of our fruitfulness, but that we make manifest we *are* His by our fruitbearing. They who bear no fruit have no vital union with Christ, and like the barren fig tree, are under His curse. Very solemn is this, and by such a criterion each of us should measure himself. That which is brought forth by the Christian is not to be restricted unto what, in many circles, is called "service" or "personal work," but has reference to that which issues from the exercise of all the spiritual graces. Thus: "Love your enemies, bless them that curse you, do good to them that hate you and pray for them which despitefully use you and persecute you; that ye may be the children of your Father which is in heaven" (Matt. 5:44, 45), that is, that you may *make it evident* to yourself and fellows that you have been made "partaker of the Divine nature."

"Now the works of the flesh are manifest, which are these," etc., "but the fruit of the Spirit is love, joy, peace, longsuffering, gentleness, goodness, faith, meekness, temperance" (Gal. 5:19, 22, 23). The reference is not directly to what the Holy Spirit produces, but rather to that which is born of the "spirit" or new nature of which He is the Author (John 3:6). This is evident from its being set over against the "works of the flesh" or old nature. It is by means of this "fruit," these lovely graces. that the regenerate make manifest the presence of a supernatural principle within them. The more such "fruit" abounds, the clearer our evidence that we have been born again. The total absence of such fruit would prove our profession to be an empty one. It has often been pointed out by others that what issues from the flesh is designated "works," for a machine can produce such; but that which the "spirit" yields is *living* "fruit" in contrast from "dead works" (Heb. 6:1; 9:14). This fruit-bearing is necessary in order to evidence the new birth.

3. *Only thus do we certify that we have been made partakers of an effectual call and are among the chosen of God.* "Brethren, give diligence to make your calling and election sure" (II Peter 1:10) is the Divine exhortation — one which has puzzled many. Yet it should not: it is not to secure it Godward (which is impossible), but to make it more certain to yourselves and your brethren. And how is this to be accomplished? Why, by acquiring a clearer and fuller evidence of the same: by spiritual growth, for growth is proof that life is present. This interpretation is definitely established by the context. After enumerating the bestowments of Divine grace (vv. 3, 4) the apostle says, now here is your responsibility: "And besides this, giving all diligence, add to your faith [by bringing it into exercise] virtue; and to virtue knowledge; and to knowledge temperance; and to temperance patience; and to patience godliness; and to godliness brotherly kindness; and to brotherly kindness love" (vv. 5-7). Faith itself is ever to be operative, but according to different occasions and in their seasons let each of your graces be exercised, and in proportion as they are, the life of holiness is furthered in the soul and there is a proportionate spiritual growth (cf. Col. 3:12, 13).

4. *Only thus do we adorn the doctrine we profess* (Titus 2:10). The Truth we claim to have received into our hearts is "the doctrine which is according to godliness" (I Tim. 6:3), and therefore the more our daily lives be conformed thereto the clearer proof do we give that our character and conduct is regulated by *heavenly* principles. It is by our fruits we are known (Matt. 7:16), for "every good tree bringeth forth good fruit." Thus, it is only by our being "fruitful in every good work" (Col. 1:10) that we make it manifest that we are the "trees of the Lord" (Ps. 104:16). "Now are ye light in the Lord, *walk* as children of light" (Eph. 5:8). It is not the character of our walk which qualifies us to become the children of light, but which demonstrates that we are such. Because we are children of Him who is light (I John 1:5) we must shun the darkness. If we have been "sanctified in Christ Jesus" (I Cor. 1:2) then only that should proceed from us which "becometh saints" (Eph. 5:3). The more we progress in godliness the more we adorn our profession.

5. *Only thus do we experience more genuine assurance.* Peace becomes more stable and joy abounds in proportion as we grow in grace

and in the knowledge of our Lord and Saviour Jesus Christ, and become more conformed practically to His holy image. It is because so many become slack in using the means of grace and are so little exercised about growing up into Christ "in all things" (Eph. 4:16) that doubts and fears possess their hearts. If they do not "give all diligence to add to their faith" (II Peter 1:5) by cultivating their several graces, they must not be surprised if they are far from being "sure" of their Divine calling and election. It is "the diligent soul," and not the dilatory, who "shall be made fat" (Prov. 13:4).

It is the one who makes conscience of obedience and keeps Christ's commandments who is favored with love-tokens from Him (John 14:21). There is an inseparable connection between our being "led [forward] by the Spirit of God" — which intimates our voluntary occurrence — and His "bearing witness with our spirit" (Rom. 8:14, 16).

6. *Only thus are we preserved from grievous backsliding.* In view of much that has been said above this should be quite obvious. The very term "backsliding" denotes failure to make progress and go forward. Peter's denial of Christ in the high priest's palace was preceded by his following Him "afar off" (Matt. 26:58), and that has been recorded for our learning and warning. The same principle is illustrated again in connection with the awful fall of David. Though it was "at the time when kings go forth to battle" he was selfishly and lazily taking his ease, and while so lax succumbed to temptation (I Sam. 11:1, 2). Unless we "follow on to know the Lord" and learn to make use of the armor which He has provided, we shall easily be overcome by the Enemy. Only as our hearts are kept healthy and our affection set upon things above shall we be impervious to the attractions of this world. We cannot be stationary: if we do not grow, we shall decline.

7. *Only thus shall we preserve the cause of Christ from reproach.* The backsliding of His people makes His enemies to blaspheme — how many have taken occasion to do so from the sad case of David! When the world sees us halting, it is gratified, being bolstered up in their idea that godliness is but a pose, a sham. Because of this, among other reasons, Christians are bidden to "be blameless and harmless, the sons of God, without rebuke in the midst of a crooked and perverse nation, among whom shine ye as lights in the world" (Phil. 2:15). If we go backward instead of forward — and we *must* do one or the other — then we greatly dishonor the name of Christ and fill His foes with unholy glee. Rather is it "the will of God that with well-doing we put to silence the ignorance of foolish men" (I Peter 2:15). The longer they remain in this world, the more apparent should be the contrast between the children of light and those who are the subjects of the Prince of darkness. Very necessary then, from many considerations, is our growth in grace.

4

Its Nature

I

WE have now arrived at what is really the most important part of our subject, but which is far from being the easiest to handle. If we are to be preserved or delivered from erroneous views at this point it is very necessary that we should form a right concept of what spiritual growth is *not* and what it actually *is.* Mistaken ideas thereon are widely prevalent and many of God's own people have been brought into bondage thereby. There are those who have made little or no advancement in the school of Christ that fondly imagine they have progressed considerably, and are very hurt if others do not share their opinion; nor is it any simple task to disillusion them. On the other hand, some who have grown considerably know it not, and even conclude they have gone backward; nor is it any easy matter to assure them they have been needlessly disparaging themselves. In either case the mistake is due to measuring themselves by the wrong standard, or in other words, through ignorance of what spiritual growth really consists.

If the reader met a half dozen people out of as many different sections of Christendom whom he is warranted in regarding as children of God, and asked them to define for him their ideas of spiritual growth, he would probably be surprised at the diversity and contrariety of the answers given. As the reception of one part of the Truth prepares us to take in another, so the admittance of error paves the way for the coming in of more. Moreover, the particular denomination to which we belong and the distinctive form of *its* "line of things" (II Cor. 10:16), has a powerful effect in determining the type of Christians reared under its influences — just as the nature of the soil affects the plants growing in it. Not only are his theological views cast into a certain mold and his concept of the practical side of Christianity largely determined thereby, but his devotional life and even his personal demeanor are also considerably affected by the same. Consequently there is much similarity in the "experience" of the great majority belonging to that particular party. This is largely the case with all the principal evangelical denominations, as it is also with those who profess to be "outside all systems."

Just as a trained ear can readily detect variations of inflection in the human voice and locate by a person's speech and accent which part of the country he hails from, so one with wide interdenominational associations has little difficulty in determining, even from a brief talk on spiritual things, which sect his companion belongs to: no label is necessary, his affiliation is plainly stamped upon him. And if in the course of the conversation he should ask his acquaintance to describe what he considered to be a mature Christian, his portrayal would naturally and necessarily be shaped by the particular ecclesiastical type he was best acquainted with. If he belonged to one particular group, he would picture a sombre and gloomy Christian; but if to a group at the opposite pole, a confident and joyous one. The kind most admired in some circles is a deep theologian; in others, the one who decries "dry doctrine" and is occupied chiefly with his subjective life. Yet another would value neither theology nor experience, considering that the soul's contemplation of Christ was the beginning and end of the Christian life; while still others would regard as eminent Christians those who were most zealous and active in seeking to save sinners.

In attempting to describe the character of Christian progress, or as it is more frequently termed, growth in grace, we shall therefore seek to avoid a mistake often made thereon by many denominational writers — a mistake which has had most injurious effects on a large number of their readers. Instead of bringing out what the Scriptures teach thereon, only too often they related their own experiences; instead of treating the essentials of spiritual growth, they dwelt upon circumstantials; instead of delineating those general features which are common to all who are the subjects of gracious operations, they depicted those exceptional things which are peculiar only to certain types — the neurotic or melancholy. This is much the same as though artists and sculptors took for their models only those with unusual deformities, instead of selecting an average specimen of humanity. True, it would be a human being that was imaged, yet it could convey only a misrepresentation of the common species. Alas that, in the religious as well as the physical realm, a freak attracts more attention than a normal person.

We shall not then relate our own spiritual history. First, because we are not now writing to satisfy the unhealthy curiosity of a certain class of readers who delight in perusing such things. Second, because we regard the private experience of the Christian as being too sacred to expose to the public view. It has long seemed to us that there is such a thing as spiritual unchastity: the inner workings of the soul are not a fit subject to be laid bare before others — "The heart knoweth his own bitterness, and a stranger doth not intermeddle with his joy" (Prov. 14: 10). Third, because we are not so conceited as to imagine our own particular conversion and the ups and downs of our Christian life are of sufficient importance to narrate. Fourth, because there are probably some features about our conversion and some things in our subsequent spiritual history which have been duplicated in very few other cases, and therefore they would only be calculated to mislead others if they should look for a parallel in themselves. Finally, because as intimated above, we deem it more honoring to God and far more helpful to souls to confine ourselves to the teaching of His Word on this subject.

But before proceeding we must anticipate an objection which is almost certain to be brought against what has been said in the last paragraph. Did not the apostle Paul describe *his* conversion. And may not, should not, we do so too? Answer: first, Paul is the only New Testament writer who gave us any account of his conversion or related anything of his subsequent experiences. It would be a reversal of all sound reasoning to make an exception into a rule or conclude that an isolated case established a precedent. The very fact that Paul's case stands alone, indicates it is *not* to be made an example of. Second, his experience was not only exceptional but unique: the means used was the supernatural appearance to him of the ascended Christ, so that he had a physical sight of Him and heard His voice with his natural ears – a thing which none has done since. Third, the account of his conversion was not made to intimate Christian friends, nor before a local church when applying for membership, but instead before his enemies (Acts 22), and Agrippa – virtually his judge – when making a defense for his life. Thus the circumstances were extraordinary and afford no criterion for ordinary cases. Finally, his experience on the Damascus road was necessary to qualify him for the apostolic office (Acts 1:22; I Cor. 15:8, 9; cf. II Cor. 12:11).

Once more it seems advisable to take up first the negative side of our subject ere turning to the positive. So many mistaken notions now hold the field that they need uprooting if the ground is to be prepared: or to drop the figure, if the minds of many are to be fitted to take in the Truth. Our readers differ so much in the type of ministry they have sat under, and some of them have formed such fallacious views of what spiritual growth consists of, that if we now described the principal elements of Christian progress, one and another would probably consider, according to what they have imbibed, that we had omitted the most important features. We shall therefore devote the remainder of this chapter to pointing out as many as possible of those things which, though often regarded as such, are *not* essential parts of spiritual growth, in fact no part thereof at all. Though this may prove rather wearisome to some, we would ask them to bear with us and offer up a prayer that it may please God to use the paragraphs which follow to the enlightenment of those who are befogged.

1. *Weight of years.* It is often considered that spiritual growth is to be measured by the calendar, that the length of time one has been a Christian will determine the amount of progress he has made. Certainly it ought to be so, yet in fact it is frequently no index at all. God often pours contempt on the distinctions made by men: out of the mouth of "babes and sucklings" has He perfected praise (Matt. 21:16). It is generally supposed that those with snowy locks are much more spiritual than young believers, yet if we examine what is recorded of the closing years of Abraham, Isaac, David, Hezekiah and others of Israel's kings, we find reason to revise or qualify such a conclusion. True, some of the choicest saints we have ever met were "patriarchs" and "mothers in Israel," yet they have been exceptions rather than the rule. Many Christians make more real progress in piety the first year than in the next ten that follow.

2. *Increasing knowledge.* We must distinguish between things that differ, namely, a knowledge of spiritual things and actual spiritual knowledge. The former can be acquired by the unregenerate: the latter is peculiar to the children of God. The one is merely intellectual and theoretical; the other is vital and effectual. One may take up "Bible study" in the same way as another would the study of philosophy or political economy. He may pursue it diligently and enthusiastically. He may obtain a familiarity of the letter of Scripture and a proficiency in understanding its terms, far in advance of the hard-working Christian who has less leisure and less natural ability; yet what is such knowledge worth if it affects not the heart, fails to transform the character and make the daily walk pleasing to God! "Though I understand all mysteries and all knowledge . . . and have not love, I am nothing" (I Cor. 13:2). Unless our "Bible study" is conforming us, both inwardly and outwardly, to the image of Christ, it profits us not.

3. *Development of gifts.* An unregenerate person taking up the study of the Bible may also be one who is endowed with considerable natural talents, such as the power of concentration, a retentive memory, a persevering spirit. As he prosecutes his study his talents are called into play, his wits are sharpened and he becomes able to converse fluently upon the things he has read, and he is likely to be sought after as a speaker and preacher: and yet there may not be a spark of Divine life in his soul. The Corinthians grew fast in gifts (I Cor. 1:4, 7) yet they were but "babes" and "carnal" (3:2, 3), and needed to be reminded of the "more excellent way" of love to God and their brethren. Ah, my reader, you may not have the showy gifts of some, nor be able to pray in public as others, but if you have a tender conscience, an honest heart, a forbearing and forgiving spirit, you have that which is far better.

4. *More time spent in prayer.* Here again, to avoid misunderstanding, we must distinguish between things that differ: natural prayer and spiritual. Some are constitutionally devotional and are attracted by religious exercises, as others are by music and painting; and yet they may be total strangers to the breathings of God's Spirit in their souls. They may set aside certain parts of the day for "a quiet time with God" and have a "prayer list" as long as their arm, and yet be utterly devoid of the spirit of grace and supplications. The Pharisees were renowned for their "long prayers." The Mohammedan with his "praying mat," the Buddhist with his "praying wheel," and the Papist with his "beads," all illustrate the same principle. It is quite true that growth in grace is ever accompanied by an increased dependence upon God and a delighting of the soul in Him, yet that does not mean that we can measure our spirituality by the clock — by the amount of time we spend on our knees.

5. *Activity in service.* In not a few circles this has been and still is made the test of one's spirituality. As soon as a young person makes a

Christian profession he is set to work. It matters not how ill qualified he is, lacking as yet (in many instances) even a rudimentary knowledge of the fundamentals of the faith, nevertheless he is required or at least expected to engage forthwith in some form of what is plausibly termed "service for Christ." But the Epistles will be searched in vain for a warrant for such things: they contain not so much as a single injunction for young believers to engage in "personal work." On the contrary they are enjoined to obey their parents in the Lord (Eph. 6:1) and the young women are to be "keepers at home" (Titus 2:5). Many have reason to lament "they [not God!] made me the keeper of the vineyards, but mine own vineyard [spiritual graces] have I not kept" (Song of Sol. 1:6).

6. *Happy feelings.* Considerable allowance needs to be made for both temperament and health. Some are naturally more vivacious and emotional than others, of a more lively and cheerful spirit, and consequently they engage in singing rather than sighing, laughter than weeping. When such people are converted they are apt to be more demonstrative than others, both in expressing gratitude to the Lord and in telling people what a precious Saviour is theirs. Yet it would be a great mistake to suppose that they had received a larger measure of the Spirit than their more sober and equable brethren and sisters. A shallow brook babbles noisily but "still waters run deep" — yet there are exceptions here as the Niagara Falls illustrate. Increasing holiness is not to be gauged by our inward comforts and joy, but rather by the more substantial qualities of faith, obedience, humility and love. When a fire is first kindled there is more smoke and crackling, but after, though the flame has a narrower compass, it has more heat.

7. *Becoming more miserable.* Yet, strange as it may sound to some of our readers, there are not a few professing Christians who regard *that* as one of the principal elements of spiritual growth. They have been taught to regard assurance as presumption and Christian joy as lightness, if not levity. Should they experience a brief season of peace "in believing" they are fearful that the Devil is deceiving them. They are occupied mostly with indwelling sin rather than with Christ. They hug their fears and idolize their doubts. They consider that the slough of despond is the only place of safety, and are happiest when most wretched. This is by no means an exaggerated picture, but sadly true to a certain type of religious life, where long-facedness and speaking in whispers are regarded as evidence of a "deep experience" and marks of piety. True, the more light God gives us the more we perceive our sinfulness, though humbled thereby, the more thankful we should be for the cleansing blood.

8. *Added usefulness.* But God is sovereign and orders His providences accordingly. Unto one He opens doors, unto another He closes them, and to His good pleasure we are called upon to submit. Some streams

He replenishes, but others are suffered to dry up: thus it is in His dealings with His people — by providing or withholding favorable openings for them to be of spiritual help to their fellows. It is therefore a great mistake to measure our growth in grace and our bringing forth of good fruit by the largeness or smallness of our opportunities of doing good. Some have larger opportunities when young than when they become older, yet if the hearts of the latter are right, God accepts the will for the deed. Some that have the most grace are stationed in isolated places and are largely unknown to their fellow Christians, yet the eye of God sees them. Shall we say that the flowers on the mountain side are wasted because no human eye admires them, or that the songs of birds in the forests are lost on the air because they regale not the ears of men!

9. *Temporal prosperity.* Though it is shared by few of our fellow ministers, yet it is the firm conviction of this writer that, as a general rule, temporal adversity and straitened circumstances in the present life of a Christian is a mark of God's displeasure, an evidence that he has choked the channel of blessing (see Ps. 84:11; Jer. 5:25; Matt. 6:33). On the other hand we should certainly be drawing an erroneous conclusion if we regard the flourishing affairs of an unregenerate professor as a proof that the smile of heaven rested upon him, rather would it be the case of one who was being fattened for the "day of slaughter" (James 5:5). Many such an one receives his good things in this world, but in the world to come is tormented in the flame (Luke 16:24, 25). Even among God's own people there may be those who yield to a spirit of covetousness, and in some cases the Lord gratifies their carnal desires, but "sends leanness into their souls" as He did with Israel of old.

10. *Liberality in giving.* We do not believe any heart can remain selfish and miserly where the love of God has been shed abroad in it, but rather that such an one will esteem it a privilege as well as duty to support the cause of Christ and minister to any brother in need, according as God has prospered him, yet it is a very misleading standard to judge a person's spirituality by his generosity (I Cor. 13:3). For some years we lived in districts where the principal denominations taught that the church's spirituality was measured by the amount it contributed to missions; yet while numbers of them raised very considerable sums, vital godliness was most conspicuous by its absence. Millions of dollars are given to the "Red Cross Society" by those making no Christian profession at all! Never were the coffers of the churches so full as they are today, and never were the churches so devoid of the Spirit's unction and blessing.

II

All sound teaching, like the safest method of reasoning, proceeds from the general to the particular, and therefore we shall attempt to show the principles from which spiritual growth issues and the main lines along which Christian progress advances, before we enter into a detailed analysis of the same. God first gave Israel His law, and then because His "commandment is exceeding broad" (Ps. 119:96) supplied amplification through the prophets and a still more specific explication of its contents through Christ and His apostles. Spiritual growth is the development of spiritual life, and spiritual life is communicated to a sinner at the new birth, so the more clearly we are enabled to understand the nature of regeneration, the better prepared we shall be to perceive the character of spiritual growth. Admittedly regeneration is profoundly mysterious, but there are at least two things which afford us help thereon: the fact that it is a "renewing" (Titus 3:5), and that it is a real and radical (though not complete or final) reversal of what happened to us at the fall. The old creation gives us some idea of the new creation, and the order in which the former was wrecked prepares us to grasp the order in which the latter is effected.

Natural man is a composite being, made up of spirit and soul and body. The "spirit" seems to be the highest part of his nature, being that which capacitates for God-consciousness or the knowledge of God — He being "spirit" (John 4:24). The "soul" or ego appears to be that which, expressing itself through the body, constitutes what is termed our "personality," and is the seat of self-consciousness, and by it man has communion with his fellows. The body or physical organism is that which provides the soul with a habitation in this world, and it is the seat of sense-consciousness, being that through which man has contact with material things. The order of Scripture is "spirit and soul and body" (I Thess. 5:23), but man with his customary perversity invariably reverses it and speaks of "body, and soul and spirit." How that reveals what man has degenerated into: the body, which he can see and feel, which occupies most of his concern, and comes first in his consideration and estimation. His "soul" receives little thought and still less care, and as to his "spirit" he is unaware that he has any.

"And God said, Let us make man in our image, after our likeness" (Gen. 1:26). God is tri-une, there being three persons in one and indivisible Divine essence. And it was in the image of the triune God that man was made, as the plural pronouns plainly connote. Thus man was made a tri-une creature. His "spirit" which is the intellectual principle and highest part, was capacitated for communion with God and was designed to regulate (by its wisdom) the soul, in which resides the emotional nature or the "affections." The soul in turn was to regulate the body, as it received through the physical senses information of the external world. But at the fall man reversed the order of his creation: making a "god" of his belly he henceforth became enslaved to the lower world, and the soul instead of directing the physical mechanism became to a large extent the lackey of its senses and demands. Communion with God being severed, the spirit no longer functioned according to its distinctive nature, and though not extinguished, was dragged down to the level of the soul.

What has just been pointed out should be clearer to the reader by pondering it in the light of Genesis 3. In assailing Eve, Satan made his attack upon her *spirit* — the principle which receives from God — for he first called into question the Divine prohibition (v. 2) and then, replying to her objection, assured her "ye shall not surely die," and added as an inducement "in the day ye eat thereof, then your eyes shall be opened, and ye shall be as gods, knowing good and evil" (vv. 4, 5), thereby seeking to weaken her faith, and flatter her ambition by promising greater wisdom. Hearkening to his lies, the woman was "deceived" (I Tim. 2:14). Her judgment became clouded through doubting God's threat, and once the light of God in her spirit was lost, all was lost. Her affections became corrupted so that she now "desired" or lusted after the forbidden fruit — not by the prompting of her spirit, but by the solicitation of her physical senses: and her will became depraved so that she "took" thereof.

Now, from the experimental side of things, regeneration is the initial work of God in reversing the effects of the fall, for its favored subject is then "renewed in knowledge, after the image of him that created him" (Col. 3:10): that is to say, spiritual perception is restored to him, so that he now has again what he lost in Adam — a vital, powerful, direct knowledge of God. In consequence of this he is brought back again into communion with God, restored to a conscious fellowship with Him. One aspect of this mysterious but blessed work is brought before us in Hebrews 4:12 where we are told, "the Word of God is quick and powerful, and sharper than any two-edged sword, piercing even to the dividing asunder of soul and spirit." We understand that last clause to signify that the regenerated person's "spirit" is now freed from its immersion into the soul and is raised to its own superior level, being placed *en rapport* (brought into harmony with) God Himself. Thus Paul declares "I serve [God] with my *spirit*" (Rom. 1:9) — not "soul"; and "my spirit prayeth" (I Cor. 14:14). In distinction therefrom "purified your *souls* [affections] in obeying the truth" (I Peter 1:22).

Though the above may sound recondite and, being new to our readers, somewhat difficult to grasp, yet it should, we think, be more or less clear that in order for us to answer to what God has wrought in us, in order to live as becometh Christians, the body should take second place to the soul and be ruled thereby: and the soul in turn be subordinated to the spirit, which is to be enlightened and controlled by God. Unless the body be made subservient to the soul, man lives his life on the same level as the animals; and unless the Christian's "affections" and emotions be regulated by wisdom from the spirit, he lives on the same plane as the unregenerate. "Seek ye first the kingdom of God and his righteousness, and all these things shall be added unto you" (Matt. 6:33). That means, make the things of the spirit your paramount concern, and your lower interests will be automatically subserved. If the mind or spirit be "stayed on God," the soul will enjoy perfect peace, and the soul at rest will act beneficially on the body. Thus, in proportion as our lives accord with what took place in us at the new birth will be our spiritual growth and prosperity.

Nothing but a knowledge of God can satisfy the spirit of man, as nought but His love can content the soul. Man's supreme happiness consists in the exercise of his noblest parts and faculties on their proper objects, and the more excellent those objects be, the more real and lasting pleasure do they give us in the knowledge and love of them. Thus it is that, when God has designs of mercy toward an individual, He begins by shining upon his understanding and attracting his heart unto Himself. As that work of grace proceeds that individual is enabled to see something of "the deceitfulness of sin" (Heb. 3:13), how it has deluded him into vainly imagining that the things of time and sense could afford him satisfaction, until he discovers that (to use the figurative language of the prophet) he has "spent his money for that which is not bread" and "labored for that which satisfieth not" (Isa. 55:2). Therefore does God say unto him, "hearken unto me, and eat ye that which is good, and let your soul delight itself in fatness." Until God becomes our "Portion" the soul is left with an aching void.

Here, then, is what occurs at regeneration: God "hath given us an understanding that we may know him that is true" (I John 5:20) – and this He does by quickening the "spirit" in us. And again we read "For God who [in connection with the first creation, Gen. 1:3] commanded the light to shine out of darkness, hath [in His work of the new creation] shined in our hearts, to give the light of the knowledge of the glory of God in the face of Jesus Christ" (II Cor. 4:6). Thus, Christian progress must consist in our advancing in a personal and experimental knowledge of God, and consequently when the apostle prayed for the spiritual growth of the Colossians he made request that they might be "increasing in the knowledge of God" (1:10). Simultaneously with this communication of a supernatural knowledge of Himself, the "love of God is shed abroad in our hearts by the Holy Spirit" (Rom. 5:5) and therefore spiritual growth consists of a deeper apprehension and fuller enjoyment of that love with a more complete response thereto; and hence when making request for the same on behalf of the Ephesians Paul prayed that they might "know the love of Christ which passeth knowledge" (3:19).

It is not our immediate design to give as full a description as our present light affords of the precise nature of regeneration, but only to point out those of its principal elements which the better enables us to grasp what spiritual growth consists of. We will therefore mention but one other feature of the new birth, or that which is at least an inseparable adjunct of it, namely, the impartation of *faith*. Nor shall we now attempt to define what faith is: sufficient for the moment to acknowledge that it is a blessed "gift of God" (Eph. 2:8), in nowise originating in the exercise of the human will, but communicated by "the operation of God" (Col. 2:12), and therefore it is a supernatural principle, active in its favored recipient, bringing forth fruit after its own kind, and thereby evidencing its Divine source. It is "by faith, not by sight" (II Cor. 5:7) the Christian walks: as said the apostle "the life which I now live in the flesh, I live by the faith of the Son of God [He being its Object], who loved me and gave himself for me" (Gal.

2:20). This it is which distinguishes all the regenerate from the unregenerate, for the latter are "children in whom is no faith" (Deut. 32:20; cf. II Thess. 3:3).

The Christian life begins by the exercise of a God-given faith, namely, an act whereby we receive Christ as our own personal Saviour (John 1:12). We are "justified by faith," and by Christ "have access by faith into this grace [i.e., accepted into God's favor] wherein we stand" (Rom. 5:1, 2). We are "sanctified by faith" (Acts 26:18), that is, made actual participants of the ineffable purity of Christ. Through the Spirit we "wait for the hope of righteousness by faith" (Gal. 5:5; cf. II Tim. 4:8). It is by "the shield of faith," and that alone, we are able to "quench all the fiery darts of the wicked" (Eph. 6:12). It is "through faith and patience" that we "inherit the promises" (Heb. 6:12). It was by faith that the Old Testament saints "obtained a good report" (Heb. 11:3) and wrought such wonders as the remainder of that chapter demonstrates. It is by faith we successfully resist the Devil (I Peter 5:9) and overcome the world (I John 5:4). From all of which it is very evident that the measure of our Christian progress will be very largely determined by the extent to which this principle be kept healthy and remains operating in us.

To sum up what has been pointed out above: regeneration is both a "renewing" and a "new creation." As a "renewing" it is a continual process, as II Corinthians 4:16 clearly shows. This aspect of it is a partial reversal of and recovery from what happened to us at the fall. It is a Divine quickening, which necessarily presupposes an entity or faculty already existing, though in need of being made alive or revived. This "renewing" is of the inner man, which includes both spirit and soul or "the mind" and "heart." It is an initial and radical act, followed by a repeated but imperceptible process whereby the nobler or immaterial parts of our beings are elevated or refined. This does not mean that "the flesh" or evil principle in us undergoes any improvement, but that our faculties are spiritualized; and thus spiritual growth will consist of the mind being more and more engaged with Divine objects, the affections being increasingly set upon things above, the conscience becoming more tender, and the human will being made more amenable to the Divine, and thereby the inner man more and more conformed to the holy image of Christ.

But regeneration is something more than a "renewing" or quickening of parts and faculties already in existence: it is also a "new creation," the bringing into existence of something which did not exist before, the actual bestowment of something to the sinner in addition to all that he had as a natural man. That "something" is variously designated in Scripture (and by theologians) according to its different relations and aspects. It is termed "life" (I John 5:12), yea life "more abundantly" (John 10:10) than unfallen Adam enjoyed. It is named "spirit" because "born of the Spirit" (John 3:6) and therefore is to be distinguished from our natural spirit; and "the spirit of power and of love and of a sound mind" (II Tim. 1:7). It is called "the earnest of the Spirit" (II Cor. 1:22), being a token or firstfruits of what will be ours when glorified; and "grace" (Eph. 4:7) as an inward principle. Theologians designate it "the new nature," and many allude to it under the composite term of "the Christian's graces," which is warranted by John 1:16, and is probably the easiest for us to comprehend. Considered thus, spiritual growth may be said to be the development of our graces: the strengthening of faith, the enlarging of hope, the increasing of love, the abounding of peace and joy: see II Peter 1:3 and carefully note verses 5-8.

Thus far we have been dwelling almost entirely upon the internal aspect of our theme, so we will now quote one verse which directs attention to the external side. "For we are his workmanship, created in Christ Jesus unto good works, which God hath before ordained that we should walk in them" (Eph. 2:10). Here is the response which we are required to make unto the new birth. God's purpose in our new creation or regeneraton is that we should "walk in good works" that we may make manifest the spiritual root which He then implanted by bearing spiritual fruit. Such was the design of Christ in dying for us: to "purify unto himself a peculiar people, zealous of good works" (Titus 2:14). From which it plainly follows that, the more zealous we are of good works and the more steadfastly we walk in them, the more do we rightly answer to what God has wrought in us. Now the performance of our daily duties are so many "good works," if they be done from faith's obedience to God's requirements and with an eye to His approbation and glory. Hence the more faithfully and conscientiously we discharge our obligations toward God and toward our fellows, the more true Christian progress we are making.

All that has been before us above receives simplification when it is viewed in the light of *conversion* and its proper sequel. Regeneration is entirely the work of God, wherein we are passive, but conversion is an act of ours; the one being the effect and consequence of the other. The word "conversion" means to turn around, it is a right-about-face. It is a turning from the world unto God, from Satan unto Christ, from sin unto holiness, from being absorbed with the things of time unto devotion to our eternal interests. At regeneration we received a supernatural knowledge of God, and as the consequence, in His light we see ourselves as depraved, lost and undone. At regeneration we received a nature which is "created in righteousness and true holiness" (Eph. 4:24), and as a consequence we now hate all unrighteousness and sin. At regeneration we were given an understanding that we might know Him that is true (I John 5:20) and our response is to yield ourselves unto His dominion and trust in His atoning blood. At regeneration we received Divine "grace" as an indwelling principle, and the effect is to make us willing to deny ourselves, take up our cross daily and follow Christ. The proper sequel to such a conversion is that we stedfastly adhere to the surrender we then made of ourselves unto the Lord Jesus, and the more we do so such will be our spiritual progress.

III

We have sought to show the principles from which spiritual growth issues and the main lines along which Christian progress advances, pointing out that spiritual growth is the development of the spiritual life communicated at regeneration. Now we shall look at the particular, seeking to set out in some detail of what that development actually consists.

1. Spiritual growth consists of *an increase in spiritual knowledge*. God works in us as rational creatures, according to our intelligent nature, so that nothing is wrought in us unless knowledge paves the way. We cannot speak a language unless we have some understanding of the same. We cannot do work with an implement or machine nor play on a musical instrument until we have a knowledge of them. The same obtains in connection with spiritual things. We cannot worship intelligently or acceptably an unknown God. He must first reveal Himself and be known by us, for we could not love or trust One with whom we had no acquaintance. Therefore does God's Word declare "They that know thy name will put their trust in thee" (Ps. 9:10). It cannot be otherwise: once God is revealed to us as a living reality, the heart at once confides itself to Him, as being definitely worthy of its fullest reliance and dependence. It is spiritual ignorance of God which lies at the foundation of all our distrust of Him, and therefore of all our doubts and fears: "Acquaint now thyself with him and be at peace" (Job 22: 21).

The Christian life begins in knowledge, for "the new man is renewed in knowledge" (Col. 3:10). "This is life eternal, that they might know thee the only true God, and Jesus Christ whom thou hast sent" (John 17:3). There has been much difference of opinion among commentators as to the scope of these words. When we wrote thereon many years ago we adopted the view of the majority of Christian writers, namely, a declaration of the way and means by which eternal life is obtained: just as the words that follow "this is the condemnation" in John 3:19 do not define the character of that condemnation, but rather tell us the *cause* of it. While we still believe in the legitimacy and soundness of the interpretation we gave formerly, yet a more mature reflection would not restrict the meaning of John 17:3 to that explanation, but would also understand it to signify that "eternal life" (of which we now have but the promise and earnest) or everlasting bliss and glory will consist of an ever-increasing knowledge of the triune God as revealed in the Person of the Mediator.

This knowledge does not consist in theological thoughts or metaphysical speculations about the Godhead, but in such spiritual understanding of Him as causes us to believe in the Lord God, to cast our souls upon Him, and center in Him as our everlasting Portion. "The renewed understanding is raised up and enlightened with a supernatural life, so that what we know of the Lord is by intuitive knowledge which the Holy Spirit is most graciously pleased to give. Hence believers are said to be called out of darkness into marvellous light, and Paul says 'ye were sometime darkness but now are ye light in the Lord.' As the knowledge of the Father, Son and Spirit is reflected upon the renewed mind in the person of Christ, so it is received into the heart" (S. E. Pierce). This spiritual apprehension of God is such as no outward means can of themselves convey: no, not even the reading of the Word or hearing it preached. In addition thereto, God by His own light and power conveys to the human spirit such an effectual discovery of Himself as radically affects the understanding, conscience, affections and will, reforming the life.

As the Christian life begins in spiritual knowledge so it is increased thereby: "But grow in grace and in the knowledge of our Lord and Saviour Jesus Christ" (II Peter 3:18), upon which we quote again from the excellent Pierce. "I conceive that by *grace* here all those faculties, graces, habits, dispositions, which are wrought in us by the Holy Spirit are to be understood. And to have our spiritual faculties, graces, habits, and dispositions exercised distinctively and supernaturally on their proper objects and subjects *is* to 'grow in grace.' What follows in the text is explanatory: 'and in the knowledge of our Lord and Saviour Jesus Christ.' He is the Object on which all our graces are to be exercised. He is the life of all our graces. Therefore growing into a greater knowledge of Him, and the Father's love in Him, is to 'grow in grace,' for thereby all our graces are quickened, strengthened, exercised and drawn forth to the praise of God." While we do not think that exhausts the meaning of II Peter 3:18, yet such an interpretation is borne out by the second verse of the Epistle: "Grace and peace be multiplied unto you *through* the knowledge of God, and of Jesus our Lord" — not by the knowledge of God alone, nor of the Lord Jesus alone, but of God in Christ the Mediator, which is also the force of John 17:3.

One of the ways by which we may ascertain what spiritual growth consists of is by attending to the recorded prayers of the apostles and noting what it was for which they made request. Being very eminent themselves in grace and holiness, it was their earnest desire that the churches and particular individuals to whom their Epistles were addressed, might increase and greatly flourish in those Divine bestowments. Accordingly in his prayer for the Ephesians we find Paul petitioning that the Father of glory would give unto them "the spirit of wisdom and revelation in the knowledge of him," that the eyes of their understanding might be enlightened that they might know what is the hope of His calling (vv. 17, 18). It should be obvious that in asking for such favors for those saints there was no implication that they were entirely devoid of them or that he sought the initial bestowment of them — any more than John 20:31 signifies the Fourth Gospel was addressed to unbelievers (1:16 proves otherwise) or that his First Epistle was sent to Christians lacking in assurance; rather does I John 5:13 connote "that ye may have a clearer and fuller knowledge that eternal life is yours."

No, in making those petitions on behalf of the Ephesian saints Paul requested that a larger degree of heavenly light might be furnished unto

their minds, that they might have a more spiritual apprehension of the
One with whom they had to do, of His wondrous perfections according
to the revelation He has made of Himself in the Word, and of his
varied relationships to them. It was that they might discern the wonders of His grace and power toward, in, and for them. It was that they
might have an enlarged conception and perception of their vivication
when they were in a state of death and sin. In like manner, he prayed
that the love of the Philippian saints might "abound yet more and more
in knowledge and all judgment" (1:9). So for the Colossians, that they
might be "increasing in the knowledge of God" (1:10), which is to be
taken in its fullest sense: increasing in the knowledge of God in the
manifestation He has made of Himself in creation, in providence and in
grace; in knowledge of God in His three Persons, in His Christ the Mediator, in His law, in His gospel; in the knowledge of His holy will.

This knowledge of God, which distinguishes the regenerate from the
unregenerate, which the apostle solicited on behalf of his converts, and
which is the basic element in all real Christian progress, is something
vastly different from and superior to the mere possession of a correct
opinion about God or any speculative view concerning Him. It is a supernatural and saving knowledge. A mere theoretical knowledge of
God is inoperative and ineffectual, but an experimental acquaintance
with Him is dynamical and transforming. It is a knowledge which deeply
affects the heart, producing reverential awe, for "the fear of the Lord is
the beginning of wisdom" (Prov. 9:10). It is such a knowledge as
strengthens the Christian's graces and calls them forth into lively exercise. Since that Divine light and power is communicated to the saint by
the Spirit through the Scriptures, it causes him to search and ponder
them as he never did previously, and to mix faith with what he reads
and takes in. It is such a knowledge as promotes holiness in the heart
and piety in the life. It is a knowledge which produces obedience to
the Divine commandments, as I John 2:3, 4 plainly teaches. Yet there
can be no such knowledge of God except as He is apprehended through
Christ (II Cor. 4:6).

Such a knowledge of God lies at the foundation of everything else in
the spiritual life, being both essential and introductory. Without such
a knowledge of God we cannot know ourselves, how to order our lives in
this world, nor what awaits us in the world to come: until made acquainted with Him who is light (I John 1:5) we are in complete darkness. Calvin evinced the profundity of his spiritual insight by com-
mencing his renowned *Institutes* in saying, "True and substantial wisdom primarily consists of two parts: the knowledge of God and the
knowledge of ourselves." Without a personal and spiritual knowledge of
God we cannot perceive the infinite evil of sin and the fearful havoc
it has wrought in us: it is only in His light that we "see light" (Ps.
36:9) and discover the horribleness and totality of our depravity. Then
it is that we both behold and feel ourselves to be just as God has described us in His Word. Equally so it is only by such knowledge of
God that we can appreciate the Divinely-provided remedy: either in dis-

covering wherein it consists or realizing our dire need of the same. "The way of the wicked is as darkness" (Prov. 4:19).

From all that has been pointed out above we may see how completely dependent the Christian is upon God: no spiritual progress is possible except as He continues to shine upon us. Neither a powerful intellect, the artificial aids of philosophy, nor a thorough training in logic, can contribute one iota unto a spiritual apprehension of Divine things. True, they are of use in enabling the teacher to discourse thereon, to express himself more readily and fluently than the illiterate, but as to discovering to him Divine truth they are of no value whatever. The reason of this is evident: celestial things are high above the reach of carnal reason, and therefore it can never attain unto an acquaintance with their true nature. Heavenly grace is required for an entrance into heavenly things, and the meanest capacity is as susceptible to heavenly grace as the most capacious mind. Moreover, the things of God are addressed to *faith*, and that is a grace of which the unregenerate, be he the most accomplished savant, is utterly devoid. Divine mysteries are hidden from the naturally wise and prudent, but they are supernaturally revealed to spiritual babes (Matt. 11:25) — revealed by the Holy Spirit through a Divinely-imparted faith.

An uneducated Christian may not be able to enter into the subtle niceties of theological metaphysics, he may not be competent to debate the Truth with ingenious objectors, but he is capable of understanding the character and perfections of God, the person and work of Christ, the mysteries and wonders of redemption so as to obtain such a gracious view thereof as to excite in his mind a holy adoration of the Father and a love for and joy in the Redeemer. And such a knowledge, and that alone, will stand us in stead in the time of trial, the hour of temptation, or the article of death. Yet it is only as the Holy Spirit is pleased to give fresh light and life to the believer's mind by bringing home anew by His own unction and efficacy what is already known that he can increase in the spiritual knowledge thereof. What God has revealed in His Word must be applied again and again by the Spirit if it is to be operative in us and bear fruit through us. The believer is as much dependent upon God for any increase of spiritual knowledge as he was for the first reception of it, and constantly does he need to bear in mind that humbling word "without me ye can do nothing."

If we added nothing to the last paragraph we should present a most unbalanced view of this point, conveying the impression that we had no responsibility in the matter. As there is a radical difference between the Christian and the non-Christian, so there is between our first spiritual knowledge of God and our increase in the same. "But grow in grace and in the knowledge of our Lord" is a Divine exhortation, intimating both our privilege and our duty. We are required to make diligent use of the means God has provided, for He places no premium on slothfulness. Though we are dependent upon the Spirit to apply the Truth to us, yet that does not signify that it will make no difference whether or not we keep the things of God fresh in our minds by daily meditation upon them. Only God can bring His Word home to our hearts in living power, nevertheless we must pray "quicken thou me according to thy Word" (Ps. 119:25). Moreover it is our obligation to abstain from whatever would grieve the Spirit and thereby weaken the assurance which enables us to say "*my* Father" and "*my* Redeemer." If we increase not in the knowledge of God the fault is ours.

2. Spiritual growth consists of *a deeper delight in spiritual things and objects.* This is ever the accompaniment and effect of spiritual knowledge — affording us another criterion by which we may test the kind of knowledge we have. A merely speculative knowledge of Divine things is cold and lifeless, but a spiritual and experimental acquaintance with them affects the heart and moves the affections. One may accept much of God's Word (through early training) in a traditional way, and even be prepared to contend for the same against those who oppose it, yet it will avail nothing when the Devil assails him. Hence we are told that when the Wicked One is revealed, whose coming is after the working of Satan, with all power and signs and lying wonders, God permits him to work "with all deceivableness of unrighteousness in them that perish," and His reason for this is stated to be: "because they received not *the love of* the truth that they might be saved" (II Thess. 2:10). At best they had only a letter acquaintance with the truth: it was never enshrined in their affections. But different far is it with the regenerate: each of them can say with the Psalmist "O how love I thy law: it is my meditation all the day" (Ps. 119:97).

Spiritual delight necessarily follows spiritual knowledge, for an object cannot be appreciated any further than it is apprehended and known. Spiritual knowledge of spiritual things imparts not only a conviction of their verity and the certainty of their reality, but it also produces the soul's adherence to them, the cleaving of the affections unto them, a holy joy in them, so that they appear inexpressibly blessed and glorious unto those granted a discovery of the same. But not having been admitted into the secret thereof, the unregenerate can form no true concept or estimate of the Christian's experience, and when he hears him exclaiming of the things of God "More are they to be desired than gold, yea, than much fine gold; sweeter also than honey or the honey-comb" (Ps. 19:10), he can but regard such language as wild enthusiasm or fanaticism. The natural man lacks both the power to discern the beauty of spiritual things and a palate to taste their sweetness. Nor is the believer's relish for God's Word confined unto the promises and comforting portions: he also declares "I will delight myself in thy *commandments*, which I have loved" (Ps. 119:47).

The more the believer advances in spiritual acquaintance with the excellency and beauty of heavenly things, the more solid satisfaction do they afford his mind. The more the Christian enters into the importance and value of God's eternal Truth the more his heart is drawn out unto the glorious objects revealed therein. The more that he actually tastes that the Lord is gracious (I Peter 2:3), the more will he delight himself in Him. The more light he is granted upon the sublime mysteries of the Faith, the more will he admire the wondrous wisdom which devised them, the power which executed them, the grace which conveyed them. The more he realizes the Scriptures are the very Word of God Himself, the more he is awed by their solemnity and impressed with their weightiness. The more the ineffable perfections of Deity are revealed to his spirit, the more will he exclaim "Who is like unto thee, O Lord, among the gods [or "mighty ones"], who is like thee, glorious in holiness, fearful in praises, doing wonders!" (Exod. 15:11). And the more his heart is occupied with the person, office, and the work of the Redeemer, the more will he enter into the experience of him who said, "I count all things but loss for the excellency of the knowledge of Christ Jesus my Lord" (Phil. 3:7).

It is true that, through slackness and folly, the believer may to a considerable extent lose his relish for spiritual things, so that his reading of the Word affords him little satisfaction and delight. One who eats and drinks unwisely upsets his stomach, and then the palate no longer finds the choicest food agreeable to him. It is thus spiritually. If the believer be out of communion with God and turns to the world for satisfaction, he loses his appetite for the heavenly manna. Wherefore we are bidden to "lay apart all filthiness and superfluity of naughtiness and receive with meekness the engrafted word" (James 1:21): there must be this "laying apart" before there can be an appreciative reception of the Word. So again I Peter 2:1 shows us that there are certain lusts which have to be mortified if we are to "as new-born babes *desire* the sincere milk of the Word that ye may grow thereby." If such exhortations be duly heeded, and the Word of Christ dwells in us richly, then shall we be found "singing with grace in our hearts to the Lord" (Col. 3:16) with an ever-deepening joy in Him.

IV

3. Spiritual growth consists in *a greater love for God*. When pointing out the various aspects of regeneration (in chap. 6) we quoted Romans 5:5: "the love of God is shed abroad in our hearts by the Holy Spirit which is given unto us." Contrary to the commentators we do not regard the reference there as being to God's love for His people, but rather one of the blessed effects or consequences of the same. First, because the scope and unity of the whole context requires such an interpretation. In 5:1-11 the apostle enumerates the sevenfold result of our being justified by faith: we have peace with God (v. 1), we are established in His favor (v. 2), we rejoice in hope (v. 2), we are enabled to benefit from trials (vv. 3, 4), we have a hope that fails not (v. 5), our hearts are drawn out to God (v. 5), we are assured of final preservation (vv. 6-10). Second, the relation of the second half of v. 5 ("because") to the first leads to the same conclusion: it is *our l*ove to God which furnishes evidence that our hope is a valid one. Third, God's love for us is in Himself, and though manifested unto us could scarcely

be said to be "shed abroad in our hearts." Verse 8 clearly distinguishes His love toward us.

By nature the elect have not one particle of love for God; nay, their very minds are "enmity" against Him (Rom. 8:7). But He does not leave them forever in that fearful state. No, having from eternity set His heart upon them, He has determined to win their hearts unto Himself. And how is that accomplished? By shedding abroad His love in their hearts, which we understand to denote, by communicating from Himself a spiritual principle of love which qualifies and enables them to love Him. Faith is His gift to them (Eph. 2:8), and the evidence of that principle being in them is that they now believe and trust in Him. Hope is also His gift to them (II Thess 2:16), for prior to regeneration we had "no hope" (Eph. 2:12), and the evidence of that principle being in us is that we have a confident expectation of the future. In like manner, love is also a Divine gift, and the evidence of that principle being in an individual is that he now loves God, loves His Christ, loves His image in His people. Note how in Romans 5 we have the Christian's faith (v. 1), hope (vv. 4, 5) and love (v. 5) — which are the three great dynamics and regulators of the Christian life.

This Divine virtue which is communicated to the hearts of all Christians is that which moves their affections to cleave unto God in Christ as their supreme Good. It is designated "the love of God" because *He* is the Bestower of it, because *He* is the Object of it, and because *He* is the Increaser and Perfecter of it. It is first stirred unto action or drawn out to God, then the soul apprehends His love for him, for "we love God because he first loved us" (I John 4:19), for so long as we feared His wrath we hated Him. This particular grace is the one which most affects the others: if the heart be kept right the head will not go far wrong; but when love cools, every grace languishes. Hence we find the apostle praying for the Ephesian saints that they might be "rooted and grounded in love" (3:17). As the Christian grows he learns to love God not only for what He has done for him but chiefly for what He is in Himself — the infinitely glorious One, the Sum of all perfection. Yet our love for Him is easily chilled — through the heart's being turned unto other objects. In fact, of all of our graces this one is the most sensitive and delicate and needs the most cherishing and guarding (Matt. 24:12; Rev. 2:5).

The force of what has just been pointed out appears in that exhortation "keep yourselves in the love of God" (Jude 21). Negatively, that means, avoid everything which would chill and dampen it: careless living soon dulls our sense of God's love. Eschew whatever would grieve the Spirit or thereby give Him occasion to convict us of our sins and occupy us with our waywardness, instead of taking the things of Christ and showing them unto us (John 16:14). Shun the embraces of the world, keeping yourselves from idols (I John 5:21). Positively, it signifies: use the appointed means for keeping your affections warm and lively, set on things above. Familiarize yourself with God's Holy Word, regarding it as a series of letters from your heavenly Father. Cultivate communion with Him by prayer and frequent meditations on His perfections. Keep up a fresh sense of His love for you, sunning your soul in the enjoyment of it. Above all, adhere strictly to the path of obedience. When the Lord Jesus bade us "continue ye in my love" he at once went on to explain how we may do so: "If ye keep my commandments ye *shall* abide in my love; even as I have kept my Father's commandments and abide in his love" (John 15:9, 10; cf. I John 5:3).

A deeper and increasing love for God is not to be ascertained so much by our consciousness of the same as by the evidences it produces. There are many who sing and talk about how much they love Christ, but their walk gives the lie to their avowals. On the other hand there are some who bemoan the feebleness of their love and the coldness of their affections whose lives make it manifest that their hearts are true to Him. Feelings are no safe criterion in this matter: it is conduct which is the surest index to it. Moreover it must be borne in mind that the holiest saint who ever walked this earth, who enjoyed the most intimate fellowship with the Lord, would be the first to acknowledge and bewail the inadequacy of his affection for Him whose love passeth knowledge. Nevertheless there *is* such a thing as a growing love for God in Christ, and the same is demonstrated by a stronger bent of soul toward Him, the mind being more stayed upon Him, the heart enjoying more communion with Him and greater delight in Him, and the conscience increasingly exercised in our care to please Him. The more we are spiritually engaged with God's love for us, the more will our affections to Him be enflamed.

4. Spiritual growth consists of *the strengthening and enlarging of our faith.* Faith is the gift of God (Eph. 2:8), by which is signified that it is a spiritual principle, grace or virtue which He communicates to the hearts of His elect at their regeneration. And as His "talents" are bestowed upon us to trade with, to profit by and increase, so the principle of faith is given us to *use* and employ to the glory of God. Its first act is to believe Christ, trust in Him, and as Colossians 2:6 bids us, "As ye have therefore received Christ Jesus the Lord, so walk ye in Him." This is a most comprehensive and summarized exhortation, and would require many details in order to furnish a full explanation of it. For example, it might be pointed out that the Christian is called upon to walk humbly, dependently, submissively or obediently; yet all of these are included in faith itself. Faith is a humbling and self-emptying grace, for it is the stretching forth of the beggar's hand to receive God's bounty. Faith is an acknowledgment of my own insufficiency and need, a leaning upon One who is mighty to save. Faith is also an act of the will whereby it surrenders to the authority of Christ and receives Him as King to reign over our hearts and lives. Thus, though there is much more in it than this, yet the prime and essential force of Colossians 2:6 is: as ye have become Christians at the first by an act of faith in Christ Jesus the Lord, *continue* trusting in Him and let your life be regulated by faith — "walk" denotes progress or going forward.

In Hebrews 10:38 we are told "now the just shall live by faith." A very elementary statement is that, yet one which is turned into a serious error the moment we tamper with or change its pronoun. We are not justified *because of* our faith, but because of the imputed righteousness of Christ, but that righteousness is not actually reckoned to our account until we believe — instrumentally we are "justified by faith" (Rom. 5:1). Nor are the justified bidden to "live *upon* their faith," though many vainly try to do so. No, the believer is to live upon Christ, yet it is only by faith that he can do so. Let us be as simple as possible: I break my fast with food, yet I partake of that food by means of a spoon. I feed myself, yet it is the food and not the spoon I eat. It was said of Esau, "*by* thy sword shalt thou live" (Gen. 27:40), not *on* thy sword — he could not eat *it*. Esau would live on what his sword brought in. The Christian makes a serious blunder when he attempts to live upon the faith he fancies he can find or feel within himself: rather is he to feed upon the Word, and this he does only so far as his faith is operative — as faith lays hold of and appropriates its holy and blessed contents.

"Now the just shall live by faith" (Heb. 10:28) may well be regarded as the text of the sermon which follows immediately in the next chapter, for in Hebrews 11 we are shown at great length and in considerable variety of detail how the Old Testament saints exercised that God-given principle, how they lived by faith, and wrought great wonders by it. Nothing is there said of their courage, zeal, patience, but all their works and triumphs are attributed to *faith*: the reason for this being that their courage, zeal, and patience were the fruits of faith. As it was with them, so it is with us: we are called to "walk by faith" (II Cor. 5:7) and the extent to which we do so will determine the measure of success or failure we have in our Christian lives. As the Lord Jesus declared unto the two blind beggars who besought His mercy, "according to your *faith* be it unto you" (Matt. 9:29) and to the father of the demon-possessed child "all things are possible to him that believeth" (Mark 9:23). If we are straightened it is not in God but in ourselves, for He ever responds to reliance in and counting upon His intervention. He has expressly promised to honor those who honor Him, and nothing honors Him more than a firm and childlike faith in Him.

"The life which I now live in the flesh, I live by the faith of the Son of God, who loved me and gave himself for me" (Gal. 2:20). Such a testimony from the chief of the apostles shows us the place which faith has in the Christian life. This expression "the faith of the Son of God" signifies that He is the grand *Object* of faith, the One on whom it is to be exercised — which should help the reader to a better understanding of "the love of God" in Romans 5:5 and our remarks thereon. The Christian life is essentially a life of faith, and in proportion as his faith is not operative does he fail to live the Christian life. A life of faith consists of faith being engaged with Christ, drawing on Him, receiving from Him the supply of every need. The life of faith begins by looking to Christ, trusting in Him, relying wholly upon Him as our righteousness before God, and it is continued by looking to and trusting in Him for everything else. Faith is to look to Christ for *wisdom* that we may be able to understand all that He has revealed concerning God, concerning ourselves, salvation, and various duties. Faith is to lay hold of His precepts and appropriate His promises. But more especially, faith is to look to Christ for *strength* to perform His precepts acceptably. As we have no righteousness of our own, so no strength: we are as dependent upon Him for the one as for the other, and each is obtained from Him by *faith*.

But at this most vital point many of the Lord's people have been grievously misled. Under the guise of debasing the creature and exalting Divine grace, they have been made to believe that they are quite helpless in this matter: that as God alone is the Imparter of faith, so He alone is the Increaser of it, and that they have to meekly submit to His will as to the measure of faith He bestows or as to what He withholds from them. The consequence is that so far from their faith increasing, they are for the most part left to spend their remaining days on earth in a state full of doubting and fears. And what is still worse, many of them feel *no blame* or reproach for the feebleness of their faith, but instead, blatantly attribute it to the sovereignty of God. If such people rebuked a godless drunkard for his intemperance, they would be justly shocked were he to reply "God has not given me grace to overcome my thirst"; and yet when they are reproved for their unbelief they virtually charge God with it, by saying that He has not granted them a larger measure of faith. What a wicked slander! What a horrible misuse of the truth of God's sovereign grace! The blame is theirs, and they should honestly acknowledge it and penitently confess it before Him.

It is perfectly true that God is the Increaser as well as the Giver of faith, but it certainly does not follow from this that *we* have no responsibility in the matter. The littleness and weakness of my faith is entirely my own fault: due, not to God's unwillingness to give me more, but to my sinful failure to *use* what He has already given me! to my not crying earnestly unto Him "Lord, increase our faith" (Luke 17:5), and to my woeful neglect in making a proper use of the means He has appointed for my obtaining an increase of it. When the disciples were filled with terror of the tempest and awoke their Master, crying "carest thou not that we perish" (Mark 4:38), He reproved them for their unbelief, saying "Why are ye fearful, O ye of little faith?" (Matt. 8:26): *that* was far from inculcating the deadly delusion that they had no responsibility concerning the measure and strength of their faith! On another occasion He said to His disciples "O fools and slow of heart to believe" (Luke 24:25), which plainly signified that they were to blame for their lack of faith and were to be admonished for their unbelief.

If I have surrendered myself to the Lordship of Christ and trusted in Him as an all-sufficient Saviour, then Christ is *mine*, and I may *know* He is mine upon the infallible authority of God's Word. Since Christ *is* mine, then it is both my privilege and duty to obtain an increasing knowledge of and acquaintance with Him through the Scriptures. It is my privilege and duty to "trust in him at *all* times" (Ps. 62:8), to make known to Him my every need and to count upon Him to graciously supply the same. It is my privilege and duty to make full use of Christ, to live upon Him, to draw from His fulness (John 1:16), to freely avail myself of His sufficiency to meet my every want. It is my privilege and duty to store up His precepts and promises in my memory that the one may direct my conduct and the other support my soul. It is the office of faith to obtain from Him strength for the former and comfort from the latter, *expecting* Him to make good His word "Ask, and ye shall receive; seek, and ye shall find; knock, and it shall be opened unto you" (Matt. 7:7). It is my privilege and duty to "mix faith" (Heb. 4:2) with every recorded sentence that fell from His sacred lips, and according as I do so shall I be "nourished up" (I Tim. 4:6) — my faith will be fed, thrive, and become stronger.

But on the other hand, if I walk by sight, if I constantly take my eyes off their proper Object, and am all the time looking within at my corruptions, I shall go backward and not forward. If I am more concerned about my inward comforts than I am about by outward walk in the pleasing of Christ, in earnestly seeking to follow the example He has left me, then the Holy Spirit will be grieved and will cease taking of the things of Christ and showing them unto me. If I form the habit of attempting to view the promises of God through the darkened and thick lens of my difficulties, instead of looking at my difficulties in the light of God's promises then defeat rather than victory will inevitably follow. If I turn my eyes from my all-sufficient Saviour and am occupied with the winds and waves of my circumstances, then like Peter of old I shall begin to sink. If I do not make it my daily and diligent business to resist the workings of unbelief in my heart and cry out to Christ for strength to enable me to do so, then faith will surely suffer an eclipse, and the fault will be entirely my own. If I neglect feeding upon "the words of faith and good doctrine" (I Tim. 4:6), then my faith will necessarily be weak and languishing.

We say again that the Christian life is a life of *faith*, and just so far as the believer is not actuated by this spiritual principle does he fail at the most vital point. But let it be said very emphatically that a life of faith is not the mystical and nebulous thing which far too many imagine, but an intensely practical one. Nor is it the monopoly of men like George Muller and those who go forth to preach the gospel in foreign lands without any guaranteed salary or belonging to any human organization, trusting God alone for the supply of their every need; rather is it the birthright and privilege of *every* child of God. Nor is it a life made up of ecstasies and rapturous experiences, lived up in the clouds: no, it is to be worked out on the common level of everyday life. The man or woman whose conduct is regulated by the Divine precepts and whose heart is sustained by the Divine promises, who performs his or her ordinary duties as unto the Lord, looking to Him for wisdom, strength and patience for the discharge thereof, and who counts upon His blessing on the same, is living a life of faith as truly as the most zealous and self-sacrificing preacher.

It is true we must be on our guard against unwarrantably exalting the means and making them a substitute for the Lord Himself. The doctrine, the precepts and the promises of Scripture are so many windows through which we are to behold *God*. It is our privilege and duty to look to Him for His blessing upon the means, and since He has appointed the same to count upon Him sanctifying them to us, expecting Him to make them effectual. But we must conclude our remarks upon this point by mentioning some of the *evidences* of a deepening and increasing faith. It is a proof of a stronger and larger faith: when the soul is more established in the truth; when there is a steadier confidence in God; when we make greater use of the promises; when we are less influenced and affected by what other professing Christians believe, resting our souls alone on a "thus saith the Lord" (I Cor. 2:5); when we live more out of ourselves and more upon Christ; when many of His unregenerate disciples are turning away from Christ and He says "Will ye also go away?" and we can answer "to whom shall we go? Thou hast the words of eternal life" (John 6:66-69); when we have become more conscientious and diligent in the performing of our duties, for faith is shown by its works (James 2:8).

5. Spiritual growth consists of *advancing in personal piety*. This matter would be sadly incomplete if we omitted all reference to progress in practical godliness. As various aspects of this will come before us under the next branch of our subject, there is the less need now to enter into much detail. As the Christian obtains an enlarged spiritual apprehension of God's perfections, not only is his heart increasingly affected by His wondrous goodness and grace, but he is more and more awed by His high sovereignty and ineffable holiness, so that he has a deeper reverence for Him and His fear a larger sphere in his heart, ever exerting a more potent influence in his approaches to Him and on his deportment and conduct. In like manner, as the Christian becomes better acquainted with the person, offices, and work of Christ, he obtains not only a fuller realization of how much he owes to Him and what he has in Him, but he is made more and more conscious of what is due unto Him and what becomes one who is a follower of the Lord of glory. The better he realizes that he is "not his own, but bought with a price," the more will he resolve and endeavor to glorify God in Christ "in his body and in his spirit" (I Cor. 6:19, 20), longing more ardently for the time when he will be able to do so without let or hindrance.

5

Its Analogy

I

An "analogy" is an agreement or correspondence in certain respects between things which otherwise differ, and just as it is often an aid to obtaining the force of a word by considering its synonyms, so it frequently helps us to a better understanding of a subject or object to compare it with another and ascertain the analogy between them. This method was frequently used by our Lord in His public teaching, when He likened the "Kingdom of heaven" to a considerable variety of things. The same principle is illustrated by the figurative names which Scripture gives to the people of God. For example, they are called "sheep," and that not only because of the relation which they sustain to Christ their Shepherd, but also because there are many resemblances between the one and the other, God having designed that in different respects this animal more than any other should shadow forth the nature and character of a Christian. Much valuable instruction is obtained by tracing those resemblances. The same Divine wisdom which designated our Saviour both "the Lamb" and "the Lion" was exercised in selecting the various objects and creatures after which His children are figuratively named, and it behooves us to follow out the analogy between them and learn the lessons they are intended in impart.

"That they might be called the *trees* of righteousness, the planting of the Lord" (Isa. 63:1). Both in the Old Testament and in the New this similitude is used of the saints. The Psalmist declared "I am like a green olive tree in the house of God" (52:8) and affirmed "The righteous shall flourish like the palm tree, he shall grow like a cedar in Lebanon. Those that be planted in the house of the Lord shall flourish" (92:12, 13). Our Saviour employed the same figure when He said "Every good tree bringeth forth good fruit," and again, "Either make the tree good and his fruit good, or else make the tree corrupt and his fruit corrupt: for the tree is known by his fruit" (Matt. 7:17; 12:23) — thus every passage where "fruit" is mentioned is also an extension of the same emblem. In Romans 11 the apostle likened the nation of Israel to a "good olive tree" and Christendom to "a wild olive tree" (vv. 24, 17) in connection with their testimony before the world. The Saviour Himself was termed "the Branch of the Lord" and as One who should grow up before him "as a tender plant and as a root out of a dry ground" (Isa. 4:2; 53:2), while He resembled Himself and His people in communion with Him to "the true vine" (John 15:1).

Now it should be obvious from the frequency with which this similitude is used in the Scriptures that it must be a peculiarly instructive one. Some of the more prominent resemblances are quickly apparent. For example, their *attractiveness*. How the countryside and the mountain slopes are beautified by the trees. And what is so lovely in the human realm as those who bear the image of Christ and show forth His praises! They may be despised by the unregenerate, but to an anointed eye God's children are "the excellent of all the earth," and how they be regarded by Him whose workmanship they are is revealed in those words "his *beauty* shall be as the olive tree" (Hos. 14:6). So, too, their *usefulness*. Trees provide a habitation for the birds, shade for the earth, nourishment for the creature, material for building, fuel for the relief of man against the cold. Many, too, are the uses which God makes of His people in this world. Among other things predicated of them, they are "the salt of the earth" — preserving the body politic from going to utter putrefaction.

Before turning to that which bears most closely upon our present theme it should be particularly noted that it is not wild but cultivated trees which is the similitude used. "Blessed is the man that trusteth in the Lord . . . for he shall be like a tree *planted* by the waters" (Jer. 17:7, 8). Observe how frequently this word "planted" occurs: "which the Lord hath planted" (Num. 24:6) and compare Psalm 92:13, 14; 104:16; Isa. 61:3. They are the property of the Heavenly Husbandman (John 15:1; I Cor. 3:7-9) and the objects of His care. That it is which gives such solemn force to our Lord's words "every plant which my heavenly Father hath not planted shall be rooted up" (Matt. 15:13). This figure of the saints being "planted" by God — transferred from one soil or position to another — has at least a threefold reference. First, to God's eternal decree, when He took them out of the creature mass and chose them in Christ (Eph. 1:3). Second, to their regeneration, when He lifts them out of the realm of death and makes them "new creatures in Christ" (II Cor. 5:17). Third, to their translation, when they are removed from earth and planted in His celestial Paradise. But it is the *growth* of "trees" we must now consider.

1. They have the principle of growth *within themselves*. Trees do not grow spontaneously and immediately from external furtherances, but from their own seminal virtue and radical sap. And it is thus with the spiritual growth of Christians. At regeneration a Divine "seed" is planted in his heart (I Peter 1:23; I John 3:9) and that "seed" contains within itself a living principle of growth. We cannot define that "seed" more closely than to say a new life or spiritual nature has been communicated to the one born again. It is that which distinguishes the living children of God from the lifeless profession all around them. The latter may from external influences — such as the appeals and exhortations of preachers, the example of Christians, the natural convictions produced from reading the Word — be induced to perform all the outward duties of Christianity, but since their works issue not from a principle of spiritual life in the soul, they are not

the fruits of holiness. That spiritual principle or Divine grace imparted is described by Christ as "the water" which He gives and which becomes within its possessor "a well of water springing up into everlasting life" (John 4:14). Thus it is the nature of Christians to grow as it is of trees with the seminal principle within them to do likewise. "The tree bearing fruit whose seed is in itself" (Gen. 1:12) — first reference to "trees"!

2. They must be *watered from above*. Though trees have within themselves a vital principle yet they are not independent of provision from their Creator, being far from self-sustaining. Their growth is not something inevitable by virtue of their own seminal power, for in a protracted drought they wither and decay. Hence, when Scripture speaks of the growth of trees it is careful to ascribe it unto God's watering of them. "I will pour water upon him that is thirsty and showers upon the dry ground [interpreted by], I will pour out my Spirit upon thy seed and my blessing upon thine offspring; and they shall spring up as among the grass, as willows by the water courses" (Isa. 44:3, 4). "I will be as the dew unto Israel: he shall grow up as the lily and cast forth his roots as Lebanon" (Hos. 14:5). Only as God waters vegetation will it thrive or even survive. It is so spiritually. The Christian is not self-sufficient and independent of God. Though he has a nature capable of growth, if left to itself that nature would die, for it is only a *creature*, even though a "new creature." Hence the believer needs to be "renewed in the inner man day by day" (II Cor. 4:16).

3. They grow *silently and imperceptibly*. The development of the small sapling into the towering tree is a process veiled in secrecy. "So is the kingdom of God: as if a man cast seed into the ground, and should sleep, and rise night and day, and the seed should spring up and grow, he knoweth not how" (Mark 4:26, 27). The growing of the tree cannot be discerned by the keenest eye, except by the consequences and effects of it. It is equally thus with spiritual growth: it is unrecognizible to either ourselves or others. No matter how closely we observe the markings of our hearts or how introspective becomes our viewpoint, we cannot perceive the actual process. It is seen only by Him by whom it is wrought. Nevertheless it is made manifest by its effects and fruits: in the case of some more clearly than others. But though the process be secret the *means* are plain: in the case of trees — nourishment from the soil, moisture from the clouds, light and heat from the sun. So with the Christian: "meditate on these things, give thyself wholly to them, that thy profiting *may appear* to all" (I Tim. 4:15) — that thy spiritual growth may be evident to those about thee.

4. They grow *gradually*. In the case of some trees it is a very slow experience; with others maturity is reached more quickly. Hence in

one passage the growth of believers is likened unto that of a "cedar" (Ps. 92:12), whereas in another — where a recovered backslider is in view — it is said, "he shall grow as the lily" (Hos. 14:5). But in the majority of cases the development of spiritual life in the saints is a protracted process, being carried on by degrees, or as the prophet expressed it, "For precept must be upon precept, precept upon precept; line upon line, line upon line; here a little and there a little" (Isa. 28:10). Our spiritual growth is produced and promoted by the gracious, wise, patient, and faithful operations of the Holy Spirit. No real Christian is ever satisfied with his growth: far from it, for he is painfully conscious of what little progress he has made and how far short of God's standard he comes. Nevertheless, if he uses the appointed means and avoids the hindrances, he *will* grow. But let us now endeavor to present the analogy more closely.

First, the growth of a tree is *upward*. The vital principle within it is drawn out unto the sun above, attracted by its rays. Though rooted in the earth its nature is to move toward heaven, slowly but surely lifting its head higher and higher. Thus the growth of a tree is ascertained first and may be measured by its *upward progress*. And does not the analogy hold good in the spiritual realm? is it not thus with the saint? It is the very nature of that new life which he received at regeneration to turn unto its Giver. The first evidence of that life being imparted to the soul is his seeking unto God in Christ. The need of Him is now felt; His suitability is now perceived, and the heart is drawn out unto Him. As yet he may not be able intelligently to articulate the newborn desire in his heart, yet if that desire were put into Scriptural language it would be expressed thus: "As the hart panteth after the waterbrooks, so panteth my soul after thee, O God" (Ps. 42:1), for none else can now satisfy the newly-created thirst within him. In view of the last two chapters there is less need for us to develop this at length.

The higher the top of a tree reaches toward heaven the further from the earth does it move. Ponder that, my reader, for it is a parable in action. Before regeneration your heart was wholly set upon this world and what it provides for its devotees; but when your heart was super-naturally illumined and you beheld "the light of the knowledge of the glory of God in the face of Jesus Christ" (II Cor. 4:6) the spell was broken, and you could no longer be content with the perishing baubles which hitherto entralled you. True, the "flesh" may still lust after them, and if you yield to their solicitations your peace and joy will be dampened, and for a season disappointment and sorrow will be your portion; yet there is that within you now that is no longer contented with childish toys and that seeks after the One who bestowed that new nature. It is the normal thing for that spiritual life to grow, and if it does not, you are living far below your privileges. Such upward growth will consist of stronger yearnings after God, more constant and frequent seekings after Him, a closer acquaintance with

Him, a warmer love for Him, more intimate communion with Him, a fuller conformity to Him, and a deeper joy in Him.

As the believer grows Godward His glory becomes more and more his concern and the pleasing of Him in all his ways the main business of his life, so that he performs even common duties with an eye increasingly upon Him. Our personal and experimental knowledge of God increases by our "following on" to know Him (Hos. 6:3), for the more we seek to *do* His will the better we come to understand (John 7:17) and admire the same. Truth is then sealed on the mind, the understanding is more quickened in the fear of the Lord, and our relish of God's ways is intensified. Holy Acts become holy habits and what was at first difficult and irksome becomes easy and pleasant. The more we "exercise ourselves unto godliness" (I Tim. 4:7) the more we are admitted into its secrets. From a dim perception of spiritual mysteries we gradually attain unto "all riches of full assurance of understanding" (Col. 2:2) of them. The more we are weaned from the world, the keener relish do we have for spiritual things and the sweeter do they become to our taste. As God is better known, our love for Him increases and we set a higher esteem on Him, a greater delight in Him is experienced and more and more the heart pants after a full fruition of Him in glory.

Not that the believer ever reaches a point where he is satisfied with his knowledge of God or pleased with his love for Him. There could be no more lamentable proof of spiritual deadness and fatal self-deception than a self-complacent view of our love for God. On the other hand, equally unwarrantable is it to conclude we are not the children of God at all because our love for Him is so feeble and faulty. It is not the love of a natural son for his father which constitutes him his child, though filial love is the proper effect of that relationship. An exalted conception of the character of the parent and of the sacredness of the relationship will render an affectionate child dissatisfied with himself and cause him to declare "I reproach myself daily that I love my father so little, and I can never repay him as I ought." That would be the language of filial relation. Yet he would not be warranted in arguing, Because I do not love him as I ought, I cannot be his child; or because I love him so little, I question very much if he loves me at all." Then why reason thus in connection with our heavenly Father! Summing up this aspect we may say that, the upward growth of a believer is expressed by his heavenly mindedness and the measure in which his affections are set upon things above.

Second, the growth of a tree is *downward*. It takes a firmer hold of the soil. More particularly is that the case in hot countries, for there the tap root of a tree has to penetrate deeper and deeper into the earth in order to find its needed moisture. An allusion to this aspect of our analogy is found in Hosea 14:6 where the Lord promises Israel that he shall "cast forth [or, better, 'strike' — see margin] his roots as Lebanon," that is, as the cedars of Lebanon struck their roots deeper into the mountain slopes — cf. "his smell as Lebanon" in the next verse where the obvious reference is to the fragrant aroma of the cedars. The spiritual counterpart of this is found in such expressions as "being rooted and grounded in love" (Eph. 3:17) and "continue in the faith, grounded and settled" (Col. 1:23), the two things being brought together in "rooted and built up in him and established in the faith" (Col. 2:7), which all speak in the language of our present similitude.

As the believer grows spiritually he takes a firmer grip on Christ and "lays hold on eternal life" (I Tim. 6:12), no longer touching merely "the hem of his garment." He becomes more settled in his knowledge and enjoyment of the Saviour's love and is established more securely in the faith so that he is less liable to be "tossed to and fro and carried about with every wind of doctrine by the slight of men and cunning craftiness whereby they lie in wait to deceive" (Eph. 4:21). The young sapling has but a shallow and feeble grip on the earth and is therefore in greater danger of being uprooted by storms and gales; but the older tree, which has survived the hostile winds, has taken deeper root and is more secure. So it is spiritually; the young Christian is more susceptible to erroneous teachings, but those who are mature and established in the truth discern and refuse human fables. The more we are rooted in the love of Christ, governed by the fear of God, and have His Word dwelling richly in us, the less shall we be swayed by the fear of man, the customs of the world, or the assaults of Satan.

But more specifically: the downward growth of a Christian consists in increasing *humility* or becoming more and more out of love with himself. And this of necessity for in exact ratio to his real growth Godward will be his growth downward. The more we grow upward, that is, the more we take into our renewed minds spiritual apprehensions of the perfections of God, the excellency of the Mediator and the merits of His work, the more are we made conscious of what is due the One and the Other, and the more deeply do we feel what a poor return we have made unto them. If it be something deeper and more influential than a merely speculative or theoretical knowledge of the Father and the Son, if instead we be granted an experimental, vital, and affecting knowledge of them, then shall we be made thoroughly ashamed of ourselves, wholly dissatisfied with our love, our devotion, our conformity to their image. Such knowledge will humble us into the dust, making us painfully sensible of the coldness of our hearts, the feebleness of our graces, the leanness of our souls, and the corruptions which still indwell us.

The more a tree grows downward, the deeper its roots become imbedded in the earth, the more firmly it is fixed and the stronger it becomes, having a greater power to resist the force of the tempest. It is neither the height nor the girth of the tree, but the depths of its roots and its clinging to the ground which gives it stability and security. So it is spiritually. For the believer to grow downward is for him to have less and less confidence in and dependence upon himself:

"when I am weak, then am I strong"; for a consciousness of my weakness causes me to turn more and more unto God and cling to Him. "O our God, wilt thou not judge them, for *we have no might* against this great company that cometh against us; neither know we what to do: but our eyes are *upon thee*" (II Chron. 20:12) — that was the language of one who had grown downward.

II

We have stated that increasing *humility* in a Christian corresponds to the downward growth of a tree. As the upward growth of a tree is accompanied by its becoming more deeply rooted in the ground, so the Christian's acquaintance with, love for, and delight in God, issues in a deeper self-depreciation and self-detestation. If the knowledge we have acquired of the Truth or if what we term our "Christian experience" has made us think more highly of ourselves and better pleased with our attainments and performances, then that is a sure proof we are completely deceived in imagining we have made any real growth upward. The grand design of the Scriptures is to exalt God and humble man, and the more we experimentally or spiritually know God the less we shall think of ourselves and the lower place shall we take before him. The knowledge which "puffeth up" is merely an intellectual or speculative one, but that which the Spirit imparts causes its recipient feelingly to own "I know nothing yet as I ought to know" (I Cor. 8:2).

The more the soul converses with God and the more it perceives His sovereignty and majesty, the more will he exclaim with Abraham, "I am dust and ashes" (Gen. 18:27). The more the believer is granted a spiritual view of the Divine perfections, the more will he acknowledge with Job, "I abhor myself" (42:5). The more the saint apprehends the ineffable holiness of the Lord, the more will he declare with Isaiah, "Woe is me? for I am undone, because I am a man of unclean lips" (6:5). The more he is occupied with the perfections of Christ, the more will he find with Daniel, "my comeliness was turned in me into corruption, and I retained no strength" (10:8). The more he discerns the exalted spirituality of God's law, and how little his inner man is conformed thereto, the more will he groan in concert with Paul, "O wretched man that I am! who shall deliver me from the body of this death" (Rom. 7:24). In God's light we see ourselves, discover the horrible corruptions of our very nature, mourn over the plague of our own heart (I Kings 8:38), and marvel at the continued longsufferance of God unto us.

The truly humble person is not the one who *talks most* of his own unworthiness and is frequently telling of how such and such an experience abased him to the dust. "There are many that are full of expressions of their own vileness, who yet expect to be looked upon as eminent saints by others as their due; and it is dangerous for any so much as to hint the contrary or to carry it towards them any otherwise than as if we looked upon them as some of the chief of Christians. There are many that are much in crying out their wicked hearts and their great shortcomings and unprofitableness, and speaking of themselves as though they looked on themselves as the meanest of the saints; who yet, if a minister should seriously tell them the same things in private, and should signify that he feared they were very low and weak Christians and that they had reason solemnly to consider of their great barrenness and unprofitableness and falling so much short of many others, it would be more than they could digest. They would think themselves highly injured and there would be danger of a rooted prejudice in them against such a minister" (Jonathan Edwards).

The same writer defined evangelical humility as the "sense that a Christian has of his own utter insufficiency, despicableness and odiousness, with an answerable frame of heart." That answerable frame of heart consists of being "poor in spirit," a sense of deep need, a realization of sinfulness and helplessness. The natural man compares himself with his fellows and prides himself that he is at least as good as his neighbors. But the regenerate person measures himself by the exalted standard which God has set before him, and which is perfectly exemplified in the example Christ has left him that he should "follow His steps"; and as he discovers how lamentably he falls short of that standard and how "far off" he follows Christ, he is filled with shame and contrition. This empties him of self-righteousness and causes him to depend wholly on the finished work of Christ. It makes him conscious of his weakness and fearful that he will suffer a sad fall, and therefore he looks above for help and cries, "Hold thou me up and I shall be safe" (Ps. 119: 117). Thus the truly humble person is the one who lives most outside of himself on Christ.

This brings us to those oft-quoted but we fear little-understood words, "grow in grace" (II Peter 3:18). Growth in grace is only too frequently confused with the development of the Christian's *graces*. That is why we selected a different title for this book than the one commonly accorded the subject. Growth in grace is but one aspect or part of spiritual growth and Christian progress. When a minister asked a simple countryside woman what was her concept of "growing in grace," she replied, "A Christian's growth in grace is like the growth of a cow's tail." Puzzled at her reply, he asked for an explanation. Whereupon she said, "The more a cow's tail grows, the nearer it comes to the ground; and the more a Christian grows in grace, the more does he take his place in the dust before God." Ah, she had been taught from above something with which many an eminent theologian and commentator is unacquainted. Growth in grace is a growth *downward*: it is the forming of a lower estimate of ourselves; it is a deepening realization of our nothingness; it is a heartfelt recognition that we are not worthy of the least of God's mercies.

What is it to enter into a personal experience of saving grace? Is it not a feeling my deep *need* of Christ and the consequent perception of His perfect suitability to my desperate case? — to be acutely conscious that I am "sick" in soul and the betaking of myself to the great "Physician"? If so, then must not any advancement in grace consist of an intensification of the same experience, a clearer and fuller realization of my need of Christ? And such growth in grace results from a closer acquaintance and fellowship with Him: "Grace and peace be multiplied unto you through the knowledge of God and of Jesus our Lord" (II Peter 1:2) — that is, a vital practical, effectual knowledge of Him. In His light we see light: we become better acquainted with ourselves, more aware of our total depravity, more conscious of the workings of our corruptions. Grace is favor shown to the undeserving; and the more we grow in grace the more we perceive our undeservingness, the more we feel our need of grace, the more sensible we are of our indebtedness to the God of all grace. Thereby are we taught to walk with God and to make more and more use of Christ.

Every Christian reader will agree that if ever there was one child of God who more than others "grew in grace" it was the apostle Paul; and yet observe how he said "Not that we are sufficient of ourselves, to *think anything* as of ourselves" (II Cor. 3:5); and again, "by the grace of God I am what I am" (I Cor. 15:10). What breathings of humility were those! But we can appeal to an infinitely higher and more perfect example. Of the Lord Jesus it is said that He was "*full* of grace and truth" (John 1:14), and yet He declared "Take my yoke upon you and learn of me, for I am meek and lowly in heart" (Matt. 11:29). Does the reader detect a slip of the pen in the last sentence? Since Christ was "full of grace and truth" we should have said "*therefore* [and not 'yet'] he declared, 'learn of me, for I am meek and lowly in heart' " — the latter was the evidence of the former! Yes, so "meek and lowly in heart" was He that, though the Lord of glory, He declined not to perform the menial task of washing the feet of His disciples! And in proportion as we learn of Him shall *we* become meek and lowly in heart. Hence "and the knowledge of our Lord Jesus Christ" is explanatory of "grow in grace" in II Peter 3:18.

True humility dwells only in a heart which has been supernaturally enlightened of God and which has experimentally learned of Christ, and the more the soul learns of Christ the more lowly will it become. Even in natural things it is the novice and not the savant who is the most conceited. A smattering of the arts and sciences fills its youthful possessor with an exalted estimate of his wisdom, but the further he prosecutes his studies the more conscious will he become of his ignorance. Much more so is this the case with spiritual things. An unregenerate person who becomes familiar with the letter of the Truth imagines he has made great progress in religion; but a regenerate person even after fifty years in the school of Christ deems himself a very babe in spirituality. The more a soul grows in grace, the more does he grow out of love with himself. In one of his early epistles Paul said, "I am the least of the apostles" (I Cor. 15:9); in a later, "who am less than the least of all saints" (Eph. 3:8); in one of his last, "sinners, of whom I am chief" (I Tim. 1:15)!

Third, trees grow *inwardly*. This brings us to what is admittedly the hardest part of our subject. We have never made a study of botany, and even though we had it is doubtful if it would stand us in much stead on this point. That there must be an inward growth of the tree is obvious, though exactly what it consists of is another matter. Yet that need not surprise us, for if the analogy holds good here too, is not this uncertainty just what we should expect? Is not the inward growth of a Christian that aspect of his progress which is the most difficult to define, desribe, and still more so to put into practice? Unless the tree grows inwardly it would not grow in any other direction, for its outward growth is but the development and manifestation of its vital or seminal principle. We must fall back then on general principles and exercise a little common sense, and say: the inward growth of a tree consists of an increase of its sap, a resisting of that which would injure, and the toughening of its tissues.

The sap is the vital juice of all plants and its free circulation the determiner of its health and growth. The analogy of this in the Christian is the grace of God communicated to his soul, and his spiritual progress is fundamentally determined by his receiving fresh supplies of grace. At regeneration God does not impart to us a supply of grace sufficient for the remainder of our lives: instead, He has made Christ to be the grand Fountain of all grace, and we are required to continue betaking ourselves to Him for fresh supplies. The Lord Jesus has issued a free invitation: "If any man thirst, let him come unto me, and drink" (John 7: 37), which must not be restricted to our first approach. As long as the Christian remains on earth he is as needy as when he drew his first spiritual breath, and his need is supplied in no other way than by his coming to Christ daily for fresh supplies of His grace. Christ is "full of grace," and that fulness is *available* for His people to draw from (Heb. 4:16). "He giveth more grace . . . unto the humble" (James 4:6), that is, to those who "thirst," who are conscious of their need and who present themselves as empty vessels to be replenished.

But there is another principle which operates and regulates our obtaining further supplies of grace: "For unto every one that hath shall be given and he shall have abundance" (Matt. 25:29; cf. Luke 8:18). The context shows that the one who "hath" is he who has traded with what had been bestowed upon him: in other words, the way to obtain more grace is to make a right and good *use* of what we *already* have. Why should Christ give more if we have not improved what He previously communicated? Faith becomes stronger by exercising it. And *how* does the Christian make a good use of grace? By heeding that all-important injunction, "Keep thy heart with all diligence, for out of it are the issues of life" (Prov. 4:23). *This* is the great task which God has assigned to each of His children. The "heart" signifies the whole inner man — the "hidden man of the heart" (I Peter 3:4). It is that which controls and gives character to all that we become and do. The man is what his heart is, for "as he thinketh in his heart, so is he" (Prov. 23:7). To guard and garrison the heart is the grand work God has appointed us: the enablement is His, but the duty is ours.

Negatively, the keeping of the heart with all diligence signifies, excluding from it all that is opposed to God. It means keeping the imagination free from vanity, the understanding from error, the will from perverseness, the conscience clear from all guilt, the affections from being inordinate and set on evil objects, the inner man from being dominated by sin and Satan. In a word it means, to *mortify* the "flesh" within us, with all its affections and lusts; to resist evil imaginations, nipping them in the bud; to strive against the swellings of pride, the workings of unbelief; to swim against the tide of the world; to reject the solicitations of the Devil. This is to be our constant concern and ceaseless endeavor. It means to keep the conscience tender to sin in its first approach. It means looking diligently after its cleansing when it has been defiled. For all of this much prayer is required, earnest seeking of God's assistance, His supernatural aid; and if it be sought trustfully it will not be sought in vain, for it is the grace of God which teaches us to *deny* "ungodliness and worldly lusts" (Titus 2:11, 12).

Positively, the keeping of our hearts with all diligence signifies, the cultivation of our spiritual graces — called "the fruit of the spirit" (Gal. 5:22, 23). For the health, vigor, exercise and manifestation of those graces we are accountable. They are like so many tender plants which will not thrive unless they are given much attention. They are like so many tendrils on a vine which must be lifted from trailing on the ground, pruned and sprayed, if they are to be fruitful. They are like so many saplings in the nursery which need rich soil, regular watering, the warmth of the sun, if they are to thrive. Go carefully over the ninefold list given in Galatians 5:22, 23 and then honestly ask the question, What sincere effort am I really making to cultivate, to foster, to develop those graces? Compare too the sevenfold list of II Peter 1:5-7 and put to yourself a similar inquiry. When your graces are lively and flourishing and Christ draws near, you will be able to say "my Beloved is gone down into his garden to the beds of spices, to feed in the gardens and to gather lilies" (Song of Sol. 6:2). God esteems nothing so highly as holy faith, unfeigned love, and filial fear (cf. I Peter 3:4; I Tim. 1:5).

"Man looketh on the outward appearance, but the Lord looketh on the heart" (I Sam. 16:7). Is that sufficiently realized by us? If it is, then we are making it our chief concern to keep our hearts with all diligence. "My son, give me thine *heart*" (Prov. 23:26): until *that* be done, God will accept nothing from you. The prayers and praises of our lips, the offerings and labors of our hands, yea, a correct outward walk, are things of no value in His sight unless the heart beats true to Him. Nor will He accept a divided heart. And if I *have* really given Him my heart, then it is to be *kept* for Him, it must be devoted to Him, it must be suited to Him. Ah, my reader, there is much head religion, much hand religion — busily engaged in what is termed "Christian service," and much feet religion — rushing around from one meeting, "Bible Conference," "Communion" to another, but where are those who make conscience of keeping their *hearts*! The heart of the empty professor is like the vineyard of "the man void of [spiritual] understanding," namely, "all grown over with thorns, and nettles had covered the face thereof" (Prov. 24:30, 31).

A very few words must suffice upon the third aspect of inward growth. In the case of a tree this consists in the toughening of its tissues or strengthening of its fibers — apparent from the harder wood obtained from an older one than from a sapling. The spiritual counterpart of that is found in the Christian attaining more firmness and fixedness of character, so that he is no longer swayed by the opinions of others. He becomes more stable, so that he is less emotional; and more rational, acting not from sudden impulse but from settled principle. He becomes wiser in spiritual things because his mind is increasingly engaged with the Word of God and his eternal concerns, and therefore more serious and sober in his demeanor. He becomes confirmed in doctrine and therefore more discerning and discriminating in whom he hears and what he reads. Nothing can move him from allegiance to Christ, and having bought the Truth he refuses to sell it (Prov. 23:23). He is not afraid of being called a bigot, for he has discovered that "liberality" is emblazoned prominently on the Devil's banner.

Fourth, the growth of a tree is *outward,* seen in the spreading of its boughs and the multiplication of its branches. We have purposely devoted a greater space to those aspects of our subject on which we felt the reader most needed help. This one almost explains itself: it is the *daily walk* of the believer, his external conduct, which is in view. If the Christian has grown upward — that is, if he has obtained an increased vital and practical knowledge of God in Christ; if he has grown downward — that is, if he has become thoroughly aware of his total depravity by nature and learned to have "no confidence in the flesh" (Phil. 3:3) to effect any improvement in himself; if he has grown inwardly — obtained fresh supplies of grace from Christ and has diligently used the same by striving against indwelling sin and by resolutely resisting his carnal and worldly lusts, and if he has improved that grace by diligently cultivating his spiritual graces in the garden of his heart; then that upward, downward, and inward growth will be (not simply "ought to be"), *must be,* clearly and unmistakably shown in his outward life.

And how will that upward, downward, and inward growth be manifested by the Christian outwardly? Why, by a life of *obedience* to his Lord and Saviour. Out of love and gratitude unto the One who suffered and did so much for him, he will sincerely endeavor to please Him in all his ways. Realizing that he is not his own but bought with a price, he will make it his highest aim and earnest endeavor to glorify God in his body and in his spirit (I Cor. 6:19, 20). The genuineness of his desire to please God and the intensity of his purpose to glorify Him, will be evidenced by the diligence and constancy with which he reads, meditates upon and studies His Word. In searching the Scriptures his main quest will not be to occupy his mind with its mysteries, but rather to obtain a fuller knowledge of God's *will for him;* and instead of hankering after an insight into its typology or its prophecies he will be far more concerned in how to become *more proficient* in performing God's will. It is in the light of His Word he longs to walk, and therefore it is His precepts and promises, His warnings and admonitions, His exhortations and aids, he will most lay to heart.

One of the New Testament exhortations is, "We request you, brethren, and beseech you by the Lord Jesus, that as ye have received of us how ye ought to walk and please God, so ye would *abound more and more*" (I Thess. 4:1). One of its prayers is, "That ye might be filled with a knowledge of his will in all wisdom and spiritual understanding: that ye might walk worthy of the Lord *unto all pleasing*, being fruitful in every good work" (Col. 1:9, 10). One of its promises is, "God is able to make all grace abound toward you, that ye always having all sufficiency in all things, *may abound* in every good work" (II Cor. 9:8). And one of its examples is, "And they [the parents of John the Baptist] were both righteous before God, walking in *all* commandments and ordinances of the law *blameless*" (Luke 1:6). In the light of those verses — each of which treats with outward growth — our duty and privilege is clear: what God requires from us and the sufficiency of His enablement for the same.

6

Its Seasonableness

"To everything there is a season, and a time to every purpose under the heaven. . . . He hath made everything beautiful in his time" (Eccles. 3:1, 11). If the whole of these eleven verses be read consecutively it will be seen that they furnish a full outline of the many and different experiences of human life in this world, each aspect of man's varied career and his reactions thereto being stated. That which is emphasized in connection with all the mutations and vicissitudes of life is that they are all ordained and regulated by God, according to His unerring wisdom. Not only has He appointed a time to every purpose under heaven, but "everything is beautiful *in* his time." Nothing is too early, nothing too late. Everything is perfectly co-ordinated, and as we learn from the New Testament made to "work together for good to them that love God, to them who are the called according to his purpose" (Rom. 8:28).

There is a predestined time when each creature and each event shall come forth, how long it shall continue, and in what circumstances it shall be: all being determined by the Lord. This is true of the world as a whole, for God "worketh all things after the counsel of his own will" (Eph. 3:11). This earth has not always existed. God was the One who decided when it should spring into being, and He created it by a mere fiat: "For he spake, and it was done; he commanded, and it stood fast" (Ps. 33:9). Nor will it last forever, for the hour is coming when its very elements "shall melt with fervent heat, the earth also and the works that are therein shall be burned up" (II Peter 3:10). How far distant, or how near, that solemn hour is, no creature has any means of knowing; yet the precise day for it is unchangeably fixed in the Divine decree.

The same grand truth which pertains to the whole of creation applies with equal force to all the workings of Divine Providence. The beginning and the end, and the whole intervening career, of each person has been determined by his Maker. So too the rise, the progress, the height attained, and the entire history of each nation has been foreordained of God. "For of him, and through him, and to him are *all* things, to whom be glory forever. Amen" (Rom. 11:36). A nation is but the aggregate of individuals comprising it; and though its corporate life be much longer than of any one generation of its members, yet it is subject to the same Divine laws. Each kingdom, each empire, has its birth and development, its maturity and zenith, its decline and

death. The Egyptian had; so had the Babylonian, Medo-Persian, Gre-
cian, and Roman.

What is stated in Ecclesiastes 3:1, 11 holds good of things in the
spiritual realm, equally so with those in the material sphere, though
we are more apt to forget this in connection with the former than
with the latter. It is a fact that in the Christian life "To everything
there is *a season* and a time to every purpose under the heaven." How
can it be otherwise seeing that the God of creation, the God of providence and the God of all grace is one. It is true there is much in
the Divine operations both in Providence and in Grace which is profoundly mysterious, for "great things doeth he which we cannot comprehend" (Job 37:5). Yet not a little light is cast upon those higher
mysteries if we seek to observe the ways and workings of God *in Nature.*
How often the Lord Jesus made use of that principle, directing the
attention of His hearers to the most familiar objects in the physical
realm.

Again and again we find the Divine Teacher using the things growing in the field to illustrate and adumbrate the things which are invisible and to inculcate lessons of spiritual value. "*Consider* the lilies."
Not only look upon and admire them, but receive instruction therefrom. "Learn a parable of the fig tree" (Matt. 24:32). Yes, *learn* from
it: ponder it, let it inform you about spiritual matters. When Christ
insisted on the inseparable connection there is between character and
conduct, He employed the similitude of a tree being known by its
fruit. When He urged the necessity of new hearts for the reception
of new covenant blessings, He spoke of new bottles for new wine.
When He revealed the essential conditions of spiritual fruitfulness, He
mentioned the vine and its branches. Yes, there is much in the material world from which we may learn valuable lessons on the spiritual
life.

Take the seasons which God has appointed for the year and how
each brings forth accordingly. The coldness and barrenness of the
winter gives place to the warmth and fertility of the spring, while the
vegetables and fruit which sprout in the spring and grow through the
summer are matured in the autumn. Each season has its own peculiar
features and characteristic products. The same principle is seen operating
in a human being. The life of man is divided into distinct seasons or
stages: childhood, youth, maturity and old age; and each of those
stages is marked by characteristic features: the innocence and shyness
of (normal) children, the zeal and vigor of youth, the stability and
endurance of maturity, the experience and wisdom of old age; and each
of these distinctive features is "beautiful in its time."

Not only has God appointed the particular seasons when each of His
creatures shall come forth and flourish, but we are obliged to *wait*
His set time for the same. If we sow seeds in the winter they will
not germinate. Plants which sprout in the spring cannot be forced, but
have to wait for the summer's sun. So it is in the human realm. "To
everything there is a season and a time to every purpose under the

heaven." We cannot put old heads on young shoulders, and such efforts will not only prove unsuccessful but issue in disastrous consequences. As everything is "beautiful *in* his time" they are incongruous and unseemly *out* of season. "When I was a child, I spake as a child . . . I reasoned as a child, but when I became a man, I put away childish things" (I Cor. 13:11).

In the light of what has been said it is both interesting and instructive to ponder the ways of God with His people during the Old Testament and New Testament eras. Much of that which obtained under the Mosaic dispensation was suited to that infantile period and was "beautiful in his time"; but now that "the fulness of time" has come such things would be quite out of place. During that kindergarten stage God instituted an elaborate ritual which appealed to the senses, and instructed by means of pictures and symbols. There was the colorful tabernacle, the priestly vestments, the burning of incense, the playing of instruments. They were all invested with a typical significance, but when the Substance appeared there was no further need of them: they had become obsolete, and to bring forward such things into Christian worship is an unseasonable lapsing back to the nursery stage.

All that has been pointed out above is most pertinent to the spiritual growth of the individual Christian, and particularly to the several *stages* of his development or progress, and if duly attended to should preserve from many mistaken notions and erroneous conclusions. As the year is divided into different seasons so the Christian life has different stages, and as there are certain features which more or less characterize the year's seasons so there are certain experiences more or less peculiar to each stage in the Christian life; and as each of the year's seasons is marked by a decided *change* in what the garden and the orchard then bring forth, so there is a variation and alteration in the graces manifested and the fruits borne by the Christian during the several stages through which he passes; but "everything is beautiful in his time" — as it would be incongruous out of its season.

Now though the earth's seasons are four in number, yet only three of them are concerned with fertility or production. The analogy pertains spiritually: in the Christian life there is a spring, a summer, and an autumn — the "winter" is when his body has been committed to the grave in sure and certain hope of resurrection, awaiting the eternal Spring. Thus we should expect to find that the more explicit teaching of the New Testament divides the spiritual life of the saint on earth into three stages; and such is indeed the case. In one of his parables of the kingdom of God, Christ used the similitude of a man casting seed into the ground (a figure of preaching the gospel), saying "The earth bringeth forth of herself: first the blade, then the ear, after that the full corn in the ear" (Mark 4:28): *there* are the three stages of growth. In like manner we find the apostle grading those to whom he wrote into three classes, namely, "fathers," "young men," and "little children" (I John 2:13).

Nothing which lives is brought to maturity immediately in this lower world: instead, everything advances by gradual growth and orderly progress. God indeed created Adam and Eve in their full perfection, but He does not regenerate us into our complete stature in Christ. All the parts and faculties of the new man come into being at the new birth, but time is needed for their development and manifestation. Moreover, as natural talents are not bestowed uniformly — to some being given five, to others two, and to yet others only one (Matt. 25:15), so God bestows a greater measure of grace to one of His people than to another. There is therefore a great difference among Christians: all are not of one stature, strength, and growth in godliness. Some are "sheep" and others but "lambs" (John 21:15, 16). Some are "strong others are "weak" (Rom. 15:1). Some are but "babes," and others are of "full age" Heb. 5:13, 14). Nevertheless, each brings forth fruit "in his season" (Ps. 1:3).

If more attention were paid to the principles which we have sought to enunciate and illustrate, some of us would be preserved from forming harsh judgments of our younger brethren and sisters and from criticizing them because they do not exercise those graces and bear those fruits which pertain more to the stage of Christian maturity. One would instantly perceive the folly of a farmer who complained because his field of grain bore no golden ears during the early months of spring: equally senseless and sinful is it to blame a babe in Christ because he has neither the mature judgment nor the patience of an experienced and long-tried believer. To that statement every spiritual reader will readily assent: yet we very much fear that some of these very persons are guilty of the same thing in another direction — *selfward*: reproaching themselves in later life because they lack the glow and ardor, the zeal and zest which formerly characterized them.

Some older Christians look back and compare themselves with the days of their spiritual youth and then utter hard things against themselves, concluding that so far from having advanced, they have retrograded. In certain cases their lamentations are justifiable, as with Solomon. But in many instances they are not warrantable, being occasioned by a wrong standard of measurement and through failing to bear in mind the seasonableness or unseasonableness of certain fruits at particular times. They complain now because they lack the liveliness of earlier days, when they had warmer affections for Christ and His people, more joy in reading the Word and prayer, more zeal in seeking to promote the good of others, more fruit for their labors. They complain that though they now spend more time in using the means of grace, others who are but spiritual babes appear to derive far greater benefit though less diligent in duties than they are.

In some cases where conversion has been more radical and clearly marked, growth is more easily perceived; but where conversion itself was a quiet and gradual experience, it is much more difficult to trace out the subsequent progress that is made. As the Christian obtains more light from God he becomes increasingly aware of his filth, and by apprehensions of his decrease he will increase in humility. As spiritual wisdom increases he measures himself by a *higher* standard, and thus becomes more conscious of his comings short thereof. Formerly he was more occupied with his outward walk, but now he is more diligent in seeking to discipline his heart. In earlier years there may have been more fervor in his prayers; but now his petitions should be more spiritual. As the Christian grows spiritually his desires enlarge and because his attainments do not keep pace he is apt to err in his judgment of himself: "there is that maketh poor, yet hath great riches" (Prov. 13:7)!

Young Christians are generally more enthusiastic and active, yet their zeal is not always according to knowledge, and at times it is unseasonable through neglecting temporal affairs for spiritual. A young Christian is ready to respond to almost any plausible appeal for money, but a mature one is more cautious before he acts lest he should be supporting enemies of the Truth. The older Christian may not perform some duties with the same zest as formerly, yet with more conscience: quality rather than quantity is what now most concerns him. As we grow older, greater and more difficulties are encountered, and the overcoming of them evidences that we have a larger measure of grace. Particular graces may not be as conspicuous as previously, and yet the exercise of new ones be more evident (II Peter 1:5-7). Measure not your growth by any one part of your life, nor by any single aspect of it, but by your Christian career as a whole.

It is by no means a simple matter to accurately classify believers as to which particular grade or class they belong to in the school of Christ, either concerning ourselves or others, for spiritual growth is rarely *uniform* — though it ought to be so. Some Christians are weak and strong at one and the same time, yet in different respects, as both experience and observation show. Some have better heads than hearts, while others have sounder hearts than heads. Some are weak in knowledge, ignorant and unsettled in the Faith, who nevertheless put to shame their better-instructed brethren by their love and zeal, and by their walk and fruitfulness. Others have a good understanding of the Truth but are veritable babes when it comes to putting it into practice. Solomon was endued with great wisdom, but ruined his testimony through yielding to fleshly lusts. "A Christian should labor for a good heart well-headed, and a head well-hearted" (Thos. Manton).

Again; it needs to be borne in mind that there are great differences in the same Christian at sundry times, yea within a single season, so that the three stages of spiritual growth may coincide in a single saint. The maturest "father" in some respects may be as weak as a new born "babe" in other regards, and tempted as violently as the "young men." The case of the godliest man is not always uniform. One day he may be rapt into the holy mount to behold Christ in His glory; and the same evening he may be tossed with winds and waves, and in his feelings be like a ship on the point of sinking. Now he may, like Paul, be caught up into Paradise and favored with revelations which he cannot express to others, and anon be afflicted with a thorn in the flesh, the messenger of Satan to buffet him. Calms and storms, peace and troubles, combats and conquests, weakness and strength, alternate in the lives of God's people; yet in each they may bring forth fruit which is "beautiful in his time."

All that has been dwelt upon above may appear to some of our readers as being so elementary and obvious that there was really no need to point out the same. Though that be the case, there are others who at least require to be reminded there. It is not so much our knowledge but the *use* we make of it that counts the most; and often our worst failures issue not from ignorance but from acting contrary to the light we have. A due recognition of the seasonableness or unseasonableness of particular spiritual fruits in the Christian life will preserve from many wrong conclusions. On the one hand it should keep him from expecting to find in a spiritual babe those fruits and developed graces which pertain to a state of maturity, and on the other hand he who regards himself as a "father" in Christ must vindicate that estimation by bringing forth far more than do young Christians.

II

The leading principle which we sought to enunciate and illustrate, namely, fruit suitable to the season, receives exemplification in that statement, "A word spoken in due season, how good is it!" (Prov. 15:23): a word of sympathy to one in trouble, of encouragement to the despondent, of warning to the careless. Hence we find the minister of Christ exhorted, "Preach the word: be instant in season, out of season; reprove, rebuke, exhort, with all longsuffering and doctrine" (II Tim. 4:2) — by the "in season, out of season" we understand, at stated times and as opportunity occurs. The same principle was exemplified by the Baptist when he said, "Bring forth therefore fruits meet for repentance" (Matt. 3:8) — praising God for His mercies at that time would have been unseasonable, rather was godly sorrow for the abuse of them called for. "There is a time to weep, and a time to laugh" (Eccles. 3:4).

Fruitfulness is an essential quality of a godly person, but his fruit should be *seasonable*. A time of suffering calls for self-examination, confession, and the exercise of patience. A season of testing and trial requires the exercise of faith and courage. When blest with revivings and spiritual prosperity, holy joy and praise are becoming. It is written "Therefore will the Lord wait that he may be gracious . . . blessed are all they that wait for him" (Isa. 30:18) — wait for the time He has appointed for the development and manifestation of particular graces. Unseasonable graces are like untimely figs, which are never full flavored. Most of us are too impatient. "No chastening for the *present* seemeth to be joyous, but grievous . . . nevertheless *afterward* it yieldeth the peaceable fruit of righteousness unto them which are *exercised* thereby" (Heb. 12:11) — exercised in conscience as to what has given occasion for the chastisement, exercising faith for the fulfilling of this promise, and patience while awaiting the same.

As we turn now to look at the characteristics which mark the three stages of the Christian life, it must be borne in mind: (1) we are not to understand that what is predicated of the "fathers" in nowise pertains to the "babes," but rather that the particular grace ascribed abounds in the former more eminently. (2) That what is said of each of the three may, in different respects, belong to a single Christian, so that "young men" who are "strong" may in another way, be as weak as the "babes." (3) We must not lose sight of God's liberty in apportioning His grace as and when He pleases: He works not uniformly, and causes some of His people to make much more rapid progress than others during the earlier years of their Christian lives, while others who seem slow at the start overtake and pass them at a later stage.

"I write unto you little children (*teknia*) because your sins are forgiven you for His name's sake" (I John 2:12). "I write unto you fathers, because ye have known him that is from the beginning. I write unto you young men, because ye have overcome the wicked one. I write unto you little children (*paidia*) because ye have known the Father" (I John 2:13). This is the classical passage on the present aspect of our theme, though its force is somewhat obscured through the translators making no distinction between the two different Greek words they have rendered "little children." I John 2:12 pertains to the whole of the "called" family of God irrespective of growth or attainment, for every believer has had his sins forgiven him for Christ's sake. The word used there for "little children" is a term of *endearment*, and was employed by Christ in John 13:33 when addressing the apostles, and occurs again in this epistle in 2:28; 3:7 etc.

Only in I John 2:13 are believers graded into three distinct classes according to the degrees of their spiritual progress: "fathers," "young men," and "little children" — or preferably "babes," to mark the distinction from the word used in verse 12. That is the order of dignity and responsibility: had it been the order of *grace*, it had been "babes, young men and fathers." As some one has said "If Christ were to enter a Christian gathering for the purpose of showing forth His favor, He would commence with the youngest and feeblest one present; but if to judge the works of His servants, He would begin with the maturest saint." For example, Christ appeared many times after His resurrection: He ended by manifesting Himself to the apostle Paul, but with whom did He begin? — with Mary Magdalene out of whom He had cast seven demons! The same principle is illustrated in the parable of the "pence" (grace) — beginning with the eleventh-hour laborer; but reversed in the parable of the "talents," where *responsibility* is in view.

As we are writing on the subject of spiritual progress, or as most writers designate it "growth in grace," we propose to inverse the order of I John 2:13 and consider first the spiritual *babes*. If any one should consider we are taking an unwarrantable liberty with the Word in so doing, we would appeal to Mark 4:28, where our Lord spoke of "first the blade, then the ear, after that the full corn in the ear." And now as we seek to grapple more closely with our present task we have to acknowledge we experience considerable difficulty in attempting to set forth with any measure of definiteness what it is which specially marks the spiritual "babe" in contrast from the "young men" and "fathers," or if others prefer, that which distinguishes the "blade," from the "ear," and "the full corn in the ear." But if we cannot satisfy our readers, we trust that we may be kept from confusing any of them.

In view of the vastly superior conditions which obtained in the days of the apostles — illustrated by such passages as Acts 2:44, 45; 11: 19-21; I Corinthians 12:8-11 — it is not to be supposed that many of the features which marked that glorious period will be reproduced in a "day of small things" (Zech. 4:10) such as that in which we are now living. The line of demarcation between the church and the world was much more plainly drawn then than it is now; the contrast between lifeless and living professors more easily perceived, and so on. Therefore it is reasonable to conclude that the distinct stages of the Christian life and the different forms which believers occupied in the school of Christ, were then more plainly marked; and though the difference be one of degree rather than of kind, yet that very difference renders it the more difficult for us to describe or identify the several grades.

In his most excellent "Letters on Religious Subjects" John Newton has three pieces entitled "Grace in the Blade," "Grace in the Ear," "Grace in the Full Corn." He began his second piece by saying "The manner of the Lord's work in the hearts of His people is not easily traced, though the fact is certain and the evidence demonstrable from Scripture. In attempting to explain we can only speak in general, and are at a loss to form such a description as shall take in the immense variety of cases which occur in the experience of believers." It is just because so many preachers have failed to take into their account that "immense variety of cases," and instead, have pictured the experience of conversion as though it were cast in a *uniform* mold, that numbers of their hearers and readers have been much stumbled, fearing they were never truly converted because their experience differed widely from that described by the preacher.

George Whitefield stated, "I have heard of a person who was in a company with fourteen ministers of the Gospel, some of whom were eminent servants of Christ, and yet not one of them could tell the time when God first manifested Himself to their soul." Then he went on to say to his hearers and readers, "We do not love the pope, because we love to be popes ourselves, and set up our own experience as a standard to others. Those that had such a conversion as the Philippian jailor or the Jews on the day of Pentecost may say, You are not Christians at all because you had not the like terrible experience. You may as well say to your neighbor, You have not had a child, for you were not in labor all night. The question is, whether a real child is born: not how long was the preceding pain, but whether it was productive of the new birth and whether Christ has been formed in your hearts!"

Some are likely to object to what is said above and say, Though the circumstantials of conversion may vary in different cases, yet the essentials are the same in all: the law must do its work before the soul is prepared for the gospel, the heart must be made sensible for its sickness before it will betake itself unto the great Physician. Even though that should be the experience of many of the saints, yet the Holy Spirit is by no means tied down to that order of things, nor do the Scriptures warrant any such restricted view. Take the cases of Peter and Andrew, his brother, and the two sons of Zebedee (Matt. 4:18-22), and there is nothing in the sacred narrative to show that *they* went through a season of conviction of sin before they followed Christ! Nor was there in the case of Matthew (9:9). Zaccheus was apparently attracted by mere curiosity to obtain a sight of the Lord Jesus, and a work of grace was wrought in his heart immediately, and he "received him *joyfully*" (Luke 19:6)!

Let us not be misunderstood at this point. We are neither casting any reflection upon those ministers who preach the law by which a knowledge of sin is obtained (Rom. 3:20), nor disparaging the importance and necessity of conviction of sin. Rather are we insisting that God is perfectly free to work as He pleases, and that I have no Scriptural reason to doubt the reality of my conversion simply because my heart was then melted by a sense of God's wondrous *love,* rather than awed by a discovery of His holiness or terrified by a realization of His wrath; and that I have no warrant to call into question the genuineness of another's conversion merely because it was not cast in a certain mold. The all-important thing is whether the subsequent walk evidences that I have passed from death unto life. In Zechariah 12:10 "mourning" *follows* and not precedes a saving looking upon Christ! There are some who taste the bitterness of sin more sharply after conversion than they did before.

Now as the Holy Spirit is pleased to use different means in connection with the converting of souls, so also there is real variety in the experiences of those newly brought to a saving knowledge of the Truth. On the other hand, as there are certain essentials found in every genuine conversion — the turning from sin, self, the world unto God in Christ, receiving Him as our personal Lord and Saviour and then following Him in the path of obedience — so there are certain characteristics in babes in Christ which distinguish them from the "young men" and "fathers." And the very name by which they are designated more or less defines those characteristics. As infants or little children they are largely creatures of impulse, swayed by their emotions more than regulated by judgment. Feelings play a large part in their lives. They are very impressionable, easily influenced, and largely unsuspecting, believing readily whatever is told them by those who have their confidence.

"I write unto you little children, because ye have known the Father" (I John 2:13). *That* is the distinguishing mark which none other than the Holy Spirit has given of the spiritual infant. It is a statement which needs to be particularly taken to heart and pondered by some of our readers for it plainly signifies that unless *we* "know the Father" we are not entitled to regard ourselves as being His children. In the natural life the very first thing which babes and young children discover is an acknowledgement – in their infantile way – of their parents, aiming to call them by their names ("papa" and "mamma") in distinguishing them from others. And thus it is also spiritually: the distinguishing act of babes in Christ is to acknowledge God to be their *Father*, and this they do by expressing, in their way, their attachment to Him, their delight in Him, and their dependence on Him, lisping out His name in their praises and petitions before the throne of grace.

What we have just pointed out is agreeable to such passages as these: "thou shalt call me, my Father and shalt not turn away from me" (Jer. 3:19). "I am a Father to [the spiritual] Israel, and Ephraim is my first born . . . Ephraim, my dear son, a pleasant child . . . I will surely have mercy upon him, saith the Lord" (Jer. 31:9, 20). In the first formal instruction which the Lord Jesus gave to His young disciples, He bade them "After this manner pray ye: *our Father* which art in heaven" (Matt. 6:9). How can we approach Him with any confidence or freedom unless we view Him in this blessed relation? If we have been reconciled to Him by Jesus Christ then God *is* our Father, and "because ye are sons, God hath sent forth the spirit of His Son into your hearts, crying, Father! Father!" (Gal. 4:6); and that spirit causes its possessor to come in a holy familiarity and childlike manner to God, and evidences itself in a desire to honor and please Him.

Not only would it be misleading to our minds for the young convert (even though old in years) to be likened unto a "little child" (Matt. 18:2, 3) unless there was a *real resemblance*, and thus a propriety in employing this figure, but it would also be a strange departure from one of the well-established "ways" of God, namely, His having so wrought in the first creation as to strikingly foreshadow His works in the new creation, the natural having been made to adumbrate the spiritual. We see that principle and fact illustrated in every direction. As in the natural so in the spiritual: there is a begetting (James 1:19), a conception or Christ being formed in the soul (Gal. 4:19), a birth (I Peter 1:23), and that birth evidenced by a "cry" (Rom. 8:15), and the newborn babe desiring "the sincere milk of the Word" (I Peter 2:2); so there are many features in common between the natural and the spiritual infant.

Little children are far more regulated by their affections than by their understanding, and the young Christian is much taken with the love of God, the grace of the Lord Jesus, and the comforts of the Holy Spirit. He delights greatly in his own experience, and to hear the experience of others. As the natural child is timorous and easily scared, so the young Christian is quickly alarmed, as was evidenced by the fearing disciples on the storm-swept sea, to whom the Saviour said "O ye of *little* faith." As the digestive system of a youngster is feeble, so the babe in Christ needs to be fed on "milk" rather than "strong meat." "I have yet many things to say unto you, but ye cannot bear them now" (John 16:12). Owing to an undeveloped understanding, babes in Christ are not "established" in the Faith: "be no more *children* – tossed to and fro and carried about with every wind of doctrine" (Eph. 4:14).

"A young convert is much taken with his own importunity in prayer, with his own enlargements and affections (they being very warm and lively), with the multitude of means and the much time he spends in the use of and observance of them; whereas a believer of longer standing and greater measure of spiritual growth values those discoveries which the Holy Spirit gives him in prayer and inward converse with the Lord, of the Father's free love, and the Son's personal, particular, and prevalent intercession on his behalf: and he is more taken with those, than with his own fervor and supplications . . . The 'babes' in Christ are particularly affected with a sense and enjoyment of pardoning mercy and calling God 'Father.' Hence, the blessings of pardon of sin, peace with God, the spirit of adoption, and an advancement in and an increased spiritual perception of these precious realities, must be a growth in grace such as is quite suited to their spiritual stature and circumstances" (S. E. Pierce).

7

Its Stages

I

In the last chapter we called attention to the fact that Christians may be graded into three classes according to their "stature" in Christ or their spiritual development and progress. In proof thereof appeal was made to Mark 4:28 and I John 2:13. In addition to those passages we may also take note of our Lord's Parable of the Wheat, wherein He represented the good-ground hearers as bringing forth fruit in varying degrees or quantities. That parable is recorded in each of the first three Gospels and there is, among others, this noticeable difference between their several statements: that Mark says of those who received the Word, they "bring forth fruit: some thirtyfold, some sixty, and some a hundred" (4:20); whereas in Matthew's account that order is reversed: "brought forth some a hundredfold, some sixty, and some thirty" (13:23). Evidently the same parable was uttered by our Lord on different occasions and He did not employ precisely the same language, the Holy Spirit guiding each Evangelist according to His particular design in that Gospel.

Since Matthew is the opening book of the New Testament it is obviously the connecting link between it and the Old, and accordingly the nature of its contents differ considerably from that of the three which follow. The prophetic element is far more prominent and its dispensational character more marked. Many have regarded the parables of Matthew 13 as supplying a prophetic outline of the history of Christendom. Personally, we still believe in that view: that, instead of its course being steadily upwards, it was to be definitely downwards, and that so far from the gospel converting the world to Christ this age would witness the whole public testimony of God being corrupted. Thus we regard the "hundredfold" of Matthew 13:23 as being descriptive of the primitive prosperity of Christianity in the days of the apostles, the "sixty" of the noticeable and lesser yield during the times of the Reformers and Puritans, and the "thirty" as that which resulted from the labors of men like Whitefield, Jon. Edwards, and later, Spurgeon; while to-day nothing is left but the mere *gleanings* of the harvest. Thus the course of this Christian dispensation has been very similar to that of the Mosaical, with its reformations in the days of David and then of Ezra, but ending as Malachi shows!

But in Mark 4:20 it is not the corporate testimony which is in view, but the spiritual experience of individual believers: "and brought forth fruit: some thirtyfold, some sixty, and some a hundred," which corresponds with the three grades of verse 28 — "first the blade, then the ear, after that the full corn in the ear," and the apostle's more definite description — "I write unto you fathers, because ye have known him that is from the beginning. I write unto you young men, because ye have overcome the wicked one. I write unto you little children [babes] because ye have known the Father" (I John 2:13). As Thomas Goodwin pointed out: John "had an advantage over all his fellow apostles in that he lived the longest of them, so that in the course of his life he went through the several ages or seasons that Christians do, and having also had an experience of other Christians and what was eminently in and proper to each age of men in Christ, writes to all sorts accordingly, and sets down what things spiritual belonged into those several stages."

In the preceding chapter we dwelt upon some of the features which characterize the "babes" or "little children," pointing out that those very designations intimate that which distinguishes them from the "young men" and "fathers," for God has made the natural to shadow forth the spiritual. "Brethren, be not children in understanding" (I Cor. 14:20). As in a young child reason is undeveloped, so in a spiritual babe there is but a feeble apprehension of the deeper things of God; yet as that exhortation shows, the believer ought soon to pass out of a state of infancy. What is said of them in I John 2:13 describes another mark: "ye have known the Father." Little children acknowledge their parents, are dear to them, hang about them, cannot endure to be long absent from them. They expect to be much noticed and fondled, and accordingly it is said of the good Shepherd "He shall gather the *lambs* with his arms and carry them in his bosom" (Isa. 40:11). Little ones must be dangled on the knees, cannot endure the frowns of a father, and are not yet strong enough for conflicts: and hence God tempers His providential dealings with them accordingly. The babe has "tasted that the Lord is gracious" (I Peter 2:3), but as yet knows not of the "fulness" there is in Him.

Now the young convert is not to remain a spiritual babe but is bidden to "grow in grace and in the knowledge of our Lord and Saviour Jesus Christ" (II Peter 3:18), yea, to "grow up into him in *all* things" (Eph. 4:15). God has made full provision for him to do so, and by his availing himself of that provision is He honored and glorified. But the sad fact is that many Christians never do so, and many others who "run well" for a while lapse back again into spiritual infancy. We are warned against this very danger by the solemn example of the Hebrews, to whom the apostle had to write, "Of whom we have many things to say and hard to be uttered, seeing ye are dull of hearing. For when for the time ye ought to be teachers, ye have need that one teach you again which be the first principles of the oracles of God, and are become such as have need of milk and not of strong meat. For every one that useth milk is unskilful in the word of righteousness: for he is a babe" (5:11-13).

Three things marked those believers who had failed to advance in the school of Christ. First, they were "dull of hearing" which connotes not slow-wittedness, but failure of affection and will to respond to the teaching they had received. They were unconcerned about what they heard, unsearched by it, and consequently it effected no change for the better in their characters and conduct. In Scripture, to "hear" God means to *heed* Him, to bring our ways and works into accord with His revealed will. God's Word is given to us as a Rule to walk by (Ps. 119:105), and walking signifies to go forward in the highway of holiness. Thus, to be "dull of hearing" is a species of self-will, it is a nonresponse to the call of God, it is to disregard His precepts. As intelligence begins to dawn, the first thing required of a little child should be subjection to the will of those who have its best interests at heart; and the first thing required by the Father of His children is loving obedience to Him.

Spiritual babes need to be taught "the first principles of the oracles of God." What were the "first principles" which God taught Adam and Eve in Eden? Why, that He was their Maker and required obedience from them. What were the "first principles" inculcated by Jehovah at Sinai? Why, that Israel must be in dutiful subjection unto the One who had redeemed them from Egypt. What were the "first principles" enunciated by Christ in His initial public address? His sermon on the mount must answer. The "first principles" of spirituality or genuine piety are personal faith in God and loving obedience to Him. While *they* be in operation the soul will prosper and make progress; as soon as they become inoperative we deteriorate. Hence, the second thing complained of is, the Hebrews were "unskilful [margin "inexperienced"] in the word of righteousness." Observe the particular title by which the Word is here called — that which emphasizes the *practical* side of things: they were not walking in "the paths of righteousness" (Ps. 23:3). They had degenerated into self-pleasers, following the by-ways of self-will.

Third, they were incapable of receiving "strong meat." The force of which may be gathered from verses 10, 11. The apostle desired to open unto the Hebrews the mystery of "Melchizedek" and bring before them deeper teaching concerning the official glories of Christ, but their state cramped him. He must suit his instruction according to the condition of their hearts, as it was evidenced by their walk. He was similarly restrained by the case of the Corinthians: "And I, brethren, could not speak unto you as unto spiritual, but as unto carnal, as unto babes in Christ. I have fed you with milk and not with meat, for hitherto (because of their perversity and naughtiness) ye were not able to bear it, neither yet now are ye able" (I Cor. 3:1, 2; see Mark 4:33). "Milk" is a figurative expression denoting precisely the same thing as "the first principles of the oracles of God" — faith, obedience. As it would be senseless to teach a child grammar before it learned the alphabet, or arithmetic before it knew the values of the numerals, so it is useless to teach Christians the higher mysteries of the Faith or to take an excursion into the realm of prophecy when they have not learned to be regulated by the practical teaching of Scripture.

Here, then, are two of the chief reasons why so few Christians really advance beyond spiritual babyhood and become "young men" that are "strong" and who "overcome the wicked one." Here are the worms which, it is to be feared, have been eating at the root of the spiritual life of some of our readers. Because they were "dull [not of intellect, but] of hearing." The Greek word for "dull" is rendered "slothful" in Hebrews 6-12. It denotes a state of slackness and inertia. It means they were too indolent to bestir themselves. They were spiritual sluggards. They were not willing to "buy the truth" (Prov. 23:23) — make it their own by incorporating it in their daily lives. They failed to "gird up the loins of their minds" (I Peter 1:13) and earnestly and resolutely set about the task God has appointed them, namely, to deny self and take up their cross daily and follow Christ. They did not lay to heart the *precepts* of the gospel and translate them into practice. They made no progress in practical godliness.

Second, lack of progress was due to their being "unskilful in the word of righteousness." The word "righteousness" means right doing, up to the required standard. God's Word is the alone Rule of righteousness, the Standard by which all our motives and actions are to be measured, the Rule by which they are to be regulated. That Word is to *govern us* both inwardly and outwardly. By that Word of Righteousness each of us will be judged in the Day to come. Now it is not said that those Hebrews were ignorant of this Word, but "unskilful in" it. The word "unskilful" here means inexperienced, that is, inexperienced in the practical *use* they made of it. I may be thoroughly familiar with its letter, understand much of its literal meaning, able to quote correctly scores of its verses, yet so far from that serving any good purpose it will only add to my condemnation if I am not *controlled* by it. To be "unskilful in the word of righteousness" means I have not yet learned how to mortify the flesh, overcome temptations, resist the Devil; and as long as that be the case, if I be saved at all, I am only a spiritual infant, undeveloped in the spiritual life.

Another thing which holds back many a young convert from spiritual progress is his making too much of his initial experience. Unless he be on his guard there is great danger of making an idol of the peace and joy which comes from the knowledge of sins forgiven. God requires us to walk by faith and not by feelings, for though the latter may for a while please us, the former is that which honors *Him*, and the faith which most honors Him is that which rests on His bare Word when there are no feelings to buoy us up. Moreover, God is a jealous God and will not long suffer us to esteem His gifts more highly than Himself. If we are more occupied with lively frames and inward comforts than we are with God in Christ, then He will take from us a sense of His comforts, and the soul will sink and be cast down under a sense of the loss of them. In such a case, Revelation 2:5 prescribes the remedy: the sin of idolatry must be penitently confessed and we must return to the Storehouse of grace as a beggar, and make Christ our all.

Many babes in Christ have their spiritual growth retarded by (negatively) the lack of suitable instruction, and (positively) by the cold water poured on their joy and ardor by their elders. It is neither necessary nor kind for some would-be wiseacres to tell them, this joy of yours will not last long: your bright sky will soon be overcast with dark clouds.

Many of them are likely to discover that soon enough for themelves, while others may live to disprove such doleful predictions. This writer was often told that he would quickly lose his assurance of God's acceptance of him in Christ, but though more than thirty-five years have passed since sovereign grace "plucked him out of the fire" (Zech. 3:2), his assurance has never wavered or weakened, for it has always rested on the unchanging Word of Him that cannot lie. Others are greatly stumbled by empty professors and the inconsistencies of some real Christians, and they allow that to keep them from striving after a closer walk with God.

Many are kept weak in faith through failure to attain unto a proper acquaintance with the person and work of Christ. They do not realize how sufficient and able He was for everything He undertook to do for them, and how perfectly He finished the same. They have no clear views of either the fulness or the freeness of His so-great salvation. Consequently, a legal spirit working with their unbelief puts them upon reasoning against their being saved freely by grace through faith. Those unbelieving reasonings gain great power from their defeats in their warfare between the spirit and the flesh, or grace and nature. They hearken to and trust more in the reports of self than to the testimony of God's Word. Thereby their faith is checked in its growth and they remain but babes in Christ. Their weak faith receives but little from Christ, and it continues weak because they have so little dependence upon the fulness of grace there is in Him for sinners. They appropriate not His promises, nor trust in His faithfulness and power. Growth in grace and in the knowledge of Christ are inseparable, and experimental knowledge of Christ is entirely dependent upon the exercise of *faith on Him.*

But we must pass on now to the second class. "I have written unto you young men because ye are strong, and the Word of God abideth in you, and ye have overcome the wicked one" (I John 2:14). Although the classification which this passage makes of the Lord's people does not regard them simply according to their natural ages, but rather to the several degrees of stature in Christ, yet the characters given them are more or less taken from and assimilated unto what prominently distinguishes each class in their natural life. Infants rejoice in the sight of their parents and in prattling to them: thus the spiritual babes are said to "know the Father." Proverbs 20:29 tells us "the glory of young men is their strength," and accordingly those who reach the second stage of Christian development are termed "young men" and it is said of them "ye are strong." Young men are renowned for their athletic vigor and are the ones called upon to fight in the defense of their country, and here they are pictured as victorious in conflict, as having "overcome the wicked one."

II

"I have written unto you young men because ye are strong, and the Word of God abideth in you, and ye have overcome the wicked one." Though these words were most certainly not written by the apostle in order to flatter, but were beyond doubt a sober statement of fact concerning those he addressed, yet — because of our dullness of understanding — they are by no means free of difficulty to us. Therefore, as the Lord is pleased to enable, we shall endeavor to supply an answer to the following questions. Wherein do the "young men" differ from the "babes"? In what sense can they be said to be "strong"? — Is there such a thing as out-growing spiritual weakness! Exactly what is signified by "the Word of God abideth in you," and are those words to be understood as explaining the preceding clause or the one which follows? In view of the many defeats which apparently all Christians experience, what is meant by "ye have overcome the wicked one"?

Wherein do "young men" differ from babes"? First, because having been longer engaged in the practice of godliness, they have learned more seriously to consider their ways in order that they may avoid sin and the occasions thereof. They have sufficiently acquainted themselves with God as to realize the need of watching, praying, striving both against inward corruptions and outward temptations. They frequently present before the throne of grace such petitions as these: "Teach me, O Lord, the way of thy statues, and I shall keep it unto the end. Give me understanding and I shall keep thy law, yea, I shall observe it with my whole heart. Make me to go in the path of thy commandments, for therein do I delight. Incline my heart unto thy testimonies and not to covetousness" (Ps. 119:33-36). Sins which formerly they regarded as blotted out by the general pardon received at conversion, are now thought of with shame and bitterness.

Second, they are more diligent in the use of means. Not that they necessarily devote more time thereto, but that they are more conscientious and spiritually exercised therein. As they have become increasingly acquainted with their corrupt inclinations, rebellious wills, the workings of unbelief and pride, they attend more closely to that basic duty "Keep thy *heart* with all diligence, for out of it are the issues of life" (Prov. 4:23), and accordingly they can truthfully say "I have inclined my heart to perform thy statutes always, even unto the end" (Ps. 119: 112), though they will often have to confess lack of power to perform their desire. That makes them the more concerned to learn how to make use of their spiritual "armor," for none so conscious of its need and so earnest to put it on as *this* grade of believers.

Third, they are better versed in the Word of God. Though not so experienced and proficient in the Word of Righteousness as the "fathers," yet they are not as unskilful as the "babes." They have learned much in how personally to appropriate the Scriptures, how to apply them to their several cases, circumstances, and needs. They long to make further progress in piety and therefore they meditate in the law of God day and night. Deeply exercised that their daily lives may be pleasing to God and adorning to the profession which they make, they are concerned to inquire "Wherewithal shall a young man cleanse his way?" and discover the answer to be "by taking heed thereto according to thy word" (Ps. 119:9). Thus they are daily furnishing themselves with spiritual knowledge and fortifying themselves against their enemies.

Fourth, they have learned to look more outside of self. They neither make so much of inward comforts nor do they lean so much unto their own understanding as once they did. They look more to Christ and live more upon Him. As formerly they trusted Him for cleansing and righteousness, now they turn to Him for wisdom and strength. They have discovered from experience that these can only be drawn from Him by the exercise of *faith*. They have realized themselves to be poor, helpless creatures, continually in need, and as having no means of their own to supply them. Thereby the Lord teaches them to live more *out of* themselves and more upon His fulness. When the enemy cometh in like a flood, they look to Christ for victory. When conscious of their impotency they do not give way to despair, but trust Christ to renew their strength. Thus by such means they pass from the weakness of infancy and become "young men."

"I have written unto you young men because ye are strong, and the Word of God abideth in you, and ye have overcome the wicked one" (I John 2:14). We have sought to describe some of the characteristic features of those whom we consider may justly be regarded as belonging to that class of Christians who are here designated "young men" particularly as they are distinguished from the "babes" or "little children." Let it be understood that what we wrote thereon was in no spirit of dogmatism, but merely an expression of personal opinion. We consider that the spiritual "young men" are believers who have acquired a considerable knowledge of the Truth and are well established in the whole plan of doctrine as set forth in the Scriptures, though as yet lacking the deeper understanding thereof as pertains to "the fathers." To which we would add, they "*know*" whom they have "believed" and "committed" their all, for we would certainly regard a Christian without assurance that Christ is *his* as still but a "babe," though we do not expect all will agree to that.

"I have written unto you young men because ye are strong, and the Word of God abideth in you, and ye have overcome the wicked one." How different are the ways of God from men's, even those of good men! Many elderly Christians today would deem it most imprudent to write or say to their younger brethren "ye are strong . . . and have overcome the wicked one," fearing that such an assertion was "dangerous" because having a strong tendency to "puff up" its recipients; which only goes to show how little some of our thoughts are formed by the Word of God and how prone we all are to fleshly reasoning. Such an attitude is but a "show of wisdom" (Col. 2:23) and a poor show at that, for it betrays both ignorance and silliness. Those who are "strong" spiritually are not at all likely to be puffed up by telling them the *truth*. Contrariwise, any who *are* puffed up by such a statement would demonstrate they were *weak!* Let us not seek to be wise above what is written, but rather set aside our proud reasonings and receive what God says as "a little child."

In making the above assertion the apostle was certainly not seeking to flatter them for he did not say "ye have made yourselves strong." Rather was he making a factual statement. In doing so, he, first, honored the Holy Spirit, by owning *His* work within them: the explanation of that statement of fact was the gracious operations of the Spirit in their hearts. Second, he was expressing his own *joy*: it was a matter of delight to him that they *had*, by the grace of God, reached this stage of spiritual health and vigor. Third, it was said by way of encouragement to them. If on the one hand it be our duty to rebuke and reprove what is evil in fellow Christians, it equally becomes us to recognize and own whatever is good in them. A word of cheer and stimulus is often a real help. If there be "a time to break down," there is also "a time to build up" (Eccles. 3:3). Paul did not hesitate to tell the Thessalonians "your faith groweth exceedingly and the charity of every one of you all toward each other aboundeth" (II Thess. 1:3).

But what did the apostle signify by his "ye are strong"? Probably the majority of Christians would promptly reply, Why, only in the sense that they were "strong in the Lord and in the power of his might" (Eph. 6:10). Yet we believe that answer is inadequate, and if the "only" in it be insisted upon, erroneous. We are in hearty accord with Thomas Goodwin who pointed out that, "There is a double spiritual strength: one that is radical in the soul itself, consisting in the strength and vigor of habitual graces; the other is assistant thereto from the Spirit, according as He is pleased to arm and fill the soul with Himself, joining with it by strengthening the graces in us, which we read of in Eph. 3:16, 'That He would grant you, according to the riches of His glory, to be strengthened with might by His Spirit in the inner man.'"

By nature the Christian was entirely devoid of spiritual power. Writing to the saints at Rome Paul said, "For when ye were yet *without* strength, in due time Christ died for the ungodly" (5:6). Now that "yet" would be quite pointless if those to whom he was writing were *still* "without strength." "For God hath not given us the spirit of fear, but of *power* and of love and of a sound mind" (II Tim. 1:7). We dishonor the work of the blessed Spirit if we view the regenerate as being in the same helpless plight as the unregenerate. At regeneration we received spiritual life, and as Goodwin pertinently asks "what is strength but life in an active vigor." Are we not told "the joy of the Lord is your strength" (Neh. 8:10), i.e., the more the believer delights himself in the Lord and rejoices in His perfections and his relation to Him, the more will his soul be invigorated and his graces quickened. Does not the Psalmist acknowledge Thou "strengthenedst me with strength *in my soul*" (138:3), so that he was no longer feeble in himself.

But let us not be misunderstood at this point. We are not arguing in favor of any kind of "strength" being imparted to the Christian which renders him in any wise self-sufficient. No indeed, perish the thought. Even the "fathers" are as completely dependent, moment by moment, upon Divine grace, as the youngest and feeblest babe in Christ. Paradoxical as it may sound to the carnal mind, the very "strength" which is communicated at the new birth makes its recipient conscious (for the first time) of his utter *weakness*. It is the purity of the new nature in the soul which makes manifest the corruptions of his flesh: it is his reception of the earnest of his inheritance which makes him poor in spirit: it is the gift of faith which causes him to be sensible of the workings of unbelief. It is the life of God in the renewed which causes them to thirst and pant after God. Nevertheless, there is a real sense in which the Christian *is strong*, both comparatively with his unregenerate impotency, and relatively in himself.

"A wise man is strong, yea, a man of knowledge increaseth strength" (Prov. 24:5). In proportion as spiritual knowledge increases so also does spiritual strength. The spirit is nourished and enriched both for spiritual work and warfare by true wisdom. As we have so often reminded the reader, growth in grace and in spiritual knowledge are inseparably connected (II Peter 3:18). There is a strength of courage, of fortitude, of resolution, which enables its possessor to stand firm against opposition, to overcome difficulties, to endure trials and afflictions. But the reverse of that is expressed in "if thou faint in the day of adversity, thy strength is small" (Prov. 24:10). If in the day of testing and trial spirits sink so that your hands hang down and your knees become weak, if when afflictions come you take the line of least resistance, neglect the means of grace and are unfitted for duties, then your "strength" is "small," and such an attitude will further weaken it. Unto such that word is especially appropriate, "Wait on the Lord: be of good courage, and he shall strengthen thine heart; wait, I say, on the Lord" (Ps. 27:4).

The order there is to be carefully noted: first, an acknowledgement of our dependency upon the Lord. Second, a being of good courage. Third, the Divine promise unto those who are of good courage. Fourth, trusting God for the fulfilment of His promise of further strength. It is unto those who have that more is given (Matt. 24:29), it is those who make use of the grace bestowed who receive larger supplies. "God more ordinarily vouchsafeth adjuvant (extra-assisting) efficacious grace to overcome temptations according to the measure of grace habitual or inherent, and therefore when men (we) are grown up to more radical inward strength He gives more effectual assisting strength, and (accordingly) He meeteth forth temptations to the ability our inward man is furnished withal, as that we are able to bear them (I Cor. 10:13). He vouchsafes His actual supplies of aiding strength according to the proportion of that inherent stock of ability He sees in the inner man, and then as the conflicts grow greater our additional aids are together therewith increased" (Thos. Goodwin).

Without further quoting verbatim from this writer we will summarize and paraphrase his next paragraph, with which we are in hearty accord. The grace of God indeed works freely, and He ties Himself absolutely to no rules and measures, but ever acts according to His own good pleasure. He takes liberty to withhold His supplies of assisting grace even from those who have most inherent grace, to show us the weakness of all our grace as it is in us, withholding from "the strong" (Rom. 15:1). His further influencing grace which moves us both to will and to do — to evidence that His grace is tied to none. This we see both in David and Hezekiah when they had grown up to this middle age in grace. Yet that alters not the fact that in His ordinary dispensations God gives more grace to those who make good use of what they already have: "every branch that *beareth fruit,* He purgeth it that it may bring forth more fruit" (John 15:2). The promise of being "made fat" is not to the sluggard but to "the soul of the diligent" (Prov. 13:4).

To sum up: by the apostle's "young men, because ye are *strong,*" we understand that through using the means of grace, by increased spiritual knowledge, by appropriating the strength which is in Christ Jesus (II Tim. 2:1), through exercising the graces of the new man, by improving (profiting from) the varied experiences through which they had passed, and by the assisting operations of the Holy Spirit, they had developed from "babes" into a higher spiritual stature and were the better qualified to use their spiritual muscles. It is written "They that wait upon the Lord [which refers not so much to an act as it is descriptive of an attitude found in all the regenerate who are in a healthy condition] shall renew their strength: they shall mount up with wings as eagles, they shall run, and not be weary; they shall walk, and not faint" (Isa. 40:31). There *is* such a thing as overcoming spiritual weakness or babyhood, but not of continual dependence on the Lord. There is such an experience as going on "from strength to strength" (Ps. 84:7). Though without Christ I can do nothing (John 15:5), yet through Him strengthening me "I can do all things" (Phil. 4:13).

"And the Word of God abideth in you." We regard that clause as connected first, with the preceding one, as casting light upon and furnishing a (partial) explanation of *why* these "young men" were "strong," as revealing to us one of the principal sources and means of their spiritual strength. And at the same time it also serves to define the nature of the strength mentioned, namely, as inherent grace, as something *within* themselves. It is by the pure milk of the Word that the babe in Christ grows (I Peter 2:2), and it is by that Word abiding in him that he becomes strong, that the faculties or graces of the new man are kept healthy and vigorous. But, second, we regard that clause as having an intimate bearing on the one that follows, seeing that it ends as well as begins with the word "and." For it was by means of the Word of God abiding in them that these young men had been enabled to "overcome the wicked one" — "by the word of thy lips have I kept me from the paths of the destroyer" (Ps. 17:4).

"And ye have overcome the wicked one." Note, first, this is not an exhortation or intimation of duty: it is not "ye ought to" but "ye have." Second, this is not predicated as a rare experience, peculiar to some exceptionally exalted saint, but is postulated of the whole of this company: "*ye* have." Third, it is not described either as a present process or a future attainment, but as an accomplished thing: not "ye are overcoming" or "will" do so, but "ye *have* overcome the wicked one." Little wonder that Goodwin said on this point, "There is a second and greater difficulty [beyond defining the "ye are strong"] namely, How and in what respect they are said more eminently [i.e., than the "babes"] to have overcome Satan? For are they not in their conflicts apt to be overcome and to yield to corrupt affections? and how far they may be overcome [by those] is not to be determined by man" — words in brackets are, in each instance, our own additions.

"Ye have overcome the wicked one." Whatever difficulty we may experience in understanding the meaning of those words, there is surely no occasion for us needlessly to add to the difficulty. We must be very careful with this verse, as with all others, not to read into it what is not there. It does not say "ye have overcome the *flesh*," that the young men had obtained victory over their inward corruptions. It is a most significant fact, and one which should exert great influence on our thinking at this point, that while this Epistle speaks of overcoming "the wicked one" and overcoming "the world" (5:4), it does not speak of believers overcoming their lusts. It is true we are bidden to mortify our members which are upon the earth (Col. 3:5), and that in varying degrees all the regenerate do so. It is also true that the grace of God effectually teaches its recipients to deny ungodliness and worldly lusts, and to live soberly, righteously and godly in this present world" (Titus 2:12), but Scripture nowhere affirms that any saint "overcame the flesh."

As intimated above, we believe that the preceding clause "and the Word of God abideth in you" throws light upon those words which have presented such a difficulty unto so many — "and ye have overcome the wicked one." First, because they declare unto us the principal *means* by which the enemy is overcome, namely, the Word of God, which is expressly designated "the Sword of the Spirit" — the one offensive weapon which is to be used against the "wicked" (Eph. 6:16, 17). Supreme demonstration of that was given by the Lord Jesus when He was attached by the Devil. He then gave proof that the Word dwelt richly in Him, that the Word of God abode in His affections and thoughts and was the Regulator of His ways. To each of Satan's temptations He replied "It is written." He did not parley with the Enemy, He did not reason or argue with him; He took His stand on the authoritative and all-sufficient Word of God and refused to turn aside therefrom, and *thereby* He overcame him. In *that* Christ has both left us an example that we should follow His steps and given us such encouragement as ensures success.

But second, it seems to us that the clause "and the Word of God abideth in you" not only signifies the means to be used, but also and perhaps chiefly, intimates the very nature of *wherein* the young men had "overcome the wicked one." In other words, the very fact that it could be said of them "the Word of God abideth in you" was itself the grand *proof* of their victory over the great Adversary. In His parable of the Sower our Lord taught that the seed sown was the Word, and that which fell by the wayside "the fowls of the air came and devoured it up." In His interpretation Christ explained that to signify: "Satan cometh immediately and *taketh away* the Word that was sown in their hearts" (Mark 4:15). That shows plainly that the primary and principal aim of the Devil is to prevent the Word of God finding a permanent abode in the human heart, and in the case of the vast majority of our fellows he is permitted to succeed. To a very large percentage of professing Christians the Lord says, as He did to the Jews, who had much head knowledge of the Scriptures, "Ye have *not* the Word of God *abiding in you*" (John 5:38).

We are living in a day of such darkness that this generation *is* "ignorant of his devices" (II Cor. 2:11). Many of God's own people seek to blame Satan for what originates with themselves. Note well the following statements: "From within, out of the heart of men, [not "from the Devil"] proceed evil thoughts, adulteries, murders . . . all these evils come from *within*" (Mark 7: 21, 23). "Now the works of the flesh [not "of the Devil"] are manifest, which are these: adultery . . . envyings, murders, drunkenness, revellings, and such like" (Gal. 5:19-21). "Every man is tempted when he is [not "assailed by the Evil one," but] drawn away of his *own* lust" (James 1:14). But pride works, and we do not wish to think that we are so evil and vile, and so we attempt to escape the onus by attributing to Satan what we ourselves are responsible for. There is no need for Satan to tempt men to such things as those passages mention. He works far more subtly and insidiously than that.

If we go back to Genesis 3, where we have the earliest mention of Satan — and the first mention of anything in Scripture invariably supplies the key to subsequent references — we are shown the realm in which he works and the central object of his attack. That realm is the *religious,* and that object is the Word of God. His opening words to Eve were "Yea hath God said?" calling into question a "thus saith the Lord." As he seeks night and day to *prevent* God's Word entering the human heart, so he labors incessantly to *remove* it when it has entered. One of his favorite tactics is to inject doubts into the minds of spiritual babes, to get them to question the inspiration and veracity of the Scriptures. Under the imposing terms of "modern thought," "scholarship," "the discoveries of science," he seeks to sap the foundation of faith. Where that fails, appeal is made to the conflicting views of the sects and denominations to discredit the inerrancy of the Word. Where that fails, recourse is had to human "tradition" in order to set aside the Oracles of God.

It is far too little realized that every attack which is made upon the Word of God, every denial of its verbal inspiration and Divine authority, every repudiation of its sufficiency as being our alone Rule of faith and practice, every corruption of its doctrine and every perversion of the ordinances and worship of the Triune God, are *from the Devil*. Many of the "babes" in Christ are severely shaken by those attacks and are tossed to and fro by various winds of erroneous doctrine. Nevertheless, Divine grace preserves them, and as they grow in grace and knowledge, as they become more cautious of whom they hear and what they read, as they become established in the Truth, they triumph over the Enemy.

He *fails* to destroy their faith in the Scriptures, to lead them astray by "damnable heresies," to catch away the Seed sown in their hearts, and therefore the Word of God abiding in them is sure *proof* that they *have* "overcome the wicked one." As the same apostle goes on to say in his fourth chapter, "many false prophets are gone out into the world," and then he added, "ye are of God little children [the term of endearment] and have *overcome*" (4:1, 4)

III

In Ephesians 4:13 there is a stature of Christ" spoken of, namely, that of "a perfect Man — unto the measure of the stature of the fulness of Christ." It would lead us too far astray from the present aspect of our subject, which is the spiritual growth of individual Christians, to enter into a full analysis and discussion of the passage in which this verse occurs (4:11-16), suffice it now to point out that it treats of the *corporeate growth* of the Church and its ultimate perfection, Verses 11, 12, state the appointment of the Christian ministry, verse 13 announces its goal, while verses 14-16 makes known the *process* by which that goal is reached. There is a "unity of the faith" among believers now, as to its "first principles," as truly as there is a saving "knowledge of the Son of God" possessed by them in this life; but that which this passage contemplates is the consummation of the same in the Body corporeate, when there will be perfect unity of faith, as there will yet be perfect knowledge and perfect holiness (Heb. 12:23), for all the saints will then be fully conformed unto the image of Christ. When the "perfect Man" is openly revealed, it will consist of a glorified Head with a glorified Body.

"The measure of the stature of the fulness of Christ" is that to which the whole of the Church is predestinated and the accomplishment thereof will be seen at the second advent of our Lord, "when He shall come to be glorified in His saints and admired in all them that believe" (II Thess. 2:10). But during this present life there are different stages of spiritual development reached by Christians, different forms in the school of Christ to which they belong, different measures of progress made by them. Broadly speaking there are three degrees of "the stature of Christ" reached by believers in this life, though the highest of them falls very far short of that which shall pertain to them in the life to come. Those three degrees are most clearly specified in I John 2:12-14, where the apostle grades the members of God's family into the "babes," the "young men" and the "fathers." We have sought to describe the principal features of the first and second, and now we are to consider what is more characteristic of and pre-eminent in the third class, the "fathers."

Note carefully how we worded the closing part of the last sentence: it is not that which is peculiar to, but rather that which is distinctive of the third class. This needs to be emphasized, or at least plainly stated, in order to prevent readers from drawing a wrong conclusion. What is predicated of each separate class is also common to the whole, though not to the same degree. In their measure the "babes" overcome the wicked one and have a real and saving knowledge of "him that is from the beginning," yet they do not "overcome" to the same extent as the "young men" nor "know" Christ so well or extensively as do the "fathers." In like manner the "fathers" rejoice in the knowledge of sins forgiven, and "know the Father" even better than they did in the days of their spiritual infancy; so too they are not only as "strong" as they were in the time of their spiritual youth, through the Word of God abiding in them, but they have progressed "from strength to strength" (Ps. 84:7), for the Word now dwells in them "richly" (Col. 3:16).

Let us remind the reader once more that in I John 2:12-14 believers are not graded according to their natural ages, nor even according to the length of time they have been Christians, but according to the spiritual growth and progress they have made in the Christian life. Some of God's elect are converted very late in life and are left in this world for but a short season at most, and though they give clear evidence of a work of grace wrought in them and bring forth fruit to the glory of God, yet they attain not to the spiritual vigor of "young men" and still less to the spiritual intelligence and maturity of the "fathers." On the other hand there are those who are regenerated in their youth and some of them make steady and constant progress, adorning the doctrine they profess and becoming useful to their fellow Christians; while others after a promising beginning, backslide, and are a grief to their brethren. It is with individual Christians as with corporeate companies of them: of the saints at Rome Paul could say "your faith is spoken of throughout the whole world" (1:8), while to the Galatians he complained "ye did run well, who did hinder you?" (5:7). To the Thessalonians he could say "Your faith groweth exceedingly" (II Thess. 1:3), but of the Ephesians it is recorded "thou hast left thy first love" (Rev. 2:4).

While it be true that the longer a person has been a Christian the more mature his spiritual character should be, the more growth in grace ought to mark him, the more intelligence he should have in the things of God, yet in many instances this is far from being actualized in experience. In only too many growth is stunted and progress is retarded, and some Christians of twenty years' standing advance no further in the school of Christ than those who entered it a few months before. We have a type of this in the contrast presented between Elihu and the aged men who took it upon themselves to counsel and criticize Job. "I said, Days shall speak and multitude of years shall teach wisdom" — *they* were given the floor first, only to exhibit their incompetency. "But there is a spirit in men, and the inspiration of the Almighty giveth them understanding. Great men are not always wise, neither do the aged understand judgment. Therefore, I said, Hearken to me" (Job 32:7-9). The "hoary head" is only a "crown of glory *if* it be found in the way of righteousness" (Prov. 16:31).

Note well, my reader, that statement in the above passage: "the inspiration of the Almighty giveth them understanding." Gracious ability comes not from the passing of the years, but by the teaching of the Holy Spirit. That gives us the Divine side: but there is also a human side — that of our responsibility. Said David "I understand more than the ancients because I *keep* thy precepts" (Ps. 119:100). Though study of and meditation upon the Word are indeed means of grace and of growth, yet spiritual understanding is obtained chiefly from personal sub-mission to God — He will not grant light on the "mysteries" of Scripture if we forsake the path of obedence. The young Christian who walks according to the Divine precepts will have more spiritual discernment and better judgment than a much older one who is lax in his "ways." "If any man will *do* His will, he *shall know* of the doctrine" (John 7: 17). The world says "Experience is the best teacher," but it errs: the child who subjects himself wholly to the Divine Rule has an all-sufficient Guide and is independent of experience. Understanding obtained through keeping God's precepts is infinitely better than knowledge se-cured by painful experience.

"I have written unto you fathers, because ye have known him [that is] from the beginning" (I John 2:14). The one thing which is here predicated of mature Christians is their *knowledge of Christ,* for the ref-erence is to the Son of God as incarnate. They have attained unto a fuller, higher, and more experimental knowledge of Christ. They are now more occupied with who He is than what He did for them. They delight in viewing Him as the One who magnified the Divine law and made it honorable, who satisfied all the requirements of Divine holiness and justice, who glorified the Father. They have a deep insight into the mystery of His wondrous Person. They have a clearer understanding of His covenant engagements and of His prophetic, priestly, and kingly functions. They have a more intimate acquaintance with Him through personal fellowship. They have a fuller experience of His love, His grace, His patience. They have obtained experimental verification of His teachings, the value of His commandments, and the certainty of His promises.

The "knowledge" which is here ascribed unto the "fathers" is far more than a speculative and historical one, with which the majority of professing Christians are content. There are several degrees of this merely theoretical knowledge. With some it is nothing more than *mem-orative,* as the Jews are said to have had "a form of knowledge" Rom. 2:20), like a map of it in their brains — acquired by retaining in their minds what they have read or heard about Divine things. With others it is an *opinionative* knowledge, so that they have not only a mental ac-quaintance with parts of the truth, but a kind of conscience and judg-ment about those things, which causes them to regard themselves as "orthodox," and yet wisdom enters not into their hearts (Prov. 1:20). A few have a yet higher degree of this knowledge, which in measure af-fects their hearts and leads to reformation of life, so that they "escape the pollutions of the world through the knowledge of *the* (not 'their') Lord and Saviour"; yet its hold on their affections is too weak to withstand strong temptations, and hence they apostatize from the Faith and re-turn to their wallowing in the mire (II Peter 2:20, 22).

In contrast from nominal professors, every regenerated soul has a su-pernatural and spiritual knowledge of God, of Christ, and the gospel, and as he grows in grace it increases. The kind of knowledge possessed by each of us may be determined by the *effects* it produces: whether it be only a bare, non-influential knowledge, or whether it be a spiritual and saving one is discovered by the *fruits* it bears. A Divinely-imparted one leads its possessor to put his trust in the Lord (Ps. 9:10), to esteem Christ superlatively (Phil. 3:8, 9), to obey Him (I John 2:3, 4). It is such as causes us to receive the truth not only in the light of it, but in the love of it (II Thess. 2:10), and thus it is an intimate, permanent, heart-affecting, and life-transforming knowledge. It is what the apostle terms "the excellency of the knowledge of Christ," and that is one which causes its possessor to count all other things but dung, and moves him to pant after a yet fuller acquaintance with Christ, a more unbroken communion with Him, a more complete conformity unto His image.

The knowledge of Christ with which the "fathers" are blest is such as fills their souls with holy awe, astonishment and admiration. They know Him through the revelation of the gospel as the One who was "set up from everlasting, from the beginning," who was "daily the Father's delight" (Prov. 8:23, 30). Thus they know Him as the One who took into union with His divine person a holy humanity. They know Him as the Image of the invisible God (Col. 1:16), as the One who has fully told out the Father. They are led into a knowledge of His Divine majesty, His Headship of the church, as the Mediator of union and communion, which floods their hearts with delight. They know Him as their Lord, their Redeemer; their Hope, their All in all. He is the grand Subject and Object of their contemplations, so that they are more and more absorbed with Him. Such knowledge finds expression in speaking well of Him to fellow-saints, by endeavoring to please Him in all things, by diligently following the example He has left us.

It must not be concluded from I John 2:13, 14 that this deeper and fuller knowledge of the Person, offices and work of Christ is the only distinguishing mark which eminently characterizes the "fathers." Hebrews 5:11-14 shows otherwise: they "teach" others, both by example and precept, giving counsel and admonition, encouragements and comfort, to their younger brethren. In that same passage they are termed "them that are of full age," and the marks of such are described as "those who by reason of use have their senses exercised to discern both good and evil," and being capacitated to masticate "strong meat," which according to the scope of that epistle has reference to the official glories of Christ, particularly His priestly. While those who cannot digest such food who find neither savour nor nourishment therein, are termed "babes," who can relish naught but "milk," that is, the simpler and more elementary aspects of the gospel.

Just as the natural infant possesses the very same faculties as the adult but has not learned to employ them, so the babe in Christ has all the "senses" or spiritual graces of the "fathers" but has not learned to use them to the same advantage. As the natural infant is incapable of distinguishing between wholesome and injurious food, so the spiritual infant has not the ability to form a correct judgment and distinguish between preachers who minister only the letter of the Word and those who are enabled to open it up spiritually. It is by "reason of use" that the spiritual senses are developed. As the muscles of the athlete or the fingers of the craftsman become fit or skillful through constant exercise, so the spiritual graces of the new man are developed by regularly calling them into play. It is by using the light we have, by practicing what we already know, which fits the soul for further disclosures of the truth and for closer communion with Christ, and which the better enables us to "discern both good and evil." Thus, a further mark of the "fathers" is wisdom, sound judgment, keen discernment.

"The old Christian has more solid, judicious and connected views of the Lord Jesus Christ, and the glories of His redeeming love: hence his hope is more established, his dependence more simple, his peace and strength more abiding and uniform than is the case of the young convert. Though his sensible feelings may not be so warm as when he was in the state of A (spiritual infancy), his judgment is more solid, his mind more fixed, his thoughts more habitually exercised upon the things within the veil. His great business is to behold the glory of God in Christ, and by beholding he is changed into the same image, and brings forth in an eminent and uniform manner the fruits of righteousness. His contemplations are not bare speculations, but have a real influence, and enable him to exemplify the Christian character to more advantage and with more consistency than can, in the present state of things, be expected from the 'babes' of 'young men' " (John Newton *Grace in the Full Ear*).

The "fathers" are such as are more diligently employed in the exercises of godliness, for having proved for themselves that obedience to God is true liberty, their practice of piety is not performed only from a sense of duty, but with joy. They more wisely manage the affairs of this life, for they have a greater measure of spiritual prudence and circumspection. They discharge their duties with increasing diligence and care, knowing that God esteems quality rather than quantity, the heart engaged therein rather than the length or measure of the performance. They are more weaned from the delights of sense, for their assurance is now based upon knowledge rather than feelings. They are more conscious than they formerly were of their frailty and ignorance, and therefore lean harder on the everlasting arms and more frequently seek wisdom from above. They are more submissive under the varying dispensations of Providence, for the trying of their faith has wrought patience (James 1:3) and therefore they are more content to meekly and trustfully leave themselves and their affairs in the hands of Him that doeth "all things well."

The "fathers" are such as have been greatly favored with light from the Spirit by His gracious opening of their understandings to perceive and their hearts to receive the teachings of Holy Writ, and they have learned that they can no more enter into the spiritual meaning of any verse in the Word without the Spirit's assistance than create a world, and therefore their daily prayer is "Open thou mine eyes, that I may behold wondrous things out of thy law." Through deep acquaintance with God their characters are more mellowed and their lives are more faithful to His praise — not necessarily in outward activities but by the exercise of their graces, thanksgiving, and adoration. Having had made to them many discoveries of the glories of Christ, received innumerable proofs of His forbearance, been partakers of countless love-tokens from Him, their testimony is, "Whom have I in heaven but thee, and there is none upon earth that I desire beside thee" (Ps. 73:25). Their minds are largely taken up with and exercised upon the wondrous perfections of Christ, both personal and official.

"But speak thou the things which become sound doctrine: that the *aged men be* sober, grave, temperate, sound in faith, in charity, in patience" (Titus 2:1, 2). Here we are informed what are the particular graces which should characterize the "fathers" in God's family. First, "be sober," or as the margin preferably has it, "be vigilant." They must not suffer increasing years to induce spiritual lethargy, rather should they issue in increasing watchfulness and alertness to danger. "Grave": not garrulous and excitable, but thoughtful and serious: less allowance will be made for *them* than younger brethren if they indulge in levity and vanity. "Temperate" or moderate in all things: the Greek word signifies "self-restrained," having their tempers and affections under control. "Sound in faith": sincere and stedfast in their profession. "In love" to Christ and their brethren. "And patience," not peevish and fretful: persevering in good works, meekly enduring trials and persecutions. "Those who are full of years should be full of grace and goodness" (Matt. Henry).

Not only does the New Testament maintain the distinction between spiritual infants and mature Christians, but it reveals how God provides *servants* of His who are specially suited unto each: "For though ye have ten thousand instructors in Christ, yet not many *fathers*" (I Cor. 4:15). The "fathers" among the ministers of Christ are not only characterized by their disinterested, affectionate, faithful, and prudent instructions, so that they are entitled to the love and respect shown unto a parent; but are Divinely and experimentally fitted to open up "the deep things of God" and edify the older as well as the young saints. Though all the true servants of Christ are commissioned by Him, yet all are not equally qualified, gifted, or useful to the church. Many are "instructors in Christ" but can go no further, being neither designed nor fitted for any thing beyond that. But a few are greatly superior to them and have more lasting importance to the flock. All are useful in their several stations, but all are not useful in the same way.

In concluding this aspect of our subject we cannot do better than call attention to the analogy between the spiritual growth of the children of God and that in the incarnate Son. Beautiful indeed is it to behold how this line of truth was exemplified in Him. The humanity of Christ was perfectly natural in its ordinary development and everything was "beautiful in his time" (Eccles. 3:1) in Him. First, we see Him as a Babe "wrapped in swaddling clothes" and cradled in a manger. Then we behold His progress from infancy to childhood and as a boy of twelve His moral perfections shone forth in being "subject to His parents," and we are told that "He increased in wisdom, and stature and in favor with God and man" (Luke 2:51, 52). When He became man His glory found other expressions, working at the carpenter's bench (Mark 6:3) followed by His public ministry. Surpremely was *He* the "Tree planted by the rivers of water" which brought forth "his fruit in his season."

8

Its Promotion

WE have now arrived at what is perhaps the most important aspect of our subject — not from the doctrinal side but from the practical standpoint. It will avail us little to discover that there is a manifold needs-be why the Christian should grow in grace and in the knowledge of the Lord, as it would advantage us nothing to be quite clear in our minds as to what Christian progress is not and what it really consists of, if we continue to be stationary. While it may awaken interest to learn that in certain fundamental respects the growth of saints is like unto trees in their upward, downward, inward and outward development, yet such information will prove of no real value unless the conscience be exercised thereby and there be definite effort on our part. Trees do not grow mechanically, but only as they derive nourishment from the soil and receive water and sunshine from above. It is instructive to find out there are different grades in God's family and to ascertain the characteristics of each, but of what service will that be to me unless I personally pass from spiritual infancy to youth and eventually become a "father" in Christ?

While there is a close analogy between the manner of a Christian's growth and that of a tree, it must not be lost sight of that there is a real and radical difference between them considered as entities, for *we* are moral agents, accountable creatures, while they are not so; and it is the exercise of our moral agency and the discharge of our responsibility which is now to engage our attention. Spiritual growth is very far from being a fortuitous thing, which occurs irrespective of the use of suitable means, nor does it take place spontaneously or apart from the availing ourselves of our privileges and the performance of our duty. Rather is it the outcome of God's blessing upon our employment of the aids which He has provided and appointed and the orderly development of the different graces He has bestowed upon us. As it is in the natural, so it is in the spiritual: there are certain things which foster and there are other things which hinder Christian progress, and it is the lasting obligation of the saint to make full use of the former and to resolutely avoid the latter. Spiritual growth will not be promoted while we remain indifferent and inactive, but only as we give the utmost diligence to attending unto the health of our souls.

In seeking to treat of the spiritual growth of a saint it needs to be borne in mind that here, as everywhere in the Christian life, there are two different agents at work, two entirely different principles are concerned: there is both a Divine and a human side to the subject, and

99

much wisdom and care are required if a proper and scriptural proportion is to be maintained. Those two agents are God and the saint; those two principles are the operations of Divine sovereignty and the discharge of Christian responsibility. The difficulty involved — admittedly a real one — is to recognize the existence of each and to maintain a due balance between the one and the other. There is a real danger that we become so occupied with the believer's duty and his diligence in using the proper means, that he takes too much credit to himself and thereby robs God of His glory — as in large measure do the Arminians. On the other hand, equally real is the danger that we dwell so exclusively on the Divine operations and our dependence on the Spirit's quickening, that a spirit of inertia seizes us and we become reduced to unaccountable non-entities — as is the case with Fatalists and Antinomians. From either extreme we should earnestly seek deliverance.

It is of vital importance at the outset that we clearly recognize that God alone can make His people grow and prosper, and that we should be deeply and lastingly sensible of our entire dependency upon Him. As we were unable to originate spiritual life in our souls, so we are equally unable to preserve or increase the same. Deeply humbling though that truth be unto our hearts, yet the declarations of Holy Writ are too implicit and too numerous to leave us in the slightest doubt upon it. "None can keep his own soul alive" (Ps. 22:29): true alike naturally and spiritually; positively, "O bless our God. . . . which holdeth our soul in life" (Ps. 68:9). "Thou maintainest my lot" (Ps. 16:5) said Christ Himself. "Thy God hath commanded thy strength" (Ps. 68:28). "From me is thy fruit" (Hos. 14:8). "Thou also hast wrought all our works in us" (Isa. 26:12). "All my springs are in thee" (Ps. 87:7). "Without me ye can do nothing" (John 15:5). Such flesh-withering statements as those cut away all ground for boasting and place the crown of honor where it rightfully belongs.

But there is another class of passages, equally plain and necessary for us to receive at their face value and be duly influenced by them: passages which emphasize the Christian's accountability, which inculcate the discharge of his responsibility, and which blame him when he fails therein: passages which show that God deals with His people as rational creatures, setting before them their duty and requiring them under pain of His displeasure and their great loss to diligently perform the same. He expressly exhorts them to "grow in grace" (II Peter 3:18). He bids them to "lay aside" the things which hinder and to desire the sincere milk of the Word that they may grow thereby" (I Peter 2:1, 2). So far from holding the Hebrews as being without excuse for not having grown, He blames them (5:11-14). Though He has promised to do good unto His people, nevertheless the Lord has declared "I will yet for this be inquired of by the house of Israel to do it for them" (Ezek. 36:37), and hesitates not to say "Ye have not, because ye ask not" (James 3:2).

At first sight it may appear impossible for us to show the meeting-point between the operations of God's sovereignty and the discharge of

Christian responsibility, and to define the relation of the latter to the former and the manner of their interworking. Had we been left to ourselves, it had indeed been a task beyond the compass of human reason; but Scripture solves the problem for us, and in terms so plain that the simplest believer has no difficulty in understanding them. "By the grace of God I am what I am: and His grace which was bestowed upon me was not in vain, but I labored more abundantly than they all; yet not I, but the grace of God which was with me" (I Cor. 15:10). It is true that the apostle was treating more immediately with his ministerial career, yet in its wider application it is obvious that the principles of the verse apply with equal propriety and force to the practical side of the Christian's life — evidenced by the Lord's people in all ages appropriating to themselves its first and last clauses: but equally important and pertinent is that which comes in between them.

In some passages "the grace of God" signifies His eternal good will unto His people; in others it connotes rather the *effect* of His favor, the "grace" which He bestows upon and infuses into them, as in "But unto every one of us is given grace according to the measure of the gift of Christ" (Eph. 4:7). Christ is "full of grace and truth . . . and of his fulness have all we received, and grace for grace" (John 1:14, 16). Just as sin is a powerful principle working within the natural man, inclining him to evil, so at regeneration God's elect have communicated to their souls Divine grace, which acts as a powerful principle working within them and inclining unto holiness. "Grace is nothing else but an introduction of the virtues of God into the soul" (T. Manton). That principle of grace which is imparted to us at the new birth is what is often termed "the new nature" in the Christian, and is designated "the spirit" because "born of the Spirit" (John 3:6); and being spiritual and holy it is opposed by indwelling sin — called "the flesh" (Gal. 5:17) — and that in turn opposes the workings of sin or the lusts of the flesh, the one being contrary to the other.

The principle of grace or new nature which is bestowed on the saint is but a *creature*, and though intrinsically holy it is entirely dependent upon its Author for strength and growth. And thus we must distinguish between the *principle* of grace and fresh *supplies* of grace for its invigoration and development. We may liken the newly-born babe and the young Christian subsequently to a fully-rigged yacht: though its sails be set, it is incapable of movement until a wind blows. The Christian is responsible to spread his sails and look to God for a breeze from Heaven, but until the wind stirs (John 3:8) he will make no progress. To drop the figure and come to the reality, what has just been said receives illustration in the apostolic benediction, wherein Paul so uniformly prayed for the saints, "Grace be unto you and peace from God our Father and the Lord Jesus Christ"; or as Peter expresses it "grace and peace be multiplied unto you," for nothing less than grace "multiplied" will enable any Christian to grow and thrive.

We must distinguish then not only between the eternal good will and favor of God to His people (Eph. 1:4, 5) and the effect or fruit of it in the actual infusion of His grace (Eph. 4:7) or bestowal of an active principle of holiness, but we must also recognize the difference between that principle and the *daily renewing* of it (II Cor. 4:16) or energizings of it by the influences of the Holy Spirit, which we deserve not. Though that new nature be a spiritual and holy one which disposes its possessor unto the pleasing of God, yet it has no sufficiency in itself to produce the fruits of holiness. Said the Psalmist "O that my ways were directed to keep thy statutes" (119:5): such a desire proceeded from the principle of grace, but having not the power in itself it needed additional Divine enablement to carry it out. So again "Quicken thou me according to thy word" (v. 25): the sparks of grace under the ashes of the flesh needed fanning into a blaze. The life of grace can only be carried on by complete dependence upon God and receiving from Him a fresh "supply of the Spirit of Jesus Christ" (Phil. 1:19).

"Ye must depend upon Christ for strength, ability to repent: all evangelical duties are done in *His* strength. Christ must give us soft hearts, hearts that are repentant; and must teach them by His Spirit before they will repent. Except He smite these rocks, they will yield no water, no tears for sin; except He break these hearts, they will not bleed. We may as well melt a flint or turn a stone into flesh as repent in our own strength. It is far above the power of nature, nay most contrary to it. How can we hate sin which naturally we love above all? mourn for that wherein we most delight? forsake that which is as dear as ourselves? It is the almighty power of Christ which only can do this: we must rely on, seek to Him for it — Lam. 5:21" (David Clarkson, 1670). The same applies just as truly to faith, hope, love, patience — the exercise of any and all of the Christian graces. Only as we are strengthened with might by the Spirit in our inner man are we enabled to be fruitful branches of the Vine.

In its final analysis the spiritual growth of the Christian turns upon the grace which he *continues to receive* from God, nor is the measure obtained determined by anything in or of us. Since it be grace, its Author dispenses it according to His own sovereign determination: "It is God which worketh in you both to will and to do of his good pleasure" (Phil. 2:13). It is God "that giveth the increase" (I Cor. 3:7): to some an increase of faith and wisdom, to others of love and meekness, to yet others of comfort and peace, to yet others strength and victory —"dividing to every man severally as He will" (I Cor. 12:11). Our concern and co-operation is equally due to enabling grace, for of ourselves we "are not sufficient to think anything as of ourselves: but our sufficiency is of God" (II Cor. 3:5). All that is good in us is but a stream from the fountain of Divine grace, and naught but an abiding conviction of that fact will keep us both humble and thankful. God it is who inclines the mind and will unto any good, who illumines our understandings and draws out our affections unto things above. Even the means of grace are ineffectual unless God blesses them to us; yet we sin if we use them not.

But let us turn now to the human-accountability-side of this subject: we are required to "grow in grace" (II Peter 3:18), it is our responsibility to obtain "more grace" (James 4:6) and the fault is entirely ours if we do not, for "the God of all grace" (I Peter 5:10) is infinitely more willing to give than we are to receive. We are plainly exhorted "Ask, and it shall be given you; seek, and ye shall find; knock and it shall be opened unto you" (Matt. 7:7) — where the reference is to our obtaining fresh supplies of grace. No fatalistic apathy is inculcated there: no sitting still with our hands folded until God "be pleased to revive us." No, the very opposite: a definite "asking," an earnest "seeking," an importunate "knocking," until the needed supply is obtained. We are expressly bidden to "*be strong* in the grace that is in Christ Jesus" (II Tim. 2:1). We are freely invited "to come boldly unto the throne of grace, that we may obtain mercy, and find grace to help in time of need" (Heb. 4:16) — pardoning grace, sanctifying grace, persevering grace, as well as grace to faithfully perform the common tasks of life.

It is then both our privilege and duty to obtain fresh supplies of grace each day. Says the apostle "let us have grace" (Heb. 12:28). But let us note the whole of that verse and observe the five things in it. "Wherefore [an inference drawn from the context] we receiving a kingdom which cannot be moved [the privilege conferred upon us], let us have grace [the enablement] whereby we may serve God acceptably [the task assigned us] with reverence and godly fear" — the manner of its performance. Such a duty as serving God acceptably we cannot possibly perform without special Divine assistance. That assistance or strength is to be definitely, diligently, constantly sought by us. To quote from John Owen on this verse — who is one of the very last to be accused of having a legalistic spirit: "to have an increase of this grace as unto its degrees and measures and to keep in exercise in all the duties of the service of God, is a duty *required of* believers by virtue of all the Gospel privileges which they receive from God. For herein consists that revenue of glory which on their account He expecteth and requireth." Alas that so many hyper-Calvinists have got so far away from that holy balance.

In order to the obtaining fresh supplies of grace we need, first, to cultivate a sense of our own weakness, sinfulness, and insufficiency, fighting against every uprising of pride and self-confidence. Second, we need to be more diligent in using the grace we already have, remembering that the one who traded with his talents was he to whom additional ones were entrusted. Third, we need to supplicate God or the same: since Christ has taught us to ask our Father for our daily bread, how much more do we need to ask Him for daily grace. There is a mediatorial fulness of grace in Christ for His people, and it is their privilege and duty to draw upon Him for the same. "Let us therefore come boldly [freely and confidently] unto the throne of grace": the verb is not in the aorist but the present tense, signifying a *continuous* coming — form the habit of so doing. It is both our privilege and duty to come, and to come "boldly." The apostle did not say none may come except they do so confidently: rather is he showing (from considerations in the context) how we *should* come. If we cannot come with boldness, then let us come asking for it.

We can advance nothing but the most idle and worthless excuses for our non-compliance with the blessed invitation of Hebrews 4:16 and our failure to "find grace to help in time of need," yea, so pointless and vain are those excuses it would be a waste of time to name and refute them. If we traced them back to their source, little as we may suspect it, it would be found that those excuses issue from a sense of self-sufficiency, as is clearly implied by those words "God resisteth the *proud,* but giveth grace unto the humble" (James 4:6). God says to me, to you, "let him take hold of my strength" (Isa. 27:5); and again, "*seek* the Lord and his strength" (I Chron. 16:11). Therefore we should come before Him with the prayer "Now therefore O God strengthen my heart" (Neh 6:9), pleading His promise "I *will* strengthen thee, yea, I will help thee" (Isa. 41:10). In an earlier paragraph we quoted the words "thy God hath commanded thy strength," yet so far from the Psalmist feeling that relieved him of all responsibility in the matter, he cried "strengthen, O God, that which thou hast wrought for us" (68:28).

And now let us show how that I Corinthians 15:10 reveals the meetingpoint between the Divine operations of grace and our improvement of the same. First, "by the grace of God I am what I am" — a brand plucked out of the fire, a new creature in Christ Jesus. Second, "and the grace which was bestowed upon me was not in vain (contrast II Cor. 6:1), but *I labored* more abundantly than they all": so far from grace encouraging unto listlessness, it stirred up to earnest endeavor and the improving of the same, so that the apostle was conscious of and shrank not from affirming his *own* diligence and zeal. Third, "yet not I but the grace of God which was with me": he disowns any credit to himself, but gives all the glory to God. It is our bounden duty to use the grace God has bestowed upon us, stirring up and exercising that holy principle, yet this is not to puff us up. As the apostle said again, "Whereunto I also labor, *striving* according to his working, which worketh in me mightily" (Col. 1:29) — he took no praise unto himself, but humbly ascribed what he had done entirely unto the Lord. Fourth, thus grace is given the Christian to make use of, to labor with — in striving against sin, resisting the Devil, running in the way of God's commandments; yet in so laboring, he must be mindful of the Source of his spiritual energy. We can only work out what God has wrought in us (Phil. 2:12, 13), but remember it is our duty *to* "work out."

Not only is it the Christian's responsibility to seek and obtain more grace for himself, but it is also his duty to stimulate and increase the grace of his brethren. Re-read that sentence and let it startle you out of your lethargy and self-complacency. It is of no avail to reply, I cannot increase my own stock of grace, let alone that of another. Scripture is plain on this point: "Let no corrupt communication proceed out of your mouth; but that which is good to the use of edifying, that it may *minister grace* unto the hearers" (Eph. 4:29) — note well that verse is addressed not specially to the ministers of the gospel, but the rank and file of God's people. Yes, you may, you *ought* to be a helper, a strengthener, a builder up of your fellow saints. Grumbling about your lot, groaning over your state, will not be any stimulus to them: rather will it depress and foster unbelief. But if you speak of the faithfulness of God, bear testimony to the sufficiency of Christ, recount His goodness and mercy to you, quote His promises, then will your hearers experience the truth of that proverb "Iron sharpeneth iron: so a man sharpeneth the countenance of his friend" (27:17).

II

It has often been said that "Everything depends upon a right beginning." There is considerable force in that adage: if the foundation be faulty, the superstructure is certain to be insecure; if we take the wrong turn when starting out on a journey, the desired destination will not be reached — unless the error be corrected. It is indeed of vital importance for the professing Christian to measure himself by the unerring standard of God's Word and make sure that his conversion was a sound one, and that his house is being built upon the rock and not upon the sand. Multitudes are deceived, fatally deceived at this vital point: "there is a generation that are pure in their own eyes, and yet is not washed from their filthiness" (Prov. 30:12). Therefore are God's children expressly bidden "Examine yourselves, whether ye be in the faith: prove your ownselves" (II Cor. 13:5). Nor is that to be done in any half-hearted way: "give *diligence* to make your calling and election sure" (II Peter 1:10) is our bounden duty.

"Prove all things": take nothing for granted, give not yourself the benefit of any doubt, but verify your profession and certify your conversion, rest not satisfied until you have clear and reliable evidence that you are indeed a new creature in Christ Jesus. Then heed the exhortation that follows: "Prove all things, *hold fast* that which is good" (I Thess. 5:21). That is no needless caution, but one which it is incumbent upon us to take to heart. There is that still within you which is opposed to the truth, yea, which loves a lie. Moreover, you will encounter fierce opposition from without and be tempted to forsake the stand you have taken. More subtle still will be the evil example of lax professors, who will laugh at your strictness and seek to drag you down to their level. For these and other reasons "We ought to give the more earnest heed to the things which we have heard, *lest* at any time we should let them slip" (Heb. 2:1) — the "at any time" imtimates we must constantly be on our guard against such a calamity.

"Let us *hold fast* the profession of our faith without wavering, for he is faithful that promised" (Heb. 10:23), and therefore we should be faithful in performing. See to it that you hide not your light under a bushel. Be not ashamed of your Christian uniform, but wear it on all occasions. Let your light so shine before men that they may see your good works. Be not a compromiser and temporizer, but out and out for Christ. "Remember therefore how thou hast received and heard, and *hold fast*" (Rev 3:3) If your conversion was a saving one you received that which was infinitely more precious than silver and gold: then prize it as such and cling tenaciously to it. Hold fast the things of God in your memory by frequent meditation thereon, keep them warm in your affections and inviolate in your conscience. "Hold fast that which thou hast, that no man take thy crown" (Rev. 3:11). If you have by grace bought the truth, see to it that you "sell it not" (Prov 23:23): be unflinching in your maintenance of it and unswerving in your devotedness to Christ and what He has entrusted to you.

Thus it is not only necessary that we begin aright, but it is equally essential that we continue right: "If ye *continue* in my word then are ye my disciples indeed" (John 8:31). A persevering attendance on Christ's instructions is the best proof of the reality of our profession. Only by a steady faith in the person and work of Christ, a firm reliance on His promises, and regular obedience to His precepts — notwithstanding all opposition from the flesh, the world and the Devil — do we approve ourselves to be His genuine disciples. "As the Father hath loved me, so have I loved you: *continue ye* in my love" (John 15:9) — continue in the believing enjoyment of it. And how is that to be accomplished? Why, by refraining from those things which would grieve that love, by doing those things which conduce to a fuller manifestation thereof. Nor is such counsel in the least degree "legalistic," as our Lord's very next words show: "If ye keep my commandments ye shall abide in my love, even as I have kept my Father's commandments and abide in his love" (v. 10).

It is perfectly true that if a soul has been regenerated by the Spirit of God that he *will* "hold on his way," yet it is equally true that holding on our way is the evidence or proof of our regeneration, and that if we do not so, then we only deceive ourselves if we suppose we are regenerated. The fact that God has promised to "perform" or "complete" the good work which He has begun in any of His people does not render it needless for *them* to perform and complete the work which He has assigned them. Not so did the apostles think or act. Paul and Barnabas spake to their followers "persuading them *to continue* in the grace of God" (Acts 13:43), which we understand to signify that they exhorted them not to be discouraged by the opposition they met with from the ungodly, nor allow the ragings of indwelling sin to becloud their apprehension of the Divine favor, but rather to go on counting upon the superabounding of God's grace and for them to more and more prove its sufficiency.

So too we find those same apostles going on to other places "Confirming the souls of the disciples and *exhorting them to continue* in the faith, and that we must through much tribulation enter into the kingdom of God" (Acts 14:22). Very far were they from believing in the mechanical idea of "once saved, always saved," which is now so rife. They insisted on the needs-be for the discharge of the Christian's responsibility and were faithful in warning him of both the difficulties and perils of the path he must steadfastly pursue if he was to enter Heaven. Yea, they hesitated not to say unto the saints that they would be presented unblameable and unreproveable in God's sight "*if ye continue* in the faith grounded and settled, and not moved away from the hope of the gospel" (Col. 1:23). So too they exhorted them "Continue in prayer and watch in the same with thanksgiving" (Col. 4:2) — watch against disinclination to prayer, be not discouraged if the answer be delayed, be persistent and importunate, be thankful for past and present mercies and expectant of future ones.

The Christian then is to continue along the same lines as he began. "As ye have received Christ Jesus the Lord, so walk ye in him" (Col. 2: 6). Observe well where the emphasis is placed: it is not "Christ Jesus the Saviour" or "Redeemer" but "Christ Jesus *the Lord.*" In order to receive Christ Jesus as "the Lord" it was necessary for you to forsake all that was opposed to Him (Isa. 55:7); continue thus and "not turn again to folly" (Ps. 85:8). It was required that you throw down the weapons of your warfare against Him and be reconciled to Him: then take them not up again, and "keep thyself from idols" (I John 5:20). It was by surrendering yourself to His righteous claims and giving to Him the throne of your heart: then suffer not "*other* lords to have dominion over you" (Isa. 26:13), but "yield yourself unto God as one that is alive from the dead" (Rom. 6:13). As Romaine pointed out, "He must be received always as He was received once." There is no change of Object and there must be no change in us. Be willing, yea glad for Him to rule over you.

But let us take note now of another word in that important verse: "As ye have received Christ Jesus the Lord, so *walk* ye in Him." Here, as in so many passages in the Epistles, the Christian life is likened unto a "walk," which denotes action, movement in a forward direction. We are not only required to "hold fast" what we have and to "continue" as we began, but we must *advance* and make steady progress. The "narrow way" has to be traversed if Life is to be entered into. There has to be a forgetting of those things which are behind (no complacent contentment with any previous attainment) and a "reaching forth unto those things which are before," pressing "toward the mark for the prize of the high calling of God in Christ Jesus" (Phil. 3:14, 15). There the figure passes from walking to running — which is more strenuous and exacting. In Hebrews 12:1, 2 the Christian life is likened unto a *race,* and in I Corinthians 9:24 we are reminded "they which run in a race run all, but one receiveth the prize," to which is added "*so* run that ye may *obtain.*"

In discussing the promotion of spiritual growth we have dwelt only on general principles; in those which immediately follow on the *means* of growth, we shall enter more into detail; but before turning to them let us connect what has been pointed out in the above paragraphs with what we emphasized earlier in this chapter. There we said that "in the final analysis the spiritual growth of a Christian depends upon the *grace* which he continues to receive from God." Now it should at once be apparent to any renewed soul that while it is obviously his duty to hold fast what he has received from God, to continue in the path of holiness, yea to go forward therein, yet he will only be enabled to discharge those duties as he receives further supplies of strength and wisdom from above. Therefore it is recorded for his encouragement, "God giveth more grace . . . giveth grace unto the humble" (James 4:6), and the "humble" are those who feel their need, who are emptied of self-confidence and self-complacency, who come as beggars to receive favors.

"Grace and peace be *multiplied* unto you" (II Peter 1:2). In connection with the apostolic salutations it needs to be borne in mind, first, they were very much more than pious forms of greeting, they were definite prayers on behalf of those to whom their Epistles were addressed. Second, since such prayers were immediately and verbally inspired by the Holy Spirit, they most certainly contained requests for those things which were "according to" the Divine will. Third, in supplicating God for what they did, the apostles set before their readers an example, teaching them what they most needed and what they should especially ask for. Fourth, thus Christians today have a sure index for their guidance and should be at no loss to decide whether they are warranted in praying for such and such a spiritual blessing. Believers today may be fully assured that it is both their privilege and duty to seek from God not only an increase, but also a multiplication of the grace which he has already bestowed upon them.

The need for increased grace is real and imperative. An active nature such as man's must either grow worse or better, and therefore we should be as deeply concerned about the increase of grace as we should be cautious against the loss of grace. The Christian life is a pulling against the current of the flesh within and the world without, and they who row against the stream must needs ply their oars vigorously and continuously, or the force of the waters will carry them backward. If a man be toiling up a sandy hill, he will sink down if he does not go forward: and unless the Christian's affections be increasingly set upon objects above, then they will soon be immersed in the things of time and sense. Very solemn and searching is that warning of our Lord's: the man who did not improve his talent lost it (Matt. 25:28) — many a Christian who once had zeal in the Lord's service and much joy in his soul, have them no more. Yet still more solemn is it to note that the call of "Let us go on unto perfection" is at once followed by a description of the state and doom of apostates (Heb. 6:1, 4).

As Manton pointed out, "It is an ill sign to be contented with a little grace. He was never good that doth not desire to grow better. Spiritual things do not cloy in the enjoyment. He that hath once tasted the sweetness of grace hath arguments enough to make him seek further grace: every degree of holiness is as desirable as the first, therefore there can be no true holiness without a desire of perfect holiness. God giveth us a taste to this end and purpose that we may long for a fuller draught." Yet He does not force the further draught upon us, but often *tests* us to see if such is really wanted by us — as Christ after communing with the two disciples on the way to Emmaus and making their hearts "burn within them" while He talked with them in the way, then "made as though He would have gone further" when they arrived at their destination; but they "constrained him, saying, Abide with us" (Luke 24:28-32). The grapes of Eshcol were a sample of what Canaan produced and fired the zeal of Joshua and Caleb to go up and possess that land; but their unbelieving brethren were content with the sample — and never obtained anything more!

In the outward part of the Christian life there may be too much, but not so in the inward. There is a zeal which is not according to knowledge, a restless energy of the flesh which spurs to activities which Scripture nowhere enjoins, but such works as those are termed "will worship" (Col. 2:22) and are often dictated by mere tradition or superstition, or are simply the imitation of what other "church members" engage in. But there cannot be too much faith in God, too much of His holy fear upon us, too much knowledge of spiritual things, too much denying of self and devotion to Christ, nor too much love for our fellow saints. For all such virtues we need "abundant grace." There are some who are far from the kingdom of God, having no deep concern for their souls (Eph. 2:13). There are others who come near to the kingdom of God (Mark 12:34), yet never enter into it (Acts 26:18). There are some who enter but who make little progress and are poor testimonials to Christ. But there are a few of whom it is said, "For so an entrance shall be ministered unto you *abundantly* into the everlasting kingdom" (II Peter 1:11), and as the context shows, *they* are the ones who "give diligence" — putting their soul's interests before everything else.

Those who improve the grace given thereby make room for more (Luke 8:18) and ensure for themselves a more ample reward in the day to come. We fully concur with Manton that "According to our measures of grace, so will our measures of glory be, for they that have most grace are vessels of a larger capacity — others are filled according to their size." We know there was not full agreement among the Puritans on this point, though we could quote from others, of them who held there will be degrees of glory among the saints in Heaven, as there will be differences of punishment among the lost in Hell. And why not? There are considerable diversities among the angels on high (Eph. 1:21, etc.). It cannot be gainsaid that God dispenses the gifts and graces of His Spirit *unequally* among His people on earth. Scripture makes it abundantly clear that God will suit our rewards according to our services, and our crowns according to the improvement we have made of His grace and of our opportunities and privileges. The reaping will be in proportion to the sowing (II Cor. 9:6, Gal. 6:8). True, every crown will be cast at the feet of Christ, but the crowns will not be in all respects alike. Labor, then, to get more grace and improve the same.

Thus there is abundant reason *why* the child of God should not only seek for more grace, but that grace may be "multiplied" unto him. If an earthly monarch should invite one of his subjects to ask a favor of him, he would not feel himself flattered if only some trifling thing were requested. Nor do we honor the Sovereign of Heaven by making petty requests — "We are coming to a King; large petitions let us bring." Does He not bid us "open thy mouth *wide*, and I will fill it" (Ps. 81:10): think you that He means not what He says? Does He not invite us "drink, yea drink *abundantly* [from the fountain of grace"], O beloved" (Song of Sol. 5:1): then why not take Him at His word? He is "the God of *all* grace" (I Peter 5:10) and has revealed to us "the riches of his grace" (Eph. 1:7), yea, "the exceeding riches of his grace" (Eph. 2:7): and for whom are they available, if not for those who feel their deep need of and trustfully seek them? "God is *able* to make all grace abound toward you" (II Cor. 9:8) and He would not have told us this if He was not also *willing* to do so.

And now let us anticipate an objection, which might be expressed thus: I realize that spiritual growth is entirely dependent on receiving fresh supplies of grace from God, and that it is my responsibility and duty to diligently and confidently seek the same. I *have* done so, yet instead of grace having been "multiplied" to me, my stock has diminished: so far from having progressed, I have gone backward; instead of my iniquities being "subdued" (Micah 7:19), my lusts rage more fiercely than ever. Several replies may be made. First, you may not have sought as earnestly as you should. Asking and seeking are not sufficient: there has to be an insistent "knocking" (Matt. 7:7), a holy *striving* with God (Rom. 15:30), a saying with Jacob, "I will not let thee go except thou bless me" (Gen. 32:26). Second, God's time to grant your request may not have arrived: "therefore will the Lord *wait* that he may be gracious unto you" (Isa. 30:18) — He waits to test your faith, and because He requires persistence and importunity from us. What is hard to obtain is valued more highly than that which comes easily.

Third, it is to be born in mind that the infusion of grace into a soul promptly evokes the enmity of the flesh, and the more grace be given us the more will sin resist it. Very soon after Christ came into the world Herod stirred up all the country against Him, seeking to slay Him; and when Christ enters a soul the whole of indwelling sin is stirred against Him, for He has come there as its Enemy. The more grace we have the more conscious are we of our corruptions, and the more we are occupied with them the less conscious are we of our grace. As grace is increased so too is our sense of need. Fourth, God does not always answer in kind. You have asked for increased holiness, and been answered with more light; for the removal of a burden, and been given more strength to carry it. You have sought for victory over your lusts, and have been given *humbling* grace so that you loath yourself more deeply. You have besought the Lord to take away some "thorn in the flesh," and He has answered by giving you grace to bear it.

9

Its Means

I

AFTER what we have said previously it may seem almost superfluous to follow with a chapter devoted to a presentation of the principal means of spiritual growth. If success in the Christian life really narrows down to our obtaining fresh supplies of grace from God, then why enumerate and describe in detail the various aids which are to be employed for the promotion of personal godliness? Because the expression "seeking fresh supplies of grace" is a far more extensive one than is commonly supposed: the "means" are really the *channels* through which that grace comes to us. When expounding Matthew 7:7 in our book *Sermon on the Mount* it was pointed out that, in seeking grace to enable the believer to live a spiritual and supernatural life in this world, though such enablement is to be sought at the Throne of Grace, yet that does not render useless nor exempt the Christian from diligently employing the additional means and agencies which God has appointed for the blessing of His people. Prayer must not be allowed to induce lethargy in those directions or become a substitute for the putting forth of our energies in other ways. We are called upon to watch as well as pray, to deny self, strive against sin, take to us the whole armor of God, and fight the good fight of faith.

In the preceding portions of His sermon Christ had presented a standard of moral excellency which is utterly unattainable by mere flesh and blood. He had inculcated one requirement after another that lies not within the power of fallen human nature to meet. He had forbidden an opprobrious word, a malignant wish, an impure desire, a revengeful thought. He had enjoined the most unsparing mortification of our dearest lusts. He had commanded the loving of our enemies, the blessing of those who curse us, the doing good to those who hate us, and the praying for those who despitefully use and persecute us. In view of which the Christian may well exclaim "Who is sufficient for these things? Such demands of holiness are far beyond my feeble strength: yet the Lord *has* made them, what then am I to do?" Here is His own answer: "Ask, and ye shall receive, seek, and ye shall find; knock, and it shall be opened unto you." The Lord Jesus knew that in our own wisdom and strength we are incapable of keeping His commandments, but He at once informed us that the things which are ordinarily impossible to men can be made possible by God.

Divine assistance is imperative if we are to meet the Divine requirements. We need Divine mercy to pardon and cleanse, power to subdue our raging lusts, quickening to animate our feeble graces, light on our

111

path that we may avoid the snares of Satan, wisdom from above for the solving of our varied problems. Only God Himself can relieve our distresses and supply all our need. His assistance, then, is to be sought: sought prayerfully, believingly, diligently and expectantly; and if it be *thus* sought, it will not be sought in vain: for the same passage goes on to assure us "What man is there of you, whom if his son ask bread, will give him a stone? Or if he ask a fish, will he give him a serpent? If ye then being evil know how to give good gifts unto your children, how much more shall your Father which is in heaven give good things to them that ask Him!" (Matt. 7:9-11). What inducement is *that!* yet other means besides prayer are to be used by us if we are to obtain that help and succor which we so sorely need.

There are three principal dangers against which the Christian needs to guard in connection with the various means which God has appointed for his spiritual growth. First, to lay too much stress upon and dependence in them: they are *but* "means" and will avail nothing unless God bless them to him. Second, going to the opposite extreme, by undervaluing them or imagining he can get above them. There are some who give way to fanaticism or persuade themselves they have been so "baptized by the Spirit" as to be independent of helps. Third, to look for that in them which can come only from God in Christ. No doubt there is room for differences of opinion as to what are the particular means which are most conducive unto Christian prosperity, and certainly there is a considerable variety of method among those who have written on this subject, some throwing their main emphasis on one aspect of it and some on another. Nor is there any agreement in the *order* in which they set forth the several aids to growth. We shall therefore present them to the reader according as they appear to us in the light of Scripture.

1. *Mortifying of the flesh.* In order to obtain fresh supplies of grace constant watchfulness needs to be exercised that we do not cut ourselves off from the Source of those supplies. If such a statement jars upon some of our readers, having to them a "legalistic" or Arminian sound in it, we fear it is because their sensibilities are not fully regulated by the teachings of Holy Writ. Would it not be foolish for me to blame the bulb for emitting no light if I had switched off the electrical current? Equally vain is it to attribute any lack of grace in me to the unwillingness of God to bestow it if I have severed communion with Him. Should it be objected that to draw such an analogy is carnal, we reply, our object is simply to illustrate. But does not the Lord Himself distinctly affirm "Your iniquities have *separated* between you and your God, and your sins have hid his face from you, that he will not hear" (Isa. 59:2): then how can I draw from the Fountain of grace if I have cut myself off from it!

None but a fanatical enthusiast will argue that a Christian may obtain a fuller knowledge of God's will and increased light on his path while he *neglects* his Bible and books and preaching thereon. Nor will the Holy Spirit open the Word to me while I am indulging in the lusts of the flesh and "allowing" sin in my heart and life. Equally clear is it that no Christian has any Scriptural warrant to expect he will receive wisdom and strength from above while he neglects the Throne of Grace, and should he keep up the *form* of "praying" while following a course of self-will and self-pleasing, answers of peace will be withheld from him. "If I regard [cherish] iniquity in my heart, the Lord will *not* hear me" (Ps. 66:18). "Ye ask and receive not because ye ask amiss, that ye may consume it upon your lusts" (James 4:3). The Holy One will be no lackey unto our carnality. "He that turneth away his ear from hearing the law [i.e., refuses to tread the path of obedience, in subjection to God's authority], even his prayer shall be abomination" (Prov. 28:9), for under such circumstances praying would be downright hypocrisy, a mocking of God.

It is therefore apparent that there is something which must take precedence of either prayer or feeding on the Word if the Christian is to make progress in the spiritual life. Whether or not we have succeeded in making that evident to the reader, Scripture is quite plain on the point. We are bidden to "receive with meekness the ingrafted Word," but before we can do so we must first comply with what immediately precedes, namely, "*lay apart* all filthiness and superfluity of naughtiness" (James 1:21). Room has to be made in our hearts for the Word: the old lumber has to be cleaned out before the new furnishings can be moved into it. We are exhorted "As new-born babes, *desire* the sincere milk of the word that ye may grow thereby" (I Peter 2:2). Ah, but there is something else *before* that, and which must needs first be attended to: "Wherefore *laying aside* all malice, and all guile, and hypocrisies, and envies, and all evil speakings" (v. 1). There has to be a purging of our corruptions ere there will be a spiritual appetite for Divine things. The natural man may "study the Bible" to become intellectually informed of its contents, but there has to be a "laying aside" of the things God hates before the soul will really hunger for the Bread of Life.

That to which we have just called attention has not been sufficiently recognized. It is one thing to read the Scriptures and become acquainted with their teaching, it is quite another to really feed upon them and for the life to be transformed thereby. God's Word is a *holy* Word, and it requires holiness of heart from the one who would be profitted by it: the soul must be attuned to its message and transmission before there will be any real "reception." And in order to holiness of soul sin has to be resisted, self-denied, corrupt lusts mortified. What we are here insisting upon is illustrated and demonstrated by the *uniform order* of Scripture. We have to "hate the evil" before we "love the good" (Amos. 5:15), and "cease to do evil" ere we can "learn to do well" (Isa. 1:16, 17). Self has to be denied and the cross taken up, before we can "follow" Christ (Matt. 16:24). We have to "cleanse ourselves from all filthiness of the flesh and spirit" if we would be "perfecting holiness in the fear of God" (II Cor. 7:1). We cannot "put on the new man" (Eph. 2:22) until we have "put off concerning the former conversation [or "manner of life"] the old man, which is corrupt according to the deceitful lusts" (Eph. 2:20)!

Sin indwells all Christians and is actively opposed to the principle of grace or "new nature." When they would do good, evil is present with them. Indwelling sin or "the flesh" — corrupt nature — has "no good thing" dwelling in it (Rom. 7:18). Its nature is entirely evil. It is beyond reclamation, being incapable of any improvement. It may put on a religious garb, as in the case of the Pharisees, but beneath is nothing but rottenness. As one has truly said "No good can be educed out of it: fire may as soon be struck out of ice as good dispositions and motions be produced in the corrupt heart of the regenerate. It will never be produced in the corrupt heart of the regenerate. It will never be prevailed upon to concur with the new principle in any of those acts which it puts forth: hence the mind of the believer is at no time wholly spiritual and holy in its acts: there is more or less of a resistance in his soul for what is holy at all seasons." As the "flesh" continually opposes what is good, so it ever disposes the will to what is evil: its desires and motions are constantly towards objects which are vain and carnal. So far as it is permitted to control the Christian, it beclouds his judgment, captivates his affections, and enslaves his will.

Now the principle of grace, "the spirit" has been communicated to the saint for the express purpose of opposing the solicitations of the flesh and for the inclining of him unto holiness. Thus the whole of his duty may be summed up in these two things: to die unto sin and to live unto God. And he can only live unto God in exact proportion as he dies unto sin. That should be self-evident, for since sin is hostile to God, entirely and inveterately so, only so far as we rise above its evil influences are we free to act Godwards. Therefore our progress in the Christian life is to be measured by the degree of our deliverance from the power of indwelling sin, and that, in turn, will be determined by how resolutely, earnestly, and untiringly we set ourselves to this great task of fighting against our corruptions. The weeds must be plucked up before the flowers can grow in the garden, and our lusts must be mortified if our graces are to flourish. Sin and grace each demand the governance of the soul, and it is the Christian's responsibility to see to it that the former is denied and the latter given the right to reign over him.

For if ye live after the flesh, ye shall die; but if ye through the Spirit do mortify the deeds of the body, ye shall live" (Rom. 8:13). That at once shows us the fundamental and vital importance of this duty: our attendance or nonattendance thereto is a matter of life or death. Mortification is not optional but imperative. The solemn alternative is plainly stated. Those words are addressed to the saints, and they are faithfully warned "if ye live after the flesh ye shall *die*," that is, die spiritually and eternally. To "live after the flesh" is to live as do the unregenerate, who are motivated, actuated, and dominated by nothing but their own fallen nature. To "live after the flesh" refers not to a single action, nor even a whole series of actions in one particular direction, but for the whole man to be regulated by the evil principle. Education and culture may produce a refined exterior; family training or other influences may lead to a "profession of religion": but the love of God prompts neither, nor is His glory the end. To "live after the flesh" is to allow our fallen nature to govern our character and guide our conduct, and such is the case with all the unregenerate.

"But if ye through the Spirit do mortify the deeds of the body, ye shall live." Note well the "if ye do": it is a duty assigned the Christian it is a task which calls for self-effort. Yet it is not a work for which he is sufficient of himself: it can only be accomplished "through the Spirit." But care has to be taken at this point lest we lapse into error. It is *not,* "if the Spirit through you," but "if *ye* through the Spirit." The believer is not a cipher in this undertaking. The Spirit is not given to relieve us of the discharge of our responsibility in this all-important matter, but rather to equip us for *our* discharge of the same. The Spirit operates by making us more sensible of indwelling sin, by deepening our aspirations after holiness, by causing the love of Christ to constrain, by strengthening us with His might in the inner man. But *we* are the ones who are required to "*mortify* the deeds of the body," that is, resist the workings of sin, deny self, put to death our lusts, refuse to "live after the flesh."

We must not under the guise of "honoring the Spirit" repudiate our accountability or under the pretext of "waiting for the Spirit to move us" or "empower us," lapse into a state of passivity. God has called us to "*cleanse ourselves* from all filthiness of the flesh and of the spirit" (II Cor. 7:1), to "put off concerning the former conversation the old man" (Eph. 4:22), to "keep yourselves from idols" (I John 5:21); and He will not accept the excuse of our inability as a valid plea. If we be His children, He has infused His grace into our hearts, and that grace is to be employed in this very task of mortifying our lusts, and the way to get more grace is to make a more diligent use of what we already have. We do not "honor the Spirit" by inertia: we honor Him and "magnify grace" when we can say with David "I kept myself from mine iniquity" (Ps. 18:23), and with Paul "But I keep under my body and bring it into subjection" (I Cor. 9:24). True, it was by Divine enablement, yet it was not something which God did for them. There was *self-effort* — rendered successful by Divine grace.

Observe it is not "If ye *have* through the Spirit mortified the deeds of the body," but "if ye *do* . . . mortify." It is not something which may be done once for all, but a continuous thing, a lifelong task which is set before the Christian. The term "mortify" is here used figuratively, inasmuch as it is a physical term applied to that which is immaterial; yet its force is easily perceived. Literally the word signifies "put to death," which implies it is both a painful and difficult task: the weakest creature may put up some resistance when its life be threatened, and since sin is a most powerful principle it will make a mighty struggle to preserve its existence. The Christian then is called upon to exert a constant and all-out endeavor to subdue his lusts, resist their inclinations, and deny their solicitations, "*striving* against sin" (Heb. 12:4) — not only against one particular form of its outbreakings, but against *all* of them, and especially against the root from which they proceed — "the flesh."

How is the Christian to set about this all-important work? First, by starving his evil nature: "make not provision for the flesh" (Rom. 13:14). There are two ways of causing a fire to go out: to cease feeding it with fuel and to pour water upon it. God does not require us to macerate our bodies nor to adopt severe external austerities, but we *are* to abstain from pampering and pleasing them. "To ask meat for our bodies is necessary, a duty; but to ask meat for our lusts is provoking to God — Ps. 78:18" (Matt. Henry). "Provision for" the flesh is anything which has the least tendency to minister unto its appetites: whatever would stir our carnal lusts must be abstained from. There are mental lusts as well as physical: such as pride, covetousness, envy, malice, presumption — these too must be starved and denied, for they are "filthiness of the spirit" (II Cor. 7:1). Avoid all excesses: be temperate in all things. Second, refuse any familiarity with worldings: "have no fellowship with the unfruitful works of darkness" (Eph. 5:11). Shun evil companions, for "a companion of fools shall be destroyed" (Prov. 13:20). "Enter not into the path of the wicked . . . avoid it, pass not by it, turn from it" (Prov. 4:13, 14). Even those "having a form of godliness" but who in practice are "denying the power thereof," God says, "from such *turn away*" (II Tim. 3:5).

Third, "Keep thy *heart* with all diligence, for out of it are the issues of life" (Prov. 4:23). Take yourself firmly in hand and maintain a strict discipline over your inner man, especially your desires and thoughts. Unlawful desires and evil imaginations need to be nipped in the bud, by sternly resisting them at our first consciousness of the same. As it is much easier to pluck up weeds while they are young or to quench a fire before it takes a firm hold, so it is much simpler to deal with the initial stirrings of our lusts than after they have "conceived" (*see* James 1:15) — refuse to parley with the first temptation, suffer not your mind to cogitate upon anything Scripture disallows. Fourth, keep short accounts with God. As soon as you are conscious of failure, excuse it not, but penitently confess it to Him. Let not sins accumulate on your conscience, but frankly and promptly acknowledge them to the Lord. Bathe daily in the Fountain which has been "opened for sin and for uncleanness" (Zech. 13:1).

It is strange that so many other writers on this subject have failed to place *first* among the means of spiritual growth this work of *mortifying* the flesh, for it should be quite obvious that it must take precedence over everything else. Of what avail can it be to read and study the Word, to spend more time in prayer, to seek to develop my graces, while I ignore and neglect that within me which will neutralize and mar all other efforts. What would be the use of sprinkling fertilizer on my ground if I allowed the weeds to grow and multiply there? Of what avail would it be my watering and pruning of a rose-bush if I knew there was a pest gnawing at its roots? Settle it then in your mind, dear reader, that no progress can be made by you in the Christian life until you realize the paramount importance and imperative necessity of waging a ceaseless warfare against indwelling sin, and not only realize the need for the same, but resolutely gird yourself for and engage in the task, ever seeking the Spirit's help to give you success therein. The Canaanites must be ruthlessly exterminated if Israel was to occupy the land of milk and honey, and enjoy peace and prosperity therein.

II

2. *Devotedness to God.* The lifelong work of mortification is but the negative side of the Christian life, being a means to an end: the positive aspect is that the redeemed and regenerated sinner is henceforth to live unto God, to wholly give up himself unto Him, to employ his faculties and powers in seeking to please Him and promote His glory. In his unregenerate days, he went "his *own* way" (Isa. 53:6) and did that which was pleasing unto himself, but at conversion he renounced the flesh, the world and the Devil, and turned unto God as his absolute Lord, supreme End, and everlasting Portion. Mortification is the daily renewing of that renunciation, a continuing to turn away from all that God hates and condemns. Devotedness to God is a living out of the decision and promise which the believer made at his conversion, when he gave himself unto the Lord (II Cor. 8:5), chose Him for his highest Good and entered into covenant with Him to love Him with all his heart and serve Him with all his strength.

In exact proportion to his strict adherence to his surrender to God at his conversion will be the believer's spiritual growth and progress in the Christian life. That mortification and devotedness unto God is the true order of the principal *means* for promoting spiritual prosperity appears, first, from the grand type furnished in the Old Testament. When God began His dealings with Israel He called them out of Egypt, separating them from the heathen, as He had their great progenitor when He called him to leave Ur of Chaldea — a figure of mortification. But that was merely negative. Having delivered them from their old manner of life and brought them over the Red Sea, He brought them unto Himself (Exod. 19:4), made known His will unto them and entered into a solemn covenant, to which they were consenting parties, declaring "all that the Lord hath said will we do and be obedient" (Exod. 24:7). Just so long as they adhered to their vow and kept the covenant all was well with them. Devotedness unto the Lord was the grand secret of spiritual success.

This order appears again in that oft-repeated word of Christ's, which contains a brief but comprehensive summary of His requirements: "If any man will come after me, let him deny himself, and take up his cross, and follow me" (Matt. 16:24). *There* are the fundamental terms of Christian discipleship and the basic principles by which the Christian life is to be regulated. Any one who "will come after me" — who chooses, decides, determines to enlist under My banner, throw in his lot with Me, become one of My disciples, "let him deny himself and take up his cross," and that "daily" (Luke 9:23) — which presents to us the work of mortification But that is only preliminary, a means to an end: the principal thing is "and *follow me*," My example. What was the grand principle which regulated *Him*? What was the unchanging end of Christ's life? This: "I came down not to do mine own will, but the will of him that sent me" (John 6:38); "I do always those things that please him" (John 8:29). And we are not following Christ unless *that* be *our* aim and endeavor.

That devotedness to God is the outstanding mark, the essential duty, the pre-eminent thing in the Christian life, is also clear from the teaching of the Epistles. "I beseech you therefore, brethren, by the mercies of God, that ye present your bodies a living sacrifice, holy, acceptable unto God, which is your reasonable service" (Rom. 12:1). That appeal is made unto Christians and *begins* the hortatory section of that Epistle. Up to that point the apostle had set forth the great facts and doctrinal contents of the gospel, and only once did he break the thread of his discourse by interjecting an exhortation, namely, in 6:11-22, the force of which is here gathered up into a concise but extensive summary. The "yield yourselves unto God as those that are alive from the dead" (6:13) and the "yield your members servants to righteousness unto holiness" (6:19) is here paraphrased as "present your bodies a living sacrifice, holy, acceptable unto God." In substance it is parallel with that word, "Son, give me thine heart, and let thine eyes observe my ways" (Prov. 23:26).

The place which is given to this precept in the New Testament intimates its paramount importance: "I beseech you therefore, brethren, by the mercies of God, that ye present your bodies a living sacrifice, holy, acceptable unto God, which is your reasonable service" (Rom. 12:1). That is the *first* exhortation of the Epistles addressed to the saints, taking precedence of all others! First, there is the duty which God requires from us. Second, the ground on which it is enforced or the motive from which it is to be performed, is made known. Third, the reasonableness of it is affirmed. The duty to which we are here exhorted is a call to the unreserved dedication and consecration of the Christian to God. But since those are terms which have suffered not a little at the hands of various fanatics we prefer to substitute for them the *devoting* of ourselves entirely to God. That word "devote" is employed in Leviticus 27:21, 28 where it is defined as "a holy thing unto the Lord" yea, "every devoted thing is most holy unto the Lord," that is, something which is set apart exclusively for His use.

Joshua 6 contains a solemn illustration of the force and implications of that term. Israel's commander informed the people that "the city [of Jericho] shall be devoted, even it, and all that are therein, to the Lord" (v. 17). Since it was His power that delivered this city of the Canaanites into their hands, He claimed it as *His*, to do with as He pleased, thereby precluding the Israelites from seizing any of its spoils for themselves. So that there might be no uncertainty in their minds, it was expressly added "But all the silver and gold, and vessels of brass and iron, are consecrated unto the Lord; they shall come into the treasury of the Lord" (v. 19). Therein lay the enormity of Achan's sin: not only in yielding to a spirit of covetousness, not only in deliberately disobeying a Divine commandment, but in taking unto himself that which was definitely devoted or set apart unto the Lord. Hence the severity of the punishment meted out to him and all his household. A monumental warning was that for all future generations of how jealously God regards that which is set apart unto Himself, and the awful seriousness of putting to a profane or common use what has been consecrated to Him!

"I beseech you therefore, brethren, by the mercies of God, that ye present your bodies a living sacrifice" signifies, then, that you devote them unto God, that you solemnly set them apart to Him, for His use, for His service, for His pleasure, for His glory. The Hebrew word for "devote" (*charam*) is rendered "consecrate" in Micah 4:13, and "dedicated" (*cherem*) in Ezekiel 44:29. The Greek word for "present" (*paristemi*) occurs first in Luke 2:22, where we are told that the parents of Jesus "brought Him to Jerusalem to *present Him* to the Lord," which in the next verse is defined as "holy to the Lord." How deeply significant and suggestive that its initial reference should be to our Great Exemplar! It is found again in II Corinthians 11:2, "that I may present you a chaste virgin to Christ." It is the term used in Ephesians 5:27, "that ye might present it to himself a glorious church." It is the same word that is translated "*yield* yourselves unto God" in Romans 6:13. It therefore means a definite, voluntary, personal act of full surrender to God.

This duty which is enjoined upon the Christian is here set forth, more or less, in the language of the Old Testament types, as the term "a living sacrifice" clearly intimates, while the word "present" is a temple term for the bringing thither of anything to God. This duty was announced in Old Testament prophecy: "they shall bring all your brethren *for an offering* unto the Lord out of all nations" (Isa. 66:20), not to be slain and burned in the fire, but to be presented for God's use and pleasure. So, too, it was revealed that when "our God shall come" He will say, "Gather my saints unto me, those that have made a covenant with me *by sacrifice*" (Ps. 50:3, 5). There were three principal things taught by the Levitical offerings. First, our sinfulness, guilt, and pollution, which could only be expiated by "a life for a life"; and that was for our humiliation. Second, the wondrous provision of God's grace: Christ a substitute and surety, dying in our stead; which was for our consolation. Third, the love and gratitude due unto God, and the new obedience which He requires from us; and that is for our sanctification.

The Christian is required to surrender the whole of his being to God. The language in which that injunction is couched in Romans 12:1 is taken from the usages of the Mosaic economy. "Present your bodies a living sacrifice" connotes, present yourselves as embodied intelligences. Our "bodies" are singled out for specific mention to show there is to be no reservation, that the entire man is to be devoted to the Lord: "The very God of peace sanctify you *wholly,* and your whole spirit and soul and body be preserved blameless" (I Thess. 5:23). When God called Israel out of Egypt He said "there shall not a hoof be left behind" (Exod. 10:26). Our "bodies are the members of Christ" (I Cor. 6:15) and therefore does He bid us "yield your members servants to righteousness unto holiness" (Rom. 6:19). It is through the body that our new nature expresses itself. As I Corinthians 6 tells us, the body is "for the Lord, and the Lord for the body" (v. 13). And again, "know ye not that your body is the temple of the Holy Spirit . . . therefore glorify God in your body" (vv. 19, 20).

This duty is expressed in Old Testament terms because the apostle was comparing Christians to sacrificial animals whose bodies were devoted as offerings to the Lord, and because he would thereby particularly emphasize that obligation which devolved upon them to be and do and suffer whatever God required. The "living sacrifice" points a parallel and not a contrast, for no animal *carcase* could be brought by an Israelite. A living victim was brought by the offerer and he laid his hand upon his head to signify he transferred to God all his right and interest in it, then he killed it before God, after which the priests, Aaron's sons, brought the blood and sprinkled it upon the altar (Lev. 1:2-5). In the application of this term to the Christian it may also include the idea of *permanency*: present your bodies a perpetual sacrifice: as in Christ "the *living* bread" (John 6:51) and "a living hope" (I Peter 1:3); it is not to be a transcient "sacrifice," but one never to be recalled. "Holy" means unblemished, and set apart solely for God's use, as the vessels of the tabernacle and temple were devoted exclusively to His service.

The Christian is called upon to give up himself to God, and that cannot be done without cost, without proving that a "sacrifice" is indeed a *sacrifice*, even though a willing one; yet it is only by so doing we can be conformed to the death of Christ (Phil. 3:10). It is to be done intelligently, *voluntarily*, as a free will offering to God, with full and hearty consent, as one gives himself or herself to another in marriage, so that the believer can now say "I am my beloved's and my beloved is mine" (Song of Sol. 6:3). Yet it is to be done *humbly*, with grief and shame for having so long delayed, for having wasted so much of my time, and strength in the service of sin. It is to be done *gratefully*, from a deep sense of Divine grace and mercy, so that the love of Christ constrains me. It is to be done *unreservedly*, with no reservation, an unqualified devoting of myself unto God. It is to be done *purposefully*, with the sincere desire, intention and endeavor to be ruled by Him in all things, ever preferring and putting His interests and pleasure before my own.

But let us notice now the ground on which this duty is enforced, or the motive by which it is to be performed. "I beseech you therefore, brethren, *by the mercies of God.*" It is not "I command you," for it is not the Divine authority to which appeal is made. "Beseech" is the tender language of loving entreaty, asking for a gracious response to the amazing grace of God. The "therefore" is a deduction made from what precedes. In the foregoing chapters the apostle had, from 3:21 onwards, set forth the gospel "mercies" or riches of Divine grace. They consist of election, redemption, regeneration, justification, sanctification, with the promise of preservation and glorification — blessings that pass knowledge. What, then, shall be our response to such inestimable favors? It was as though the apostle anticipated his Christian brethren being so overwhelmed by such lavish displays of God's goodness to them, they would exclaim "What shall I render unto the Lord for all his benefits"? What possible return can I make to Him for His surpassing love? Here, says Paul is the answer to such a query, to such a heart longing.

"I beseech you therefore, brethren, by the mercies of God, that ye present your bodies a living sacrifice, holy, acceptable unto God." It is *thus* you will manifest your gratitude and evince your appreciation of all God has done for, to, and in you. It is *thus* you will exhibit the sincerity of your love for Him. It is thus you will prove yourselves to be "followers" of Christ and adorn His gospel. It is thus you will please Him who has done everything for you: not merely by vocal thanksgiving, but by personal thanks*living*. Thus did the apostle begin to present and press those obligations which are involved by the blessed favors and privileges set forth in the preceding chapters. Those doctrinal disclosures are not so many speculative things to engage our brains, but are precious discoveries for the inflaming of our hearts. The contents of Romans 3 to 8 are given not only for the informing of our understandings, but also for the *reforming* of our lives. We should never abstract privilege from duty, nor duty from privilege, but take them together. The "therefore" of 12:1 points the practical application to all that goes before.

"Acceptable unto God, which is your reasonable service." Poor and paltry as is such a return to the Divine munificence, yet God is pleased to receive the offering up of ourselves and to announce that such an offering is agreeable to Him. That is in striking and blessed contrast from "the sacrifice of the wicked is an *abomination* unto the Lord" (Prov. 15:8). The words "reasonable service" are susceptible of various renditions, though we doubt if any are better than that of the Authorized Version. Logical or rational are warrantable alternatives, for God certainly requires to be served intelligently and not blindly or superstitiously. Literally, it may be translated "your service according to the Word." "Service" may be rendered "worship," for it is an act of homage and a temple service which is here in view, and thus accords with the idea of "sacrifice": God requires the worship of our body as well as of the mind. But in the light of the preceding "therefore" we prefer "reasonable service."

"Which is your reasonable service." And is it not so? "Those that obey not the Word are called 'fools' (Jer. 8:9) and 'unreasonable men' (II Thess. 2:3), because lacking in wisdom to discern the excellency and equity of God's ways. What can be more reasonable than that He who made all things for Himself should be served by the creatures that He made? That we should live unto Him who gave us being? That the Supreme should be obeyed, the infallible Truth believed, that He who can destroy should be feared, that He who doth reward should be loved and trusted in?" (E. Reynolds, 1670). It is reasonable because it is what Omniscience requires of us: this is the fundamental part of our covenant when we choose Him as our God: "One shall say, I am the Lord's . . . and another shall subscribe with his hand unto the Lord" (Isa. 44:5). By our own solemn consent we acknowledge God's right in us and yield to His claims. He requires that His right be confirmed by our consent: "*take* my yoke upon you" — He forces it on none.

"Which is your reasonable service." And again we ask, Is it not so? Does not a change of masters involve a changed order of life? Should not those who have been recovered from sin to God show the reality of that change in being as earnest in holiness as before they were in sin? Talk is cheap, but actions speak louder than words. If God gave Christ to us as a sin-offering, is it too much to ask that we devote ourselves to Him as a thank-offering? Christ was content to be nothing that God might be all, and is it not "reasonable" that our judicial oneness with Christ should have for its complement practical conformity to Him. If we have by regeneration passed from death unto life, is it not reasonable and meet that we devote ourselves as a "living sacrifice" to God and walk in newness of life? Are not the "mercies of God," appropriated by faith and realized in the heart, sufficient inducement to move His people to give up themselves entirely to His will, to be ordered, employed, and disposed of according to His good pleasure?

Are any inclined to ask, What has all the above to do with spiritual growth or Christian progress? We answer, much every way. Genuine conversion is a giving up of ourselves to God, an entering into covenant with Him that He should be *our God*, and His promises are made to "such as *keep* his covenant and to those that remember his commandments to *do* them" (Ps. 10:3). But if we turn from devoting ourselves to God to sin and the world, and thereby break the covenant, what possible spiritual prosperity can we enjoy or progress make? Christ died for all His people "that they which live should not henceforth live unto themselves, but *unto Him* who died for them, and rose again" (II Cor. 5:15). If then I relapse into a course of self-pleasing, so far from advancing in the Christian life, I have backslidden, repudiated the initial dedication of myself to God and have cast Christ's yoke from off me. Spiritual growth consists of *increasing* devotedness to God and being more and more conformed unto Christ's death.

It is one of the most effectual means for spiritual growth to live in the daily realization that Christ has "redeemed us *to God*" (Rev. 5:9): to restore His rights over us, to admit us to His favor and friendship, to enjoy fellowship and communion with Him, that we may be for His pleasure and glory; then to conduct ourselves accordingly. Only as we are wholly devoted to His service and praise, only as all our springs and joy are in Him, do we actualize the design of our redemption. No progress in the Christian life can be made any further than as we are regulated by the fact "ye are not your own, for ye are bought with a price" (I Cor. 6:19, 20). When that is really apprehended in the heart, the soul will become the consecrated priest and his body will be the living sacrifice offered unto God daily through Jesus Christ. Then will it be the devotedness not of constraint but of *love*. The more fully we are conformed to Christ's death, the more closely we be following the example He has left us, the more (and the *only*) true Christian progress are we making.

III

3. *Honoring the Word.* By which we mean according to God's holy and infallible Word the place which is due it in our affections, thoughts, and daily lives. But we shall only do so as we are deeply impressed with *whose* Word it is and the reasons for which it has been given to us. God has "magnified his word above all his name" (Ps. 138:2), and if we be in our right minds we shall value it far more highly than anything else (Ps. 119:72). Apart from the Word we are in total darkness spiritually (Eph. 5:8). Without the Scriptures we can know nothing about the character of God, His attitude toward us, or our relation to Him. Without the Scriptures we are ignorant of the nature of sin and its infinite demerits, nor are we capable of discovering how to be saved from the love, guilt and pollution of it. Without the Scriptures we know not whence we sprang, whither we are going, nor how to conduct ourselves in the interval between. Even as Christians, we have no other means for ascertaining God's will for us, the path we should tread, the enemies we must fight, the armor we require, and how to obtain grace to help in time of need.

All who profess to be Christians will give at least a mental assent to what has just been pointed out. But when it comes to the applying or working out of the same, there are wide differences of practice. In the matter of *what use* is to be made of God's Word there is considerable diversity of opinion. Rome does all she can to *withhold* the Scriptures from the people, forbidding the reading of them; or, where that is deemed impolitic, seeking to discourage the same. Her evil leaven has spread far and wide, for multitudes of nominal "Protestants" who do not formally accept the dogmas of the Papacy suppose that the Bible is a mysterious Book, quite beyond the comprehension of the uninitiated and that "the church" alone is competent to explain its teachings. Therefore they are quite content to receive their religious instructions secondhand, accepting what the prelate or preacher tells them from the pulpit, and since they do not "search the Scriptures" for themselves, they are unable to *test* what he tells them, and are liable to be deceived concerning their eternal interests. Thus there is no difference in this respect between them and the infatuated Papists.

But there are others who "read the Bible" for themselves: but here there are many types. Some do so *traditionally*, because their parents and grandparents read a portion each day, yet in few cases do they give evidence of possessing a saving knowledge of the truth. Others read it *superstitiously*, regarding the Bible as a sort of religious charm: when in great perplexity or deep sorrow they turn to the Book they generally neglect, hoping to find guidance or solace from it. Many read it *educationally*. If their closest friends are more or less "religious" they would feel ashamed if unable to take an intelligent part in the conversation, and so seek a general acquaintance with its contents. Others read it *denominationally*, that they may be equipped to defend "our Articles of Faith" and hold their own in controversy, seeking texts which will refute the beliefs of others. A few read it *professionally*: it is their textbook. Their principal quest is material suitable for sermons and "Bible readings." Some read it *inquisitively*, to satisfy curiosity and feed intellectual pride: they specialize on prophecy, the types, numerics, and so on.

Now one may read the Bible from such motives as those until he is as old as Methuselah and his soul be profited nothing! One may read and re-read the Bible through systematically from Genesis to Revelation, he may "search the Scriptures" diligently — comparing passage with passage, he may become quite an accomplished "Bible student," and yet, spiritually speaking, be not one whit better off for his pains. Why so? Because he failed to realize the chief reasons why God has given us His Word and to act accordingly, because his motive is faulty, because the end he had in view is unworthy. God has given the Word to us as a revelation of Himself: of His character, of His government, of His requirements. Our motive in reading it, then, should be to become better acquainted with Him, with His perfections, with His will for us. Our end in perusing His Word should be to learn how to please and glorify Him, and that, by our characters being formed under its holy influence and our conduct regulated in all its details by the rules He has there laid down. The mind needs instructing, but unless the conscience be searched, the heart influenced, the will moved, such knowledge will only puff us up and add to our condemnation.

In the preceding chapters we pointed out that in order to spiritual growth the Christian must needs engage daily in mortifying the flesh and in devoting himself as a living sacrifice to God, giving our reasons for placing them first and second among the principal aids to prosperity. Obviously giving due place to the Word comes next, for only by its instructions can we learn *what* has to be mortified and *how* to please God in our walk. Some thought was required on how best to formulate this third grand help. Many have described it as *studying* the Word, but as pointed out above one may "study" it (as the "scribes" of our Lord's day had) and yet be none the better for it. Others use the expression *feeding* on the Word, which is better, though today there are thousands who think they *are* feeding thereon and yet give little or no sign their souls are being nourished or that they are becoming more fruitful branches of the Vine. We have therefore chosen *honoring* the Word as being a more comprehensive term.

Now in order to honor the Word we must ascertain the purposes for which God has given it to us, and then regulate our efforts accordingly. The Word expressly informs us the chief ends for which it *was* written. "All Scripture is given by inspiration of God, and is profitable for doctrine, for reproof, for correction, for instruction in righteousness" (II Tim. 3:16). Since they are inspired by God it naturally and necessarily follows that they are "profitable," for He could not be the Author of what was purposeless and useless to its recipients. *For what* are the Scriptures "profitable"? First, *for doctrine,* that is, for sound and wholesome doctrine, "doctrine which is according to godliness" (I Tim. 6:3). The word doctrine means "teaching" or instruction, and then the principle or article received. In the Scriptures we have the truth and nothing but the truth on every object and subject of which they treat, such as no mere creature could have arrived at or invented. The unfolding of the doctrine of *God* is a revelation of His Being and character, such as had never been conceived by philosophers or poets. Their teaching concerning *man* is such as no physicist or psychologist had ever discovered by his own unaided powers. Such, too, is its doctrine of sin, of salvation, of the world, of Heaven, of Hell.

Now to read and ponder the Scriptures for "doctrine" is to have our *beliefs* formed by its teachings. So far as we are under the influence of prejudice, or receive our religious ideas on human authority, and go to the Word not so much with the desire to be instructed on what we know not, but rather for the purpose of finding something which will confirm us in what we have already imbibed from man, be it right or wrong, so far we exercise a sinful disregard to the Sacred Canon and may justly be given up to our own deceits. Again; if we set up our own judgment so as to resolve not to accept anything as Divine truth but what we can intellectually comprehend, then we despise God's Word and cannot be said to read it either for doctrine or correction. It is not enough to "call no man Master": if I exalt my reason above the infallible dictates of the Holy Spirit, then my *reason* formulates my *creed*. We must come to the Word conscious of our ignorance, forsaking our own thoughts (Isa. 55:7), with the earnest prayer "that which I see not, teach thou me" (Job 34:32), and that, so long as we remain on earth.

First and foremost then the inspired Scriptures are profitable for *doctrine*: that our thoughts, ideas and beliefs concerning all the subjects of Divine revelation may be formed and regulated by their infallible teachings. How that rebukes those who sneer at theological instruction, who are prejudiced against the doctrinal exposition of the gospel, who ignorantly account such "dry" and uninteresting, who are all for what they term "experimental religion." We say "ignorantly," for the distinction they seek to draw is an unscriptural and invalid one. The Word of God nowhere draws a line between the doctrinal and the experimental. How could it? when true experimental piety is nothing but the *influence of truth* upon the soul under the agency of the Holy Spirit. What is godly sorrow for sin but the influence of the truth upon the conscience and heart! Is it anything else than a realization or feeling sense of the heinousness of sin, of its contrariety to what ought to be, of its being committed against light and love, dissolving the heart to grief? Until those truths are realized there will be no weeping over your sin. Peace and joy in believing: yes, but you must have an Object to believe in;

take away the great doctrine of the Atonement and all your faith and peace are annihilated.

Yes, first and foremost the Scriptures are "profitable for doctrine": God says so, and those who declare otherwise are liars and deceivers. That refutes and condemns those who are prejudiced against the doctrine of the gospel on the pretense that it is unfriendly to the *practical* side of the Christian life. That personal piety or holy living may be neglected through an excessive attachment to favorite theological tenets is readily granted, but that doctrinal instruction is inimical to following the example which Christ has left us, we emphatically deny. The whole teaching of Scripture is "the doctrine which is according to godliness" (I Tim. 6:3): that is to say, it is the doctrine which inculcates "godliness," which supplies motives to godliness, and which therefore promotes it. If Divine truth be received according to the lovely proportions in which it is presented in the Word, so far from such a reception of it enervating practical godliness, it will be found to be the *life* of it. Doctrinal, experimental and practical religion are so necessarily connected together, they could have no existence apart from each other. The influence of the truth upon our hearts and minds is the source of all our spiritual feelings, and those feelings and affections are the springs of every good word and work.

Second, the inspired Scriptures are profitable "for *reproof*" or conviction. Five times the Greek word is rendered "rebuke" and once "tell him his fault" (Matt. 18:15). Here is the chief reason why the Scriptures are so unpalatable to the unsaved: they set before him a standard concerning which he knows he falls far short: they require that which is thoroughly distasteful to him and prohibit those things which his evil nature loves and craves. Thus, their holy teachings roundly condemn him. It is because the Word of God inculcates holiness and censures every form of evil that the unregenerate have such a disrelish for it. It is because the Word *convicts* its reader of his sins, upbraids him for his ungodliness, blames him for his inward as well as outward lack of conformity thereto, that the natural man shuns it. Flesh and blood resent interference, chafe against being censured, and is angry when told his or her faults. It is much *too humbling* for the pride of the natural man to be rebuked for his failures and chided for his errors. Therefore he prefers "prophecy" or something which pricks not his *conscience!*

"Profitable for reproof." Are you, am I, willing *to be reproved?* Are we really, honestly desirous of having made known to us everything in us which is contrary to the law of the Lord and is therefore displeasing to Him? Are we truly agreeable to be searched by the white light of the truth, to bare our hearts to the sword of the Spirit? The true answer to that question reveals whether or no we are regenerate, whether a miracle of grace has been wrought in us or whether we are still in a state of nature. Unless the answer be in the affirmative, there cannot possibly be any spiritual growth for us. Of the wicked it is said "They despised all my reproof" (Prov. 1:30). On the one hand we are told "he that hateth reproof is bruitish" and "shall die" (Prov. 12:1; 15:17); on the other, "reproofs of instruction are the way of life," "he that heareth reproof getteth understanding" (Prov. 6:23; 15:32). If we are to profit from the Scriptures we must ever approach them with an honest desire that all amiss in us may be rebuked by their teachings and be humbled into the dust before God in consequence thereof.

Third, the Scriptures are profitable "*for correction.*" The Greek word occurs nowhere else in the New Testament, but signifies "setting right." The reproving is but a means to an end: it is a showing us what is wrong that it may be put right. Everything about us, both within and without needs correcting, for the fall has put man all out of joint with God and holiness. Our thoughts on everything are wrong and need readjusting. Our affections are all disorderly and need regulating. Our character is utterly unlike Christ's and has to be conformed to His image. Our conduct is wayward and demands squaring with the Rule of righteousness. God has given to us His Word that under its guidance we may regulate our beliefs, renovate our hearts and reform our lives. Hence it answers but a poor end to read a chapter once or twice a day for the sake of decency, without any definite intention of complying with the mind of God as revealed therein. Since He has given us the Scriptures "for correction" we should ever approach them with a sincere purpose of bringing into harmony with them everything that is disorderly within us and irregular without us.

Fourth, the Scriptures are profitable "for *instruction in righteousness.*" *That* is the end for which the other three things are the means. As Matthew Henry pointed out: the Scriptures are "profitable to us for all the purposes of the Christian life. They answer all the ends of Divine revelation. They instruct us in that which is true, reprove us for all that which is amiss, direct us in all that which is good." "Instruction in righteousness" refers not to the imputed righteousness of Christ, for that is included in "doctrine," but relates to integrity of character and conduct — it is inherent and practical righteousness, which is the fruit of the imputed. For *that* we need "instructing" out of the Word, for neither reason nor conscience are adequate for such a task. If our judgment be formed or our actions regulated by dreams, visions, or supposed immediate revelations from Heaven, rather than by the plain meaning of the Holy Scriptures, then we slight them and God may justly give us up to our own delusions. If we follow the fashion, imitate our fellows, or take public opinion for our standard, we are but heathen. But if the Word of God is the only source of our wisdom and guidance, we shall be found treading "the paths of righteousness" (Ps. 23:6).

The Bible is something very different from a picture-book for amusing children, though it contains beautiful types and depicts scenes and events in a manner no artist's brush could convey. It is something more than a precious mine of treasure for us to dig into, though it contains wonders and riches far more excellent than any unearthed at Kimberley. It has not been sufficiently realized that God has given us His Word for the *ordering of our daily lives.* "The secret things belong unto the Lord our God: but the things which are revealed belong unto us and to our

children forever, *that* we may DO all the words of this law" (Deut. 29:
29). How very rarely do we hear or see that *last* clause quoted! Is
not the omitting of it a significant and solemn comment on our times?
God has given us His Word not for intellectual entertainment, not for
the merely curious to exercise his imagination upon, not for making it a
battleground of theological strife, but to be "a lamp unto our feet and a
light unto our path" (Ps. 119:105) — to point out the way in which we
should walk and to sedulously avoid those by-ways which lead to certain
destruction.

"For what things were written aforetime were written for our learning, that we through patience and comfort of the Scriptures might have
hope" (Rom. 15:4). Thus the whole of the Old Testament is for our instruction "in order that by patiently cleaving to the Lord in faith and
obedience, amid all our trials and temptations, and by taking comfort
from the daily perusal of the Scriptures we might possess a joyful hope
of Heaven, notwithstanding past sins and present manifold defects" (T.
Scott). "Now all these things [concerning Israel's sins in the wilderness
and God's judgments upon them] happened unto them for ensamples,
and they are written for *our* admonition" (I Cor. 10:11) or warning:
for us to take to heart, to heed, to avoid. We shall meet with similar
temptations and there is still the same evil nature in us as was in them,
and unless it be mortified, the same awful fate will overtake us. "Make
me to go in the path of thy commandments" (Ps. 119:35). It will
profit us nothing, nay, it will add to our condemnation, if we read the
preceptive parts of the Scriptures without attention and determination,
through God's help, to conform our conduct thereto.

"My little children, these things write I unto you that ye sin not" (I
John 2:1). *That* is the design, bearing, and end not only of this Epistle
but of all the Scriptures. *That* is the object at which every doctrine,
every precept, every promise aims: "that ye *sin not*." The Bible is the
only book in the world which pays any regard to sin against God. The
revelation which it makes of God's omniscience — "Thou knowest my
downsitting and mine uprising, thou understandest my thoughts afar
off" (Ps. 139:2) — says to me, *sin not*. So of His omnipresence — "The
eyes of the Lord are in every place, beholding the evil and the good"
(Prov. 15:3) — says to me, sin not. Are we taught the holiness of
God? it is that we should be holy. Is the truth of resurrection revealed?
it is that we "awake to righteousness and sin not" (I Cor. 15:34). For
what purpose was the Son of God manifested? that "He might destroy
the works of the Devil" (I John 3:8). Precious promises are given us
with the express design that we should "cleanse ourselves from all filthiness of the flesh and spirit, perfecting holiness in the fear of God" (II
Cor. 7:1).

"Desire the sincere milk of the word that ye may grow thereby" (I
Peter 2:2). In order to be nourished by the Word we must desire it,
and like every other *desire* that one may be cultivated or checked — as
after a time the manna was loathed by those who lusted for the
flesh-pots of Egypt. The aim of that desire for the Word is "that ye may

grow thereby": grow in knowledge, in grace, in holiness, "grow up into Christ in *all* things" (Eph. 4:15); grow in fruitfulness to God and helpfulness to your fellows. The Word must not only be desired, but "received with *meekness*" (James 1:21): that is, with yieldedness of will and pliability of heart, with readiness to be molded by its holy requirements. It must also be "mixed with *faith*" (Heb. 4:2): that is, received unquestioningly as God's own Word to me, appropriated and assimilated by me. It must be approached humbly and *prayerfully*, as the Hebrews had to bow down or go upon their knees to obtain the tiny manna on the ground. "Teach me thy statutes" (Ps. 119:12): their meaning, their application to all the details of my life, how to perform them.

If we would read the Scriptures to advantage, if our souls are to be nurtured by them, if we are to make true Christian progress, then it must be by earnest prayer and constant *meditation*. It is only by pondering the words of God that they become fixed in our minds and exert a salutary influence upon our thoughts and actions. Things forgotten have no power to regulate us, and Scripture *is* soon forgotten unless it be turned over and over in the mind. A wondrous blessing is pronounced upon the man who *meditates* in God's law day and night: "He shall be like a tree planted by the rivers of water, that bringeth forth his fruit in his season, his leaf also shall not wither, and whatsoever he doeth shall prosper" (Ps. 1:3). "These things write we unto you that your *joy* may be full" (I John 1:4). Holiness and happiness are inseparably connected. Destruction and misery are in the ways of the wicked (Rom. 3:16), but Wisdom's ways are "ways of pleasantness and all her paths are peace" (Prov. 3:17).

IV

4. *Occupation with Christ.* Clearly this comes next. We must have the Scriptures before we can have Christ, for they are they which testify of Him (John 5:39): where the Bible has not gone Christ is unknown. But in the Scriptures He is fully revealed: in the volume of the Book it is written of Him. In Him all its teachings center, for they are "the doctrine of Christ" (II John 9). In Him all its precepts are perfectly fulfilled. In Him all its promises are certified (II Cor. 1:20). In Him all its prophecies culminate, for "the testimony of Jesus is the spirit of prophecy" (Rev. 19:10). Divorce doctrine from Christ and it is indeed "dry." Separate precepts from Christ and we have no perfect exemplification of them. Sever the promises from Christ and they are no longer "Yea and Amen." Part asunder the prophecies from Christ and they are of no profit to the soul, but rather enigmas for useless speculation. Christ is the Alpha and Omega of the written Word: "Jesus Christ" is the first name mentioned in the New Testament (Matt. 1:1) and the last (Rev. 22:21), and the Old is filled with foreshadowings and forecasts of Him.

If the Christian desires the milk of the Word that he may grow thereby, it is that he "may grow up *into him* in all things, which is the Head, even Christ" (Eph. 4:15). It is unto the image of God's Son that the saint is predestinated to be conformed. It is upon Christ, now seated at God's right hand, he is to steadfastly set his affection (Col. 3:1). It is with his eyes fixed upon Christ that he is to run the race which is set before him (Heb. 12:2). It is of Christ he is to learn (Matt. 11:29), from His fulness he is to receive (John 1:16), by His commandments be directed (John 14:15). It is on Christ he is to feed, as Israel did on the manna in the wilderness (John 6). It is to Christ he is to go in all his troubles (Matt. 14:12), for He is a High Priest who can be touched with the feeling of our infirmities. It is for the honor and glory of Christ he is ever to aim (Phil. 1:20). In short, the Christian is so to act that he can say "For to me to live is *Christ.*"

Now in order to have fellowship with another there must be three things: that other must be known, he must be present, and I must have a free and familiar access to him. Thus it is with the soul and Christ. First, I must be personally acquainted with Him: He must be a living reality to my soul. Therefore it follows that if I am to have close fellowship with Him I must become better acquainted with Him, and in proportion as I do so, such will be my true progress. We agree with Pierce that the words "grow in grace" are explained (in part, at least) by the clause which immediately follows: "and in the knowledge of our Lord and Saviour Jesus Christ" (II Peter 3:18), for the second verse of that epistle tells us that grace and peace are multiplied unto us "*through* the knowledge of God and of our Lord Jesus." One of the chief things which retards the Christian, which renders him weak in faith and causes his graces to languish, is his failure to increase in the knowledge of his Lord and Saviour, and thereby attain to a deeper and more intimate acquaintance with Him. How can we fully trust or set our affections upon One who is well nigh a stranger to us?

Though the Christian believes in an *unseen* Christ, he does not — he could not — trust in an *unknown* Christ. No, his testimony is "I know whom I have believed" (II Tim. 1:12), which does not mean I know Him because I have believed, but rather I believed in Him because He stood revealed to my heart. Take the experience of the one who penned those words. There was a time when Paul was ignorant of Christ. Before his conversion the apostle knew Him not, and consequently he then had no faith in Him, no love for Him, no pantings after Him. And it is thus with all before regeneration: they knew not the things which belong to their everlasting peace. Paul was a great scholar, a strict moralist, a devout religionist, yet he was completely ignorant of the Lord Jesus Christ, whom to know is life eternal. He was trained by Gamaliel the famous teacher of that day, was deeply versed in the contents of the Old Testament, and had listened to the sermon of dying Stephen; and yet was a total stranger to the Christ of God. Nor did his theological training, philosophic mind or acquaintance with the Scriptures, lead him to a saving knowledge of Christ.

All that Paul knew of Christ was by teaching from above. It was God who enlightened his mind with a saving knowledge of the truth and who drew his heart unto the Lord Jesus by His own invincible grace and love. And thus it is with each one whom the Lord God omnipotent calleth. Every person in his natural state is altogether ignorant of the true God and is an utter stranger to the alone and all-sufficient Mediator, the righteous Redeemer, who is mighty to save. And *how* are they brought into an acquaintance with Him? It is wholly of grace and through the supernatural operations of the Holy Spirit upon their souls. As the Spirit of wisdom and revelation He is pleased to quicken the soul with spiritual life and to illumine the mind with a knowledge of Divine Truth, imparting an inward spiritual perception of Christ to the heart thereby. The outward revelation of Christ to us is in the written Word, which sets Him forth and testifies of Him, in which He is clearly, freely, and fully exhibited. But that external revelation has no saving effect upon us until the Holy Spirit shines upon our blind minds, removes the veil which is over our hearts (II Cor. 3:14, 16), and opens our understandings that we might understand the Scriptures (Luke 24: 45) and what is written therein concerning Christ.

It is only as the soul is regenerated that it is capacitated to take in spiritual views of the person, office and work of Christ, to obtain a real and satisfying knowledge of His Godhood and manhood, the purpose and design of the Father in His miraculous incarnation, life, obedience, death, and resurrection. It is the great office and work of the Holy Spirit to "testify" of the Son (John 15:26), to "glorify" Him (John 16:14), to take of the things of Christ and "show unto" those for whom He died (John 16:15), to make Him known unto the hearts of poor sinners. He does this in and by the Word, after He has fitted the soul to receive it. Hence the apostle said "We know that the Son of God is come" (I John 5:20). How did John and those to whom he wrote "know" that? His next words tell us: "and hath given us an understanding that we may know him that is true." A spiritual understanding, which is the gift of God, is a principal part of the Holy Spirit's work in regeneration, and it is by that spiritual understanding the quickened soul is enabled to receive from the Word a spiritual and supernatural knowledge of Christ, just as it is by means of the eye — and that alone — we can see and admire the glorious shining of the sun.

If it be asked, What are those sights which the Holy Spirit gives us whereby He begets faith in the heart or whereby He makes a discovery of Christ unto the soul? The answer is, the Spirit gives us no other views of Christ than what are in exact accordance with the revelation made of Him in the Scriptures of truth. But more specifically: the first discovery which the Spirit makes of Christ to the poor sinner is as a fully-suited and all-sufficient Savior, whose person and perfections are eternal and infinite, who was born into this world and called Jesus that should "save his people from their sins" (Matt. 1:21). He makes known to the soul the wondrous love and amazing grace of Christ, His robe of righteousness, His efficacious blood which was shed for those deserving of naught but Hell. He thereby takes of the things of Christ and makes such a discovery of them that the soul is captivated, the will captured and the heart won to Him, and thereby the sinner is led to believe in His person, surrender to His scepter, and rest on His finished work. The Spirit enlightens the understanding, brings the will to choose Him as his absolute Lord, his heart to love Him, and his conscience to be satisfied with His sacrifice, and his whole being yields to be governed and guided by Him.

Thus Christ is revealed in the hearts of His people (Gal. 1:16) as their one hope of eternal glory. The Word of God is the sole rule and ground of their faith. Christ is exhibited therein as the immediate Object of it, and as the Spirit takes of the things of Him and reveals them to the renewed soul He draws forth its acts upon Christ as He is made known, and thereby He becomes real and precious to the soul; thereby the heart is brought into the enjoyment of His love, to delight in His perfections, to behold Him as "altogether lovely." As Christ is made the Object of faith, faith is a spiritual perception of Him and thereby He has become a living and present Reality. As the heart is engaged with Him, as the thoughts are exercised upon His person, His titles, His offices, His perfections, His work, the soul exclaims, "my meditation of him shall be sweet: I will be glad in the Lord" (Ps. 104:34). Believers love not an unknown Christ, nor do they trust in One with whom they are unacquainted. Though unseen by the natural eye, when faith is in exercise that one can say "I *know* that my Redeemer liveth."

Now it is from this personal, inward, and spiritual knowledge of Christ, received from the Word, as taught by the Spirit, that faith in Christ takes its rise and love to Him springs therefrom as its proper cause. But all believers do not possess an equally clear and full knowledge of Christ. To some He is more fully revealed, whilst others have a vaguer view and lesser apprehension of Him, which constitutes the difference between a strong and a weak Christian. The weak believer knows but little of Christ and therefore does not trust or delight in Him so much as does a stronger one, for the latter differs from him in that he is led into a closer and fuller acquaintance with the Saviour. That may be accounted for both from the Divine side of things and from the human. As we cannot see the sun but in his own light, so neither can we see the Sun of righteousness but in His light (Ps. 36:9). As we cannot see temporal things and objects without light, so faith cannot see Christ but as the Holy Spirit shines upon and enlightens it. Nevertheless, Christ is not capricious in His shining, nor is the Spirit arbitrary in His illumination.

Christ has declared "He that hath my commandments and keepeth them, he it is that loveth me . . . and I will love him and will *manifest myself* to him" (John 14:21). But if the Christian yields to a spirit of self-pleasing, and for a season keeps not the commands of his Lord, then such precious manifestations of Him to his soul will be withheld. It is the office and work of the Spirit to take of the things of Christ and show them to the renewed, but if the believer disregards that injunction "grieve not the Holy Spirit of God" (Eph. 4:30) and allows things in his life which are displeasing to Him, so far from regaling him with fresh views of Christ He will withhold His cordials and comforts, and make him wretched until he is convicted of his backsliding and brought to full confession thereof. On the one hand the Christian who is favored with a deeper knowledge and clearer acquaintance with Christ frankly disavows any personal credit and freely ascribes his blessings wholly unto distinguishing grace; but on the other hand, the Christian who makes little progress in the school of Christ and enjoys but little intimate fellowship with Him, must take the entire blame to himself — a distinction which ever needs to be borne in mind.

Concerning Israel of old and the supply of food which God gave them in the wilderness it is recorded "and gathered some more, some less" (Exod. 16:17). The manna (type of Christ) was freely given, made accessible to all alike: if then some were more indolent to appropriate as goodly a portion as others, they had only themselves to blame. So it is with the saint and Christ. We are instructed to pray that we may be "increasing in the knowledge of God" (Col. 1:10), but if we are negligent to do so, or offer the petition only half-heartedly, we shall have not. We are assured "then shall we know if we follow on to know the Lord" (Hos. 6:3). The Hebrew word for "follow on" signifies "persevere," "follow after": it is a forceful word, connoting earnestness and diligence. The way and means are there described: we must highly value and steadfastly endeavor after the same, making it our principal quest (*see* Prov. 2:1-4; Phil. 3:12-15), and then if we perform the prescribed duty we may certainly expect the promised blessing. But if we be lethargic and rest on our oars, no progress is made, and the fault is entirely ours.

Since the believer owes his salvation to Christ and is to spend eternity with Him, surely he should make it his chief business and absorbing concern to obtain a clearer and better knowledge of Him. No other knowledge is so important, so blessed, so satisfying. We do not mean a bare, theoretical, speculative and uninfluential knowledge of Him, but a supernatural, spiritual, believing, and transforming one. Said the apostle "I count all things but loss for the excellency of the knowledge of Christ Jesus my Lord" (Phil. 3:9). Observe how *comprehensive* is this knowledge: "Christ, Jesus, Lord" — comprising the principal aspects in which He is set forth in the Word: "Christ," respecting His person and office; "Jesus," His work and salvation; "Lord," His dominion and rule over us. Note too it is an *appropriating* knowledge: "Christ Jesus *my* Lord" — to apprehend Him as mine, on good grounds, is the excellency of this knowledge. The demons know Him as Prophet, Priest and King, but they apprehend Him not with personal appropriation to themselves. But this knowledge enables its possessor to say "Who loved me, and gave himself for me" (Gal. 2:20).

This spiritual and saving knowledge of Christ is an *effectual* one. As Hebrews 6:9 speaks of "things that accompany salvation," so there are things which accompany this knowledge. "They that know thy name [the Lord as revealed] *will* put their trust in him" (Ps. 9:10): it cannot be otherwise, and the better they know Him, the firmer and fuller will be their trust. "He that seeth the Son and believeth on him may have everlasting life" (John 6:40) — seeing the Son is put before believing as the cause which produces the effect. The more we study and meditate upon the glorious person of Christ and His perfect salvation, the more we realize the everlasting sufficiency of His life and death to save us from all our sins and miseries, the more will faith be fed and spiritual graces nourished. So too the more will our hearts be enflamed and our affections drawn out to Him. It must be so, for "faith worketh by *love*" (Gal. 5:6). The more Christ is trusted the more He is endeared to the soul. The more we live in sights and views of all He has done for us, of all His office relations to us, the more glorious will He be in our esteem. It is a spiritual view of Christ by faith which removes guilt from the conscience, produces a sense of peace and joy in the heart, and enables the soul to say "my beloved is mine, and I am his."

As this knowledge is accompanied by faith and love, so also is it with *obedience*. "Hereby we do know that we know him, if we keep his commandments" (I John 2:3) — we *know* no more than we practice! "*As* ye have received Christ Jesus the Lord, *so* walk ye in him" (Col. 2:6) — submitting to His authority, believing His gospel, leaning on His arm, counting on His faithfulness, looking to Him for everything. To walk "in him" means to act in practical union with Him. The "walk" is to be regulated by His revealed will, to tread the path He has appointed for us. To submit to His will is the only true liberty, as it is the secret of solid peace and joy. To take His yoke upon us and learn of Him ensures genuine rest of soul. But as we only enjoy the good of Christ's promises as they are received by faith (appropriated to myself and relied upon), so with His precepts — they must be personally taken to myself and submitted to. Hence we read of "the obedience of faith" (Rom. 1:5). So, too, they only can be performed by *affection*: "if ye love me keep my commandments."

In order to commune with Christ there must be a spiritual knowledge of Him and an *acting faith upon Him*. Said the one who most perfectly exemplified the Christian character "the life that I now live in the flesh I live by the faith of the Son of God who loved me and gave himself for me" (Gal. 2:20). Christ was his all-absorbing Object, the Object of his faith and love. Christ was the One who had won his heart, whom he longed to please and honor, whose name and fame he sought to spread abroad, whose example he endeavored to follow. It was upon Him he fed by faith and unto Him he lived in all his actions. It was from Him he had received his spiritual life, and it was to glorify Him that he desired to spend and be spent. All our fellowship with Christ is by faith. It is faith which makes Him real — "seeing him who is invisible" (Heb. 11:27). It is faith which makes Him present: "Abraham rejoiced to see my day and he saw and was glad" (John 8:56). It is faith which brings Christ down from heaven into the heart (Eph. 3:17). It is faith which enables us to prefer Him above all things and to say "there is none upon earth I desire besides thee" (Ps. 73:25).

"Of his fulness have all we received and grace for grace" (John 1:

16). The "we" are those spoken of in verses 12, 13. In verse 14 "full of grace and truth" has reference to His own personal perfections, but in verse 16 it is His mediatorial fulness which God has given Him for His people to draw upon. The word "fulness" is sometimes used for abundance, as in "the earth is the Lord's and the fulness thereof" (Ps. 24:1), but as one of the Puritans pointed out, that is too narrow for its meaning here. In Christ there is not only a fulness of abundance, but of redundancy — an overflowing fulness of grace. There is a communication of this fulness of Christ to all believers, and they have it in a way of "receiving" (cf. Rom. 5:11; Gal. 3:2; 4:5). That which believers receive from Christ is here said to be "grace for grace," by which is meant grace answerable to grace — as "an eye for an eye and a tooth for a tooth" (Matt. 5:38) signifies an eye answerable to an eye. Whatever grace or holiness there is in Jesus Christ, there is something in the saint answerable thereto — there is the same Spirit in the Christian as in Christ.

There is in Christ, as the God-man mediator, a "fulness of grace" which is available for His people. There is laid up in Him, as in a vast storehouse, all that the believer needs for time and eternity. Of that fulness they have received regenerating grace, justifying grace, reconciling grace; from that fulness they *may* receive sanctifying grace, preserving grace, fruit-bearing grace. It is available for *faith* to *draw upon*: all that is required is that we expectantly bring our empty vessels to be filled by Him. There is a fulness of grace in Christ which infinitely exceeds our fulness of sin and want, and from it we are freely invited to draw. "Jesus stood and cried saying, "If any man thirst, let him come unto me, and drink" (John 7:37). Those words are *not* to be limited to the sinner's first coming to Christ nor is the "thirst" to be understood in any restricted sense. If the believer thirsts for spiritual wisdom, for purity, for meekness, for any spiritual grace, then let him come to the Fountain of grace and "drink" — what is drinking but "receiving," our emptiness ministered unto by His fulness.

When poor Martha, weighed down by her "much serving" fretfully asked the Saviour to chide her sister, He answered "But one thing is needful, and Mary hath chosen that good part which shall not be taken away from her" (Luke 10:40-42). What was that "good part" which she had chosen? This, she "sat at Jesus' feet and heard his word" (v. 39). Mary had a felt sense of her need: she knew where that need could be supplied: she came to receive out of Christ's fulness. And He declared that *that* is "the one thing needful," for it includes everything else. Put yourself in that posture of soul, that expectation of faith, whereby you can receive from Him. To be occupied with Christ was "the good part" which would never be taken from her. But in this restless age "sitting at the feet of Jesus" is a lost art. Instead of humbly recognizing their *own* deep need of being ministered to, puffed up with a sense of their importance and actuated by the energy of the flesh, they are "cumbered with much *serving*" — looking after the vineyards of others, but neglecting their own (Song of Sol. 1:6).

If the Christian is to make real progress he must needs be more occupied with Christ. As He is the sum and substance of all evangelical truth then an increasing acquaintance with His person, offices, and work cannot but nourish the soul and promote spiritual growth. Yet there must be constantly renewed acts of faith on Him if we are to draw from His fulness and be more conformed to His image. The more our affections be set on Him, the lighter shall we hold the things of this world and the less will carnal pleasures appeal to us. The more we spiritually meditate upon His humiliations and sufferings, the more will the soul learn to loathe sin and the more shall we esteem our heaviest afflictions but "light." Christ is exactly suited to our every case and Divinely qualified to supply our every need. Look less within and more to Him. He is the only One who can do you good. Abhor everything which competes with Him in your affections. Be not satisfied with any knowledge of Christ which does not make you more in love with Him and conforms you more to His holy image.

10

Its Decline

I

First, *its nature*. That which we are here to be concerned with is what some writers term "backsliding" — a lucid and expressive word that is not employed so often as it should be or once was. Like most other theological terms this one has been made the occasion of not a little controversy. Some insist that it ought not to be applied to a Christian since the expression occurs nowhere in the New Testament. But that is childish: it is not the mere word but the thing itself which matters. When Peter followed His Master "afar off," warmed himself at the enemy's fire, and denied Him with oaths, surely he was in a backslidden state — yet if the reader prefers to substitute some other adjective we have no objection. Others have argued that it is impossible for a Christian *to* backslide, saying that the "flesh" in him is never reconciled to God and that the "spirit" never departs from Him. But that is mere trifling: it is not a nature but the *person* who backslides, as it is the person who acts — believes or sins.

It is not because the word backslide is a controversial one that we have preferred "decline," but because the former is applied in Scripture to the unregenerate as well as the regenerate — to professors as such, and here we are confining our attention to the case of a child of God whose spirituality diminishes, whose progress is retarded. There are, of course, degrees in backsliding, for we read of "the backslider in heart" (Prov. 14:14) as well as those who are such openly in their ways and walk. Yet to the great majority of the Lord's people a "backslider" probably connotes one who has wandered a long way from God, and whom his brethren are obliged to sorrowfully "stand in doubt of." As we do not propose to restrict ourselves to such extreme cases, but rather cover a much wider field, we deemed it best to select a different term and one which seems better suited to the subject of spiritual growth.

By spiritual decline we mean the waning of vital godliness, the soul's communion with its Beloved becoming less intimate and regular. If the Christian's affections cool, he will delight himself less in the Lord and there will be a languishing of his graces. Hence spiritual decline consists of a weakening of faith, a cooling of love, a lessening of zeal, an abatement of that whole-hearted devotedness to Christ which marks the healthy saint. The perfections of the Redeemer are meditated upon with less frequency, the quest of personal holiness is pursued with less ardor, sin is less feared, loathed and resisted. "Thou hast left thy first love" (Rev. 2:4) describes the case of one who is in a spiritual decline. When that be the case the soul has lost its keen relish for the things of God, there is much less pleasure in the performance of duty, the conscience is no longer tender, and the grace of repentance is sluggish. Consequently there is a diminishing of peace and joy in the soul, disquietude and discontent more and more displacing them.

When the soul loses its relish for the things of God there will be less diligence in the quest of them. The means of grace though not totally neglected, are used with more formality and with less delight and profit. The Scriptures are then read more from a sense of duty than with a real hunger to feed on them. The throne of grace is approached more to satisfy conscience than from a deep longing to have fellowship with its occupant. As the heart is less occupied with Christ the mind will become increasingly engaged with the things of this world. As the conscience becomes less tender a spirit of compromise is yielded to and instead of watchfulness and strictness there will be carelessness and laxity. As love for Christ cools, obedience to Him becomes difficult and there is more backwardness to good works. As we fail to use the grace already received, corruptions gain the ascendancy. Instead of being strong in the Lord and in the power of His might, we find ourselves weak and unable to withstand the assaults of Satan.

A born-again Christian will never sink into a state of unregeneracy, though his case may become such that neither himself nor spiritual on-lookers are warranted in regarding him as a regenerate person. Grace in the Christian's heart will never become extinct, yet he may greatly decline with respect to the health, strength, and exercise of that grace, and that from various causes. The Christian may suffer a suspension of the Divine influences to him. Not totally so, for there is ever such a working of God as maintains the being of the spiritual principle of grace (or "new nature") in the saint, yet he does not at all times enjoy the enlivening operations of the blessed Spirit on that principle, and its activities are then interrupted for a season, and in consequence, he becomes less conversant with spiritual objects, his graces languish, his fruitfulness declines, and his inward comforts abate. The flesh takes full advantage of this and acts with great violence, and in consequence the Christian is made most miserable and wretched in himself.

If it be asked, *Why* does God withdraw the gracious operations of His Spirit from His people or suspend His comforting influences, which are so necessary for their walking in Him? Answer may be made both from the Divine side of things and the human. God may do this in *a sovereign way*, without any cause in the manner of their behavior toward Himself. As He gives five talents to one and only two to another according as seems good in His sight, so He varies the measure of grace bestowed on one and another of His people as best pleases Himself. Should any one be inclined to murmur against this, then let him pay attention to His silencer: "Is it not lawful for me to do what I will with mine own" (Matt. 20:15). God is supreme, independent, free, and distributes His bounties as He chooses, in nature, in providence, and in grace. God takes counsel with none, is influenced by none, but "worketh all things after the counsel of his *own* will" (Eph. 1:11). As such He is to be meekly and cheerfully submitted to.

But it is not only from acting according to His own imperial right that God withdraws from His people the vitalizing and comforting influences of His Spirit. He does so also that He may give them a better knowledge of themselves and *teach them* more fully their entire dependency upon Himself. By so acting God gives His children to discover for themselves the strength of their corruptions and the weakness of their grace. Though saved from the love, guilt, and dominion of sin, they have not yet been delivered from its power or presence. Though a holy and spiritual nature has been communicated to them, yet that nature is but a creature — weak and dependent — and can only be sustained by its Author. That new nature has no inherent strength or power of its own: it only acts as it is acted upon by the Holy Spirit. "In the Lord have I righteousness and strength" (Isa. 45:21): every believer is convinced of the former, but usually it is only after many a humiliating experience that he learns his strength is not in himself but in the Lord.

It is rather in a way of *chastisement* that, in the great majority of instances, God withholds from His people the gracious operations of the Spirit; and that brings us to the human side of things, wherein *our* responsibility is involved. If the saint becomes lax in his use of the appointed means of grace — which are so many channels through which the influences of the Spirit customarily flow — then he will necessarily be the loser and the fault is entirely his own. Or if the Christian trifles with temptations and experiences a sad fall, then the Spirit is grieved and His comforting operations are withheld as a solemn rebuke. Though God still loves his person; He will let him know that He hates his sins, and though He will not deal with him as an incensed Judge, yet He will discipline him as an offended Father; and it may be long before he is again restored to the freedom and familiarity that he formerly enjoyed with Him. (See Isa. 59:2; Jer. 5:25; Hag. 1:9, 10.)

Though God draws not His sword against His erring saints, yet He uses the rod upon them. "If his children forsake my law and walk not in my judgments, if they break my statutes and keep not my commandments, then will I visit transgression with the rod and their iniquity with stripes; nevertheless my loving kindness will I not utterly take from him nor suffer my faithfulness to fail. My covenant will I not break nor alter the thing that has gone out of my lips" (Ps. 89:30-34). *Then* it is our wisdom to "hear the rod" (Micah 6:9), to humble ourselves beneath His mighty hand (I Peter 5:6) and forsake our folly (Ps. 85:8). If we do not duly repent and amend our ways, still heavier chastisements will be our portion; but "if we confess our sins he is faithful and just to forgive us our sins and to cleanse us from all unrighteousness" (I John 1:9). When the Spirit's influences are withheld from the Christian, it is always the safest course for him to conclude he has displeased the Lord and to cry "Show me wherefore thou contendest with me" (Job 10:2).

Second, *its causes.* The root cause is failure to mortify indwelling sin, called "the flesh" in Galatians 5:17, which makes constant opposition against "the spirit" or the principle of grace in the soul of believers. A carnal nature is ever present within them, and at no time is it inactive, whether they perceive it or no. Yea, they are often unconscious of many of its stirrings, for it works silently, secretly, subtilely, deceptively, prompting not only to outward acts of disobedience, but producing unbelief, pride and self-righteousness, which are most offensive to the Holy One. This enemy in the soul possesses great advantages because its power to rule was unopposed by us all through our unregeneracy, because of its cursed cunning, because of the numerous temptations by which it is excited and the variety of objects upon which it acts. Yet it is our responsibility to keep our hearts with all diligence, to jealously watch over its workings, for the principal part of the "fight" to which the Christian is called consists of continually resisting the uprisings and solicitations of his evil principle: in other words, to *mortify* them.

The more carefully the believer observes the many ways in which indwelling sin assails the soul, the more will he realize his need of crying to God for help that he may be watchful and faithful in opposing its lustings. But alas we become slack and inattentive to its serpentine windings and are tripped up before we are aware of it. This is stupid folly, and it costs us dearly. By our slothfulness we get a sore wound in the soul, our graces droop, our conscience is defiled, our relish for the Word is dulled, and we lag in the performance of duty. Grace cannot thrive while lust is nourished, for the interests of the flesh and of the spirit cannot be promoted at the same time. And if our corruptions be not resisted and denied, they will, they must, flourish. If the daily work of mortifying the flesh be not diligently attended to, sin will most certainly become predominant in its actings in our hearts. If we fail there, we fail everywhere.

True, the lustings of the flesh cannot be rendered inactive, but we must refuse to provide them with fuel: "make not provision for the flesh unto the lusts thereof" (Rom. 13:14). Those lusts cannot be eradicated, but they can (by the Spirit's enablement) be refused. *There* is where the responsibility of the Christian comes in. It is his bounden duty to prevent those lusts occupying his thoughts, engaging his affections, and prevailing with the will to choose objects which are agreeable to them. Take covetousness as an example – a lusting after the empty things of this world. If the mind permits itself to have anxious thoughts for material riches, and the affections to be drawn unto them and pleasing images are formed in the imagination, the lust has prevailed and our conduct will be ordered accordingly. An earnest pursuit after corrupt things preys upon the vitals of true spirituality. The preventative for that is to set our affection upon things above, to make Christ our satisfying portion, and having "food and raiment . . . therewith be content" (I Tim. 6:8).

It is very evident then that the Christian should spare no pains in seeking to ascertain and be sensibly affected by the real causes of his spiritual decline, for unless he knows from what causes his spiritual decays proceed, he cannot "remember therefore from whence he is fallen" nor truly "repent" of his failures or again "do the first works" (Rev. 2:5); and unless and until he does these very things he will deteriorate more and more. It is equally clear that if there be certain appointed means the use of which promotes spiritual growth and prosperity, then the slighting of those means will inevitably hinder that growth. As the first of those means is the mortifying of the flesh it will be found that slackness at *that* point is the place where all failure begins. It is sin unmortified and unresisted, yielded to and allowed, and — what is still worse — unrepented of and unconfessed, which brings a blight upon the garden of the soul. Sin unmourned and unforsaken in our affections is more heinous and dangerous than the actual commission of sin.

Closely connected with the mortifying of sins is the Christian's devoting of himself entirely to God. Christian progress is largely determined by continuing as we began — by the measure in which we steadfastly adhere to the surrender we made of ourselves to Christ at our conversion and to the vows we took upon us at baptism. If our conversion was a genuine one we then renounced the world, the flesh and the devil, and received Christ as our only Lord and Saviour. If our baptism was a Scriptural one and the believer entered intelligently into the spiritual import and emblematic purport of that ordinance, he then professed to have put off the old man, and as he emerged from the water — as one symbolically risen with Christ — he stood pledged to walk in newness of life. As the adult Israelites were "baptized unto Moses" (I Cor. 10:1, 2) — accepting him as their lawgiver and leader, so those who have been "baptized" unto Christ, have put on Christ" (Gal. 3:27) — having enlisted under His banner, they now wear His uniform.

The more consistently the believer acts in harmony with the public profession he made in his baptism, the more real progress will he make. Since Christ be "the Captain" of his salvation, he is under bonds to fight against everything opposed to Him, for "they which live should not henceforth live unto themselves, but unto Him which died for them and rose again" (II Cor. 5:15). Each day the saint should renew his consecration unto God and live in the realization that "he is not his own, for he is bought with a price" — no longer free to gratify his lusts. The more Christ's purchase of him be kept fresh in his mind, the more resolutely will he conduct the work of mortification. It is forgetfulness that we belong to God in Christ which makes us slack in resisting what He hates. It is such forgetfulness and slackness that explains the call "remember therefore from whence thou art fallen" (Rev. 2:5) — i.e., your dedication to God and your baptismal avowal of identification with Christ in His death, burial, and resurrection.

While there be a healthy desire after God and a delighting of ourselves in Him, an earnest seeking to please Him and the enjoyment of communion with Him, there is necessarily an averseness for sin and a zeal against it. While we have a due sense of our obligations to God and high valuation of His grace to us in Christ, we continue to find duty pleasant and direct our actions to His glory. But when we become less occupied with His perfections, precepts, and promises, other things steal in and little by little our hearts are drawn from Him. The light of His countenance is no longer enjoyed and darkness begins to creep over the soul. Love cools and gratitude to Him wanes and then the work of mortification becomes irksome, and we shelve it. Our lusts grow more unruly and dominant and the garden of the soul is overrun with weeds. In such a case we must "repent" and return to "the first works" (Rev. 2:5) — contritely confess our sinful failures and re-dedicate ourselves unto God.

Again; if the Christian accords not to the Word of God that honor to which it is so justly entitled, he is certain to be the loser. If the Word holds not that place in his affections, thoughts and daily life which its Author requires, then sad will be the consequences. If the soul be not nourished by this heavenly bread, if the mind be not regulated by its instructions, if the walk be not directed by its precepts, disastrous must be the outcome. We must expect God to hide His face from us if we seek Him not in those ways wherein He has promised to meet with and bless us, for such a neglect is both a violation of His ordinance and a disregard of our own good. I may spend as much time in reading the Bible today as ever before, but am I doing so with a definite and solemn treating with God therein? If not, if my approach be less spiritual, if my motive be less worthy, then a decline has already begun, and I need to beg God to revive me, quicken my appetite, and make me more responsive to His injunctions.

Finally; it requires few words here to convince a believer that if there be a decreasing occupation of his heart with Christ, his fine gold will soon become dim. If he ceases to grow in a spiritual knowledge of his Lord and Saviour, if he become lax in desiring and seeking real communion with Him, if he fails to draw from the fulness of grace which is available for His people, then a blight will fall upon all his graces. Faith in Him will weaken, love for Him will abate, obedience to Him slacken, and He will be "followed" at a greater distance. His own words on this point are too clear to admit of mistake: "He that abideth in me and I in him [note the order: we are always the first to make the breach], the same bringeth forth much fruit [his graces are healthy and his life abounds in good works], for severed from me [cut off from fellowship] ye can do nothing" (John 15:5). The same things which opposed our first coming to Christ will seek to hinder our cleaving to Him, and against those enemies we must watch and pray.

"Faith which worketh by love" (Gal. 5:6). Since it is "with the heart man believeth" (Rom. 10:10), saving faith and spiritual love cannot be separated — though they may be distinguished. Faith engages the heart with Christ, and therefore its affections are drawn out unto Him. Thus faith is a powerful dynamic in the soul, and acts (to borrow the words of Thomas Chalmers) as "the impulsive power of a new affection." A little child may be amusing itself with some filthy or dangerous object, but present to him a luscious pear or peach and he will speedily relinquish it. The world absorbs the heart and mind of the unregenerate because he is of the world and so knows nothing better, for the Christ of God is a Stranger to him. But the regenerate has a new nature and by faith becomes occupied with Him who is the Center of Heaven's glory, and the more the mind be stayed upon Him, the less appeal will the perishing things of time and sense make upon him. It is faith in exercise upon its glorious Object which overcometh the world.

II

We have pointed out the deep importance of ascertaining the *causes* from which spiritual decays proceed, in order to bring us to a due compliance with the injunctions of Revelation 2:5. We cannot turn from that which is injurious and avail ourselves of the remedy until we are conscious of and sensibly affected by those things which have robbed of spiritual health. But let not the young Christian assume a defeatist attitude and conclude that ere long he too will suffer a decline. Prevention is better than cure. To be forewarned is to be forearmed. This aspect of the theme should serve a dual purpose: a warning against such a calamity and as furnishing instruction for those whose graces have already begun to languish. Thus far we have dwelt only on what will be the inevitable consequences if the believer fails to make a diligent and full use of the chief aids to spiritual growth; now we proceed to point out other things which are among the causes of decline.

A *slackening in the prayer life* will soon lower the level of one's spiritual health. This is so generally recognized among Christians that there is the less need for us to say much thereon. Prayer is an ordinance of Divine appointment, being instituted both for God's glory and our good. It is an owning of His supremacy and an acknowledgment of our dependency. On the one hand the Lord requires to be waited on, to be asked for those things which will minister unto our wellbeing; and on the other hand, it is by means of prayer that our hearts are prepared to receive or be denied those things which we desire — for it is essentially a holy exercise in which our wills are brought into harmony with the Divine. A considerable part of our religious life consists in praying, either in public or in private, either orally or mentally; and our spiritual prosperity ever bears a close proportion to the degree of fervor and constancy with which this important duty is attended to. Prayer has been rightly termed "the breath of the new creature," and if our breathing be impeded then the whole system suffers — true alike spiritually and naturally.

But prayer is more than a duty: it is also one of the two principal means of grace, and without it the other (the Word) profits us little or nothing. Since prayer be the breath of the new creature, we need to live in its own element — the atmosphere of Heaven. In order thereto a new and living way has been opened to the throne of grace, whither we may come with boldness and confidence, and there find help. Help for what? For everything needed in the Christian life, more particularly, for enablement to comply with the Divine precepts. That which God requires from us may be summed up in one word, *obedience,* and it is only through prayer we obtain strength for the performance thereof. That is partly the meaning of "For the law was given by Moses, but grace and truth came by Jesus Christ" (John 1:17). The law reveals man's duty, but it conveys no power for the discharge of it. But *grace* (as well as truth) comes to us by Jesus Christ as the previous verse tells us, yet there is no other way of receiving out of His fulness except by the prayer of faith.

Prayer is even more than a means of grace: it is a holy privilege, an unspeakable boon, an inestimable favor, and it should be the most delightful of all spiritual exercises. It is by prayer we have access to God and converse with Him, whereby He becomes more and more a living Reality unto the soul. It is then that we draw near to Him and He draws near to us, and there is a sacred converse the one with the other. Thereby we commune with and delight ourselves in Him. It is while we are thus engaged that the Spirit graciously fulfills His office work as the Spirit of adoption, whereby we cry "Father! Father!" We then find He is more ready to hear than we are to speak. Pleading the merits of Christ we enjoy most blessed fellowship with Him and obtain fresh foretastes of the everlasting bliss awaiting us on high. It is to a reconciled Father we come, and as "his dear children." If we approach in the spirit of the prodigal son, the same welcome awaits us and the same tokens of love are received by us. It is then we are made to exclaim "Thou anointest my head with oil, my cup runneth over" and that we pour out our hearts before Him in praise and adoration.

Now contemplate a slackening of the prayer life in the light of the three things pointed out above, and what must be the inevitable consequences! How can I prosper if I shirk my duty? How can the blessing of God rest upon me if I largely refuse that which He requires from me? If prayer also be one of the chief means of grace and I neglect it, am I not "forsaking my own mercies"? If it be the only channel through which I obtain fresh supplies of grace from Christ shall I not necessarily be feeble and sickly? If my strength be not renewed, how can I successfully resist my spiritual foes? If no power from on high be received, how shall I be able to tread the path of obedience? And if prayer be the principal channel of communion and converse with God, and that holy privilege be lightly esteemed, will not God soon become less real, my heart grow cold, my faith languish, and my joy vanish? Yes, a slackening in the prayer life most certainly entails spiritual decline, with all that accompanies the same.

Sitting under an unedifying ministry. God has appointed and equipped certain men to act as His shepherds to feed His sheep. He speaks of them as "pastors according to mine heart, which shall feed you with knowledge and understanding" (Jer. 13:15). In the ordinary course of events it is His method to employ human instrumentality, and therefore He has provided gifted servants "for the perfecting of the saints" (Eph. 4:11, 12). Satan knows that, and hence he raises up false prophets to deceive and destroy. II Corinthians 11:13-15 warns us that "such are false apostles, deceitful workers, transforming themselves into the apostles of Christ." Nor should we be surprised at this, "for Satan himself is transformed as an angel of light. Therefore it is no great thing if his ministers also be transformed as the ministers of righteousness." Those ministers of his have long held most of the professors' chairs in the seminaries, thousands have occupied the pulpits of almost every denomination, and the great majority of those who sat under them were corrupted and fatally deluded by a specious mixture of truth and lies; and real Christians who attended; injuriously affected.

It is because of the presence of these disguised ministers of Satan that God bids His people "Beloved, believe not every spirit, but try the spirits whether they be of God, for many false prophets are gone out into the [professing] world" (John 4:1). "Try" them by the unerring standard of Holy Writ: "To the law and to the testimony: if they speak not according to this word, it is because there is no light in them" (Isa. 8:20). God holds you responsible to "prove all things" (I Thess. 5:21) and *commends* those who *have* "tried those who say they are apostles and are not, and hast found them liars" (Rev. 2:2). His urgent command to each of His children is, "*Cease,* my son, to hear the instruction that causeth thee to err from the words of knowledge" (Prov. 21:27). That is not optinal but obligatory, and we disregard it at our peril. Listening to false doctrine is highly injurious, for it causes to err from right beliefs and right practices. The ministry we sit under affects us for good or evil, and therefore our Master enjoins us "Take heed what ye hear" (Mark 4:24).

It is of far greater moment than young Christians realize that they *heed* that which has just been pointed out. The reading matter we peruse and the religious instruction we imbibe has as real an influence and effect upon the mind and the soul as that which we eat and drink does on the body: if it be corrupt and poisonous its effects will be identical in each case. Proof of that is found in the history of the Galatians. To them the apostle said, "Ye did run well: who did hinder you that ye should not obey the truth?" (5:7), and the answer was, heretics, Judaizers, who perverted the gospel. And the saint to-day is hindered ("driven back," margin) if he attends the preaching of error. Therefore "*shun* profane and vain babblings, for they will increase unto more ungodliness and their word will eat as doth a canker" (II Tim. 2:16, 17). The teaching of heretics diffuses a noisome influence, till it eats away the life and power of piety, as a gangrene spreads through a limb.

But one may sit under what is termed a "sound" ministry and, through no fault of his own, derive no benefit from the same. There is a "dead orthodoxy," now widely prevalent, where the truth is preached, yet in an unctionless manner, and if there be no life in the pulpit there is not likely to be much in the pew. Unless the message comes fresh from God, issues warmly and earnestly from the preacher's heart, and be delivered in the power of the Holy Spirit, it will neither reach the heart of the hearer nor minister that which will cause him to grow in grace.

There is many a place in Christendom where a living, refreshing, soul-edifying ministry once obtained, but the Spirit of God was grieved and quenched, and a visit there is like entering a morgue: everything is cold, cheerless, lifeless. The officers and members seem petrified, and to attend such services is to be chilled and become partaker of that deadening influence. A ministry which does not lift the soul Godwards, produce joy in the Lord, and stimulate to grateful obedience, casts the soul down and soon brings it into the slough of despond.

Only the Day to come will reveal how many a babe in Christ had his growth arrested through sitting under a ministry which supplied him not with the sincere milk of the Word. Only that Day will show how many a young believer, in the warmth and glow of his first love, was discouraged and dismayed by the coldness and deadness of the place where he went to worship. No wonder that God so rarely regenerates any under such a ministry: those places would not prove at all suitable as nurseries for His little ones. Many a spiritual decline is to be attributed to this very cause. Then take heed, young Christian, where you attend. If you cannot find a place where Christ is magnified, where His presence is felt, where the Word is ministered in the power of the Spirit, where your soul is actually fed, where you come away as empty as when you went, — then far better to remain at home and spend the time on your knees, feeding directly from God's Word, and reading that which you *do* find helpful unto your spiritual life.

Companionship with unbelievers. "Enter not into the path of the wicked and go not in the way of wicked men" (Prov. 4:14). "I have written unto you not to keep company — with the world" (I Cor. 5:10, 11). The word for "company" there means *to mingle*: we cannot avoid contact with the unregenerate but we must see to it that our hearts do not become attracted to them. Indeed the Christian is to have good will toward all he encounters, seeking their best interests (Gal. 6:10); but he is to have no pleasure in or complacency toward those who despise his Master. It is forbidden to walk with the profane in a way of friendship. "Be not unequally yoked together with unbelievers" (II Cor. 6:14), for familiarity with them will speedily dull the edge of your spirituality. "Be not deceived: evil communications corrupt good manners" (I Cor. 15:33). We cannot disregard these Divine precepts with impunity. "Know ye not that the friendship of the world is enmity with God?" (James 4:4). "A companion of fools shall be destroyed" (Prov. 13:20).

But it is not only the *openly* profane and lawless who are to be shunned by the saint: he needs especially to avoid *empty professors.* By which we mean, those who claim to be Christians but who do not *live* the Christian life; those who are "church members" or "in fellowship" with some assembly, but whose conduct is careless and carnal; those who attend service on Sunday, but who may be found at the movies or the dance-hall during the week. The empty professor is far more dangerous as a close acquaintance than one who makes no profession: the Christian is less on his guard with the former, and having some confidence in him is more easily influenced by him. Beware of those who say one thing but do another, whose talk is pious but whose walk is worldly. The Word of God is plain and positive on this point: "Having a form of godliness, but [in action] denying the power [reality] thereof: *from such turn away*" (II Tim. 3:5). If you do not, they will soon drag you down with themselves into the mire.

O young Christian, your "companions," those with whom you most closely associate, exert a powerful influence upon you for either good or evil. Far better that you should tread a lonely path with Christ, than that you offend Him by cultivating friendship with religious worldlings. "He that liveth in a mill, the flour will stick upon his clothes. Man receiveth an insensible taint from the company he keepeth. He that liveth in a shop of perfumes and is often handling them carrieth away some of their fragrancy: so by converse with the godly we are made like them" (A Puritan). "He that walketh with wise men shall be wise" (Prov. 13:20). In selecting your closest friend, let not a pleasing personality allure: there are many wolves in sheep's clothing. Be most careful in seeing to it that what draws you to and makes you desire the Christian companionship of another is his or her love and likeness to Christ, and not his love and likeness to yourself.

"I am a companion of all that fear thee and of them that keep thy precepts" (Ps. 119:63) should be the aim and endeavor of the child of God, though such characters indeed are very scarce these evil days. They are the only companions worth having, for they alone will encourage you to press forward along the "narrow way." It is not those who profess to "believe in the Lord," but those who give evidence they *revere* Him; not those who merely profess to "stand for" His precepts, but who actually perform them, that you need to seek out. So far from sneering at your "strictness" they will strengthen you therein, give salutary counsel, be fellow helpers in prayer and piety: the godly will quicken you to more godliness. Their conversation is on sacred topics, and that will draw out your affection to things above. If you are unable to locate any of these characters, then make it your earnest prayer "Let those that fear thee *turn unto me* and those that know thy testimonies" (Ps. 119:79).

An undue absorption with worldly things. "Worldly" is a term that means very different things in the minds and mouths of different people. Some Christians complain that their minds are "worldly" when they simply mean that, for the time being (and often rightly so), their thoughts are entirely occupied with temporal matters. We do not propose to enter into a close defining of the term, but would point out that the performing of those duties which God has assigned us in the world, or the availing ourselves of its conveniences (such as trains, the telegraph, the printing press), or even enjoying the comforts which it provides (food, clothing, housing), are certainly not "worldly" in any evil sense. That which *is* injurious to the spiritual life is, time wasted in worldly pleasures, the heart absorbed in worldly pursuits, the mind oppressed by worldly cares. It is the *love of* the world and its things which is forbidden, and very close watch needs to be kept on the heart, otherwise it will glide insensibly into this snare.

The case of Lot supplies a most solemn warning against this evil. He yielded to a spirit of covetousness and so consulted temporal advantages that the spiritual welfare of his family was disregarded. When Abraham invited him to make choice of a portion of Canaan for himself and his herds, instead of remaining in the vicinity of his uncle, upon whom the blessing of the Most High rested, he "lifted up his eyes (acting by sight rather than by faith) and beheld all the plain of Jordan that it was well watered everywhere . . . then Lot chose him all the plain of Jordan and Lot journeyed east." Thus, he even went outside the land itself, for we are told "Abraham dwelt in the land of Canaan and Lot dwelt in the cities of the plain and pitched his tent toward Sodom" (Gen. 13:8-10). Nor did that content him: he became an alderman in Sodom (Gen. 18:1) and discarded the pilgrim's "tent" for a "house" (v. 3). How disastrous the sequel was both to himself and his family is well known.

One form of worldliness which has spoiled the life and testimony of many a Christian is *politics*. We will not now discuss the question whether or not the saint ought to take *any* interest in politics, but simply point out what should be evident to all with spiritual discernment, namely, that to take an eager and deep concern in politics must remove the edge from any spiritual appetite. Clearly, politics are concerned only with the affairs of *this* world, and therefore to become deeply absorbed in them and have the heart engaged in the pursuit thereof, will inevitably turn attention away from eternal things. Any worldly matter, no matter how lawful in itself, which engages our attention inordinately, becomes a snare and saps our spiritual vitality. We greatly fear that those saints who spent several hours a day in listening to the speeches of candidates, reading the newspapers on them, and discussing party politics with their fellows during the recent election, lost to a considerable extent their relish for the Bread of Life.

III

Having dwelt at some length on the nature of spiritual decline and pointed out some of the principal causes thereof, a few words should be said on its *insidiousness*. Sin is a spiritual disease (Ps. 103:3) and, like so many others, it works silently and unsuspected by us, and before we are aware of it our health is gone. We are not sufficiently on our guard against "the deceitfulness of sin" (Heb. 3:13): unless we resist its first workings, it soon obtains an advantage over us. Hence we are exhorted "Take good heed therefore unto yourselves that ye love the Lord your God" (Josh. 23:11), for all spiritual decline may be traced back to a diminution of our love for Him. The love of God is of heavenly extraction, but being planted in an unfriendly soil, it requires guarding and watering. We are not only surrounded with objects which attract our affections and operate as rivals to the blessed God, but have an inward propensity to depart from Him.

In the early stages of the Christian life love is usually fresh and fervent. The first believing views of the gospel fill the heart with amazement and praise to the Lord, and a flow of grateful affection is the spontaneous outcome. The soul is profoundly moved, wholly absorbed with God's unspeakable gift, and weaned from all other objects. This is what God terms "the kindness of thy youth, the love of thine espousals" (Jer. 2:2). It is then that the one who has found such peace and joy exclaims, "I love the Lord because he hath heard my voice, my supplications [for mercy], because he hath inclined his ear unto me: therefore will I call upon him as long as I live" (Ps. 116:1, 2). At that season the renewed soul can scarcely conceive it possible to forget Him who has done such great things for it or to lapse back in any measure to his former loves and lords. But if after twenty years of cares and temptations have passed over him without producing this effect, it will indeed be happy. There *are* some who experience no decline, but that is far from being the case with all.

There are those who speak of the Christian's departing from his first love as a matter of course, who regard it as something inevitable. Not a few elderly religious professors who have themselves become cold and carnal (if they ever had life in them), will seek to bring young and happy Christians to this doleful and God's dishonoring state of mind. With a sarcastic smile they will tell the babe in Christ, though you are on the mount of enjoyment to-day, rest assured it will not be long until you come down. But this is erroneous and utterly misleading. Not so did the apostles act towards young converts. When Barnabas visited the young Christians at Antioch, he "saw the grace of God and was glad," and so far from leading them to expect a state of decline from their initial fervor, assurance, and joy, he "exhorted them all, that with purpose of heart they would cleave unto the Lord" (Acts 11:23). While the great Head of the church, informed the Ephesian saints that He had it *against* them "because thou hast left thy first love" (Rev. 2:4).

There is no reason or necessity in the nature of things why there should be any abatement in the Christian's love, zeal, or comfort. Those objects and considerations which first gave rise to them have not lost their force. There has been no change in the grace of God, the efficacy of Christ's blood, the readiness of the Spirit to guide us into the truth. Christ is still the "Friend of sinners," able to save them unto the uttermost that come to God by Him. So far from there being good or just reason why we should decline in our love, the very opposite is the case. Our first views of Christ and His gospel were most inadequate and defective: if we follow on to know the Lord, we shall obtain a better acquaintance with Him, a clearer perception of His perfections, His suitability to our case, His sufficiency. He should, therefore, be more highly esteemed by us. Said the apostle "this I pray, that your love may abound yet more and more in knowledge and in all judgment" (Phil. 1:9). So far from himself relapsing, as he neared the end of his course, forgetting the things that were behind, he reached forth to those that were before.

To decline in our love is quite unnecessary and to be lamented, but to attempt a vindication of it is highly reprehensible. It would be tantamount to arguing that we were once too spiritually minded, too tender in conscience, too devoted to God. That we were unduly occupied with Christ and made too much of Him: that we overdid our efforts to please Him. It is also practically to say, we did not find that satisfaction in Christ which we expected, that we obtained not the peace and pleasure in treading Wisdom's ways that we looked for, and, therefore, that we were obliged to seek happiness in returning to our former pursuits, and thereby we confirmed the sneer of our old companions at the outset, that our zeal would soon abate and that we would return again to them. To such renegades God says "O my people, what have I done unto thee? and wherein have I wearied thee? testify against me" (Mic. 6:3).

The fact remains, however, that many do decline from their first love, though they are seldom aware of it until some of its effects appear. They are like foolish Samson, who had trifled with temptations and displeased the Lord, and who "awoke out of his sleep and said, I will go out as at other times before, and shake myself. And he *wist not* that the Lord was departed from him" (Judg. 16:20). Yielding to sin blinds the judgment, and we are unconscious that the Spirit is grieved and that the blessing of God is no longer upon us. Our friends may perceive it and feel concerned because of the same, but we ourselves are not aware of it. Then it is those solemn words accurately describe our case: "strangers have devoured his strength, and he knows it not; yea, gray hairs are here and there upon him, yet he *knoweth not*" (Hos. 7:9)! "Gray hairs" are a sign of the decay of our constitution and of approaching decrepitude: so there are some signs which tell of the spiritual decline of a Christian, but usually he is oblivious to their presence.

We will turn now and point out some of the *symptoms* of spiritual decline. Since sin works so deceitfully and Christians are unconscious of the beginnings of retrogression, it is important that the signs thereof should be described. Once again we find that the natural adumbrates the spiritual, and if due attention is paid thereto, much that is profitable for the soul may be learned therefrom. Constipation is either due to self-neglect or a faulty diet, and when sin clogs the soul it is because we have neglected the work of mortification and failed to eat "the bitter herbs" (Exod. 12:8). Loss of appetite, paleness of countenance, dullness of eye, absence of energy, are so many evidences that all is not well with the body and that we are on the way to a serious illness unless things soon are righted: and each of those has its spiritual counterpart. Irritability, inability to relax, and loss of sleep, are the precursors of a nervous breakdown, and the spiritual equivalents are a call "return unto thy *rest* O my soul" (Ps. 116:7).

In cases of leprosy, real or supposed, the Lord gave orders that the individual should be carefully examined, his true state ascertained, and judgment given accordingly. And just so far as a spiritual disease is more odious and dangerous than a physical one, by so much is it necessary for us to form a true judgment concerning it. Every spot is not a leprosy! and every imperfection in a Christian does not indicate he is in a spiritual decline. Even the apostle Paul groaned over his inward corruptions, and confessed he had not yet attained nor was he already perfect, but pressed forward to the mark for the prize of the high calling. Yet those honest admissions were very far from being acknowledgments that he was a backslider or that he had given way to an evil heart of unbelief in departing from the living God. Great care has to be taken on either side, lest on the one hand we call darkness light and excuse ourselves, or on the other call light darkness and needlessly write bitter things against ourselves.

Undoubtedly more are in danger of doing the former than the latter. Yet there *are* Christians, and probably not a few, who wrongly depreciate themselves, draw erroneous conclusions and suppose their case is worse than it is. For instance, there are those who grieve because they are no longer conscious of that energetic zeal, of those fervent and tender affections, which they were sensible of in the day of their espousals. But a change in their natural constitution, from an increase of years, will account for that. Their animal spirits have waned, their natural energy has diminished, their mental faculties are duller. But though there be less tender and warm feelings, there may be more stability and depth in them. Many things relating to the present world, which in our youth would produce tears, will not have that effect as we mature, though they may lay with greater weight on our spirits. To confuse the absence of the brightness and excitement of youth with spiritual decline and coldness is a serious mistake.

On the other hand every departure from God must not be reckoned a mere imperfection, which is common to all the regenerate. Alas, the tendency with writer and reader alike is to flatter himself that *his* "spot" is only "the spot of God's children" (Deut. 32:5), or such as the best of Christians are subject to; and therefore to conclude there is nothing very evil or dangerous about it. Though we may not pretend or deny that we have any faults, yet are we not ready to regard them lightly and say of some sin, as Lot said of Zoar "is it not a little one?" Or to exclaim unto one we have wronged, "What have we done *so much* against thee?" But such a self-justifying spirit evidences a most unhealthy state of heart and is to be steadfastly resisted. The apostle Paul spoke of a certain condition of soul which he feared he should find in the Corinthians: that of having sinned and yet *not* repented for their deeds, and where *that* is the case spiritual decay has reached an alarming stage. Here are some of the symptoms of spiritual decline.

1. Waning of our love for Christ. If the Lord Jesus is less precious to our souls than He was formerly, in His person, office, work, grace, and benefits, whatever we may think of ourselves, we have assuredly gone back. If we have a lower esteem of the Lover of our souls, if our delight in Him was decreased, if our meditation upon His perfections are more infrequent, if we commune less with Him, then grace in us has certainly suffered a relapse. It is the nature of certain plants to turn their faces towards the light: so it is of indwelling grace to strongly in-

cline the heart unto heavenly objects and to take pleasure therein. But if we neglect the means of grace, are not careful to avoid sinful pleasures, or suffer ourselves to be weighted down by the concerns and cares of this life, then will our affections indeed be dampened and our minds rendered vain and carnal. As it is only by acts of faith on the glory of Christ that we are changed into His image (II Cor. 3:18), so a diminishing of such views of Him will cause our hearts to become chilled and lifeless.

2. Abatement of our zeal for the glory of God. As the principle of grace in the believer causes him to have assurance of Divine mercy to him through the Mediator, so it inspires concern for the Divine honor. As that principle is healthy and vigorous it will cause us to refuse whatever displeases and dishonors God and His cause, and inspire us to practice those duties with a peculiar pleasure which are most conducive to the glory of God, and which give the clearest evidence of our subjection to the royal scepter of Christ. If the new nature be duly nourished and kept lively, it will influence us to bring forth fruit unto the praise of God; but if that new nature be starved or become sickly, our concern for God's glory will greatly decrease. If we have become less conscientious than formerly of whether our conduct become or bring reproach upon the holy Name we bear, then that is a sure mark of our spiritual decline.

3. Loss of our spiritual appetite. Was there not a time, dear reader, when you could truly say "Thy words were found and I did eat them, and thy Word was unto me the joy and rejoicing of my heart" (Jer. 15: 16)? If you cannot honestly affirm that to-day, then you have retrograded. You may indeed be a keener "Bible student" than ever before and spend more time than previously in searching the Scriptures, but that proves nothing to the point. It is not an intellectual interest but a spiritual relish for the Bread of life that we are now treating of. Do we really *savor* the things that be of God: the precepts as well as the promises, the portions that search and wound as well as comfort? Do we not merely wish to understand its prophecies and mysteries, but really "hunger and thirst after *righteousness*"? If we prefer ashes to the heavenly manna, the "husks" which the swine feed on to the fatted calf — secular literature than sacred — then that is an evident sign of spiritual decline.

4. Sluggishness or drowsiness of mind. One is in a sad frame when exercise before God and communion with Him are supplanted by carnal ease. In spiritual torpor it is much the same as in the natural: our senses are no longer exercised to discern good and evil, we neither see nor hear as we ought, nor can we be impressed and affected by spiritual objects as we should be. While in such a condition spiritual duties are neglected, or at most performed perfunctorily and mechanically, so that we are none the better for them. If spiritual duties be attended to from

custom or conscience rather than from love, they neither honor God nor profit ourselves. Though the outward exercise be gone through, the spirit of it is lacking, the heart is no longer in them. Those who read the Bible or say their prayers as a matter of form or habit perceive no change in themselves: but those who are accustomed to *treat with God* in them, and then discover a disinclination thereto, may know that grace in them has languished. If we have no delight in them we are in a sad case.

5. Relaxing in our watchfulness against sin. The want of alertness in guarding against all that is evil, under a quick and tender sense of its loathsome nature, is a sure sign of spiritual decline. Refusing to keep our hearts with all diligence, indifference to the working of our corruptions, trifling with temptations without, are certain evidences of the decay of personal holiness. When the new nature is healthy and vigorous sin is exceedingly sinful to the saint, because he then has a clear and forcible apprehension of its malignity and contrariety to God, and that maintains in him a holy indignation against it. While the mind is engaged in considering the awful price which was paid for the remission of our sins, a detestation of evil is stirred up in the heart, and that is attended with strict watchings, for the renewed soul cannot countenance that which was the procuring cause of his Savior's death. Such an exercise of grace has been obstructed if sin now appears less heinous and there is less care in maintaining a watch against it.

6. Attempting to defend our sins. There are some sins which all know are indefensible, but there are others which even professing Christians seek to justify. It is almost surprising to see what ingenuity people will exercise when seeking to find excuses where *self* is concerned. The cunning of the old serpent which appeared in the excuses of our first parents seems here to supply the place of wisdom. Those possessing little perspecuity in general matters are singularly quick-sighted in discovering every circumstance that appears to make in their favor or serves to extenuate their fault. Sin, when we have committed it, loses its sinfulness, and appears a very different thing from what it did in others. When a sin is committed by *us*, it is common to give it another name — covetousness becomes thrift, malignant contentions fidelity for the truth, fanaticism zeal for God — and thereby we become reconciled to it and are ready to enter on a vindication, instead of penitently confessing and forsaking it.

7. Things of the world obtaining control of us. In proportion as the objects of this scene have power to attract our hearts, to that extent is faith inoperative and ineffectual. It is the very nature of faith to occupy us with spiritual, heavenly, and eternal objects, and as they become real and precious our affections are drawn out to them, and the baubles of time and sense lose all value to us. When the soul is communing with God, delighting itself in His ineffable perfections, such trifles as

our dress, the furnishing of our homes, the glittering show made by the rich of this world, make no appeal to us. When the Christian is ravished by the excellency of Christ and the inestimable portion or heritage he has in Him, the pleasures and vanities which charm the ungodly will not only have no allurement but will pall upon him. It therefore follows that when a Christian begins to thirst after the things of time and sense and evinces a fondness for them, his grace has sadly declined. Those who find satisfaction in anything pertaining to this life have already forsaken the Fountain of living waters and hewed them out broken cisterns that hold no water (Jer. 2:13).

11

Its Recovery

I

WE shall attempt little more here than seeking to show *the necessity for* recovery from a spiritual decline. Nor will that be an easy task: not because of any inherent difficulty in this aspect of our subject, but owing to the variety of cases which need to be considered, and which should be dealt with separately. There are some physical ailments which if handled promptly call for comparatively mild treatment, but there are others that demand more drastic means and remedies. Yet as any doctor will testify, many are careless about what are deemed trifling disorders and delay so long in attending to the same that their condition so deteriorates as to become dangerous and often fatal. In the last chapter we pointed out that every spot was not leprosy: yet it should be remembered that certain spots which resembled that disease aroused suspicion, and required that the patient be examined by the priest, isolated from others, and kept under his observation until the case could be more definitely determined — depending upon whether there was a further deterioration or spreading of the spot (Lev. 13:4-8).

It is much to be doubted if there is any Christian on earth who so retains his spiritual vitality and vigor that he *never* stands in need of a "reviving" of his heart (Isa. 58:15); that there is no time when he feels it requisite to cry "quicken thou me according to thy word" (Ps. 119: 25). Yet it must not be concluded from this statement that every saint experiences a definite relapse in his spiritual life, and still less that a life of ups and downs, decays and recoveries, backslidings and restorations, is the best that can be expected. The experiences of others is *not the Rule* which God has given us to walk by. Crowded dispensaries and hospitals do indeed supply a warning, but they certainly do not warrant my lapsing into carelessness or fatalistically assuming I too shall ere long be physically afflicted. God has made full provision for His people to live a holy, healthy, and happy life, and if I observe many of them failing to do so, it should stimulate me to greater watchfulness against the neglect of God's provision.

After what has been discussed in previous chapters it should scarcely be necessary to remind the reader that unless the Christian maintains close and steady communion with God, daily intercourse with and drawing from Christ's fulness, and regular feeding on the Word, the pulse of his spiritual life will soon beat more feebly and irregularly. Unless he often meditates on the love of God, keeps fresh before his heart the humiliation and sufferings of Christ, and frequents the throne of grace, his affections will soon cool, his relish for spiritual things will decrease, and obedience will neither be so easy nor pleasant. If such a deterioration be ignored or excused, it will not be long ere his heart glides imperceptibly into carnality and worldliness: worldly pleasures will begin to attract, worldly pursuits absorb more of his attention, or worldly cares weight him down. Then, unless there be a return to God and humbling of the heart before Him, it will not be long — unless providence hinder — before he be found in the ways of open transgression.

There are degrees of backsliding. In the case of a real child of God it always commences in the heart's departure from Him, and where that be protracted, evidences thereof will soon appear in the daily walk. Once a Christian becomes a backslider outwardly he has lost his distinguishing character, for then there is little or nothing to distinguish him from a religious worldling. Backsliding always presupposes a profession of faith and adherence unto Christ, though not necessarily the existence or reality of the thing professed. An unregenerate professor may be sincere though deluded and he may, from various considerations, persevere in his profession to the end. But more frequently, he soon wearies of it, and after the novelty has worn off or the demands made upon him become more intolerable, he abandons his profession, and like the sow returns to his wallowing in the mire. Such is an apostate, and with very rare exceptions — if indeed there be any at all — his apostasy is total and final.

Up to the beginning of this chapter we have confined ourselves to the spiritual life of the regenerate, but we have now reached the stage where faithfulness to souls requires us to enlarge our scope. Under our last division we dwelt upon spiritual decline: its nature, its causes, its insidiousness and its symptoms. It is pertinent therefore to enquire now, What will be *the sequel* to such a decline? A general answer cannot be returned, for as the decline varies considerably in different cases — some being less and some more, acute and extended than others — the outcome is not always the same. Where the relapse of a Christian be marked — if not to himself, yet to onlookers — he has entered the class of "backsliders" and that will cause the spiritual to stand in doubt of him. It is this consideration which requires us to enlarge the class to which we now address our remarks, otherwise, unregenerate professors who have deteriorated in their religious life would be likely to derive false comfort from that which applies only to those who have been temporarily despoiled by Satan.

Unless spiritual decline be arrested it will not remain stationary, but become worse, and the worse it becomes the less are we justified in regarding it *as* a "spiritual decline," and the more does Scripture require us to view it as the exposure of a worthless profession. Hence it is that any degree of spiritual deterioration is to be regarded not complacently, but as something serious and if not promptly corrected, as highly dangerous in its tendency. But Satan will attempt to persuade the Christian that though his zeal has abated somewhat and his spiritual affection cooled, there is nothing for him to worry about; that even if his health has begun to decline, yet, seeing he has not fallen into any great sin, his condition is not at all serious. But every decay is dangerous, especially such as the mind is ready to excuse and plead for a continuance therein. The nature and deadly tendency of sin is the same in itself, whether it be in an unregenerate, or a regenerate person, and if it be not resisted and mortified, repented of and forsaken, the outcome will be the same. "When lust hath conceived, it bringeth forth sin, and sin, when it is finished, bringeth forth death. Do not err, my beloved brethren" (James 1:15, 16).

Three stages of spiritual decline are solemnly set before us in Revelation 2 and 3. First, to the Ephesian backslider Christ says, "I have against thee, because thou hast left thy first love" (2:4). That is the more striking and searching because there was much here that the Lord commended: "I know thy works and thy labor and thy patience . . . and for my name's sake hast labored and hast not fainted." Yet He adds, "Nevertheless, I have against thee." In this case, things were still all right in the external life, but there was an inward decay. Observe well that this Divine indictment "I have *against thee* because thou hast left thy first love" is an unmistakably plain intimation that Christians are held accountable for the state of their love Godwards. There are some who seem to conclude from those words "the love of God is shed abroad in our hearts by the Holy Spirit which is given unto us" (Rom. 5:5) that they have no personal responsibility in connection therewith, and who attribute to the sovereignty of God their coldness of heart, rather than blaming themselves for the waning of their affections. But that is highly reprehensible: being an adding of insult to injury.

It is as much the duty of a saint to maintain a warm and constant affection to Christ as it is to preserve his faith in regular exercise, and he is no more warranted in excusing his failure in the one than in the other. We are expressly bidden, "Keep yourselves in the love of God" (Jude) and "set your affection on things above" (Col. 3:1), and it is a horrible perversion and abuse of a blessed truth if I attribute my *not* doing so unto God's sovereign withholding from me the inclination. Those words of Christ's "I have against thee" is the language of censure because of failure, and He certainly had not used it unless he was to blame. Observe He does not merely say "Thou hast *lost* thy first love," as it is so frequently misquoted — man ever tones down what is unpalatable! No, "thou hast *left* thy first love" — something more serious and heinous. One may "lose" a thing involuntarily, but to *leave* it is deliberate action! Finally, let us duly note that our Lord regarded that departure not as an innocent infirmity, but as a culpable sin, for He says "repent"!

In his faithful sermon on Revelation 2:4 C. H. Spurgeon pointed out that we ought to feel alarmed if we have left our first love, and ask the question, "Was I ever a child of God at all?" going on to say: "Oh, my God, must I ask *myself* this question? Yes, I will. Are there not many of whom it is said, they went out from us because they were not of us? Are there not some whose goodness is as the morning cloud and as the early dew — may that not have been *my* case? I am speaking for you all. Put the question: may I not have been impressed under a certain sermon, and may not that impression have been a mere carnal excitement? May it not have been that I thought I repented, but did not really repent? May it not have been the case that I got a hope somewhere, but had not a right to it? and never had the loving faith that unites me to the Lamb of God? And may it not have been that I only thought I had love to Christ, and never had it; for if I really had love to Christ should I be as I now am? See how far I have come down! may I not keep on going down until my end shall be perdition and the fire unquenchable? Many have gone from heights of a profession to the depths of damnation, and may I not be the same? Let me think, if I go on as I am, it is impossible for me to stop; if I am going downwards, I may go on doing so. And O my God, If I go on backsliding for another year — who knows where I may have backslidden to? Perhaps into some gross sin. Prevent, prevent it by Thy grace! Perhaps I may backslide totally. If I am a child of God I know I cannot do that; but still may it not happen that I only thought I was a child of God?"

Searching as is the complaint of Christ to the Ephesian backslider, His word to the Sardinian is yet more drastic: "I know thy works, that thou hast a name that thou livest, and art dead" (3:1). That does not signify that He was here addressing an unregenerate person, but rather one whose conduct belied his name. His life did not correspond with his profession. He had a reputation for piety, but there was no longer evidence to justify it, no fruit to warrant it any longer. Not only had there been deterioration within, but also *without*. The salt had lost its savor, the fine gold had become dim, and hence his profession brought no honor and glory to Christ. He bids him "Be watchful," for that was the very point at which he had failed. "And strengthen the things which remain, that are ready to die," which shows the "art dead" of verse 1 does not mean dead in sins. "For I have not found thy works perfect before God" — not "complete" or "full." Good works were not yet totally abandoned, but many of them were lacking. Part of his duty was listlessly performed, the other part neglected, and even the former was "ready to die."

Thus it will be seen that the case of the Sardinian backslider is much worse than that of the Ephesian. There is no remaining stationary in Christianity: if we do not advance, we retrograde; if we are not fruit-bearing branches of the Vine, we become cumberers of the ground. Decay of grace is not a thing to be regarded lightly, and treated with indifference. If it is not attended to and corrected, our condition will grow worse. If we do not return to our first love — by heeding the injunctions laid down in Revelation 2:5 — then we may expect to become like the Sardinian backslider: one whose witness for Christ is marred. Unless our hearts are kept right, our affection to Christ warm, then the life will soon deteriorate — our works will be deficient both in quality and quantity, and those around us will perceive it. Ere long a "name to live" is all we shall have: the profession itself will be invalid, worthless, "dead."

But worst of all is the Laodicean professor (3:15-20). What makes his case so fearfully solemn is that we are at a loss where to place him, how to classify him — whether he is a real Christian who has fearfully backslidden, or naught but an empty professor. To him Christ says "thou art neither hot nor cold," neither one thing nor the other, but rather an unholy mixture. Such are those who vainly attempt to serve two masters, who are worshippers of God one day, but worshippers of mammon the other six. To him Christ goes on to say "I would thou wert cold or hot": that is either an open and avowed enemy or a faithful and consistent witness for Me. Be one thing or the other: a foe or a friend, an utter worldling or one who is in spirit and in truth a "stranger and pilgrim" in this scene. Corrupt Christianity is more offensive to Christ than is open fidelity. If he who bears His name does not depart from iniquity, *His* honor is affected. "Because thou art lukewarm . . . I will spue thee out of my mouth": in thy present condition thou art an offense to me, and I can no longer own thee.

It is the figure of an emetic which Christ there uses: the mingling together of what is hot and cold, thus producing a "lukewarm" draught which is nauseating to the stomach. And that is exactly what an "inconsistent Christian" is to the Holy One. He who runs with the hare and hunts with the hounds, who is one man inside the church and a totally different one outside; he who seeks to mix godliness with worldliness "I will spue thee out of my mouth" — instead of confessing his name before the Father and His holy angels. But observe what follows: "thou sayest, I am rich, and increased with goods, and have need of nothing." Exactly opposite is this estimation of his from Christ's. No longer "poor in spirit" (Matt. 5:3), he declares himself to be "rich." No longer coming to the throne of grace as a beggar to obtain help, he deems himself to be "increased with goods." No longer sensible of his ignorance, weakness, emptiness, he feels himself to "have need of nothing." That is what makes his case so dangerous and desperate: he has no sense of personal need.

"And knowest not that thou art wretched, and miserable, and poor, and blind, and naked." As carnality and worldliness increase, so also does pride and complacency, and where they dominate spiritual discernment becomes non-existent. Phariseeism and self-sufficiency are inseparable. It was to those who prayed, "God, I thank thee, that I am not as other men, extortioners, unjust, adulterers," and who asked Christ, "are we blind also?" to whom He said, "ye say, We see: therefore your sin remaineth" (John 15:41). The Pharisee boasted "I fast twice in the week, I give tithes of all that I possess": in his own esteem and avowal he was "rich and increased with goods, and had need of nothing," and for that very reason he knew not that he was "wretched and miserable and poor." That too is another form of the nauseating mixture which is so abhorrent to Christ: orthodox in doctrine, but corrupt in practice. One who is loud in claiming to be sound in the faith but who is tyrannical and bitter toward those who differ from him, who holds "high doctrine" but cannot live in peace with his brethren, is as offensive to Christ as if he were thoroughly worldly.

Can such a character as the one who has just been before us be a real though a backslidden Christian? Frankly, we know not, for we are unable to say just how far a saint may fall into the mire and foul his garments before God recovers him, by answering him with "terrible things in righteousness" (Ps. 65:5). Before He made good that awful threat and spued out the Laodicean professor, Christ made a final appeal to him. "I counsel thee to buy of me gold tried in the fire, that thou mayest be rich; and white raiment, that thou mayest be clothed and the shame of thy nakedness do not appear; and anoint thine eyes with eyesalve, that thou mayest see." But though we do not feel capable of deciding whether or not "the root of the matter" really is in him, two things are plain to us. First, that if I have "left my first love" it will not be long before my profession will become "dead," and unless it is revived I shall soon be a Laodicean. Second, that while any person is in a Laodicean state he has no Scriptural warrant to regard himself as a Christian, nor should others consider him as such.

There are many professing Christians who have declined in their practice of piety to a considerable extent, yet who comfort themselves with the idea that they will be brought to repentance before they die. But that is not only an unwarrantable comfort, but is presumptuously tempting God. As another has pointed out, "Whosoever plunges into the gulf of backsliding or continues easy in it under the idea of being recovered by repentance, may find himself mistaken. Both Peter and Judas went in, but only one of them came out! There is reason to fear that thousands of professors are now lifting up their eyes in torment, who in this world reckoned themselves good men, who considered their sins as pardonable errors, and laid their accounts of being brought to repentance: but, ere they were aware, the Bridegroom came and they were not ready to meet him." They of whom it is said, they are "slidden back by a perpetual backsliding they hold fast deceit, they refuse to return" (Jer. 8:5) are the ones "who draw back unto perdition" (Heb. 10:39). And my reader, if you have left your first love, you have "departed from the living God," and until you humbly and penitently return to Him can have no guarantee that you will not be a *"perpetual* backslider."

We should carefully distinguish between the sin which indwells us and our falling into sin. The former is our depraved nature, which God holds us accountable to make no provision for, to resist its workings and refuse its solicitations. The latter is, when through lack of watching against indwelling corruptions, sin breaks forth into open acts. It is an injurious thing to fall into sin, whether secretly or openly, and sooner or later the effects will certainly be felt. But to *continue* therein, is much more evil and dangerous. God has denounced a solemn threatening against those who persist in sin: He "woundeth the head of His enemies, the hairy scalp of such a one as *goeth on still* in his trespasses" (Ps. 68:21). For those who have known the way of righteousness to pursue a course of sin is highly offensive to God. He has provided a remedy (Prov. 28:13): but if instead of confessing and forsaking our sins, we sink into hardness of heart, neglect prayer, shun the company of the faithful, and seek to efface one sin by the committal of another, we are in imminent danger of being abandoned by God and are "nigh unto cursing, whose end is to be burned" (Heb. 6:8).

Let us return to the point where we almost began and ask again, What will be the *sequel* to a decline? It should now be still more evident that a general answer cannot be returned. Not only does God exercise His sovereignty here, using His own good pleasure and not acting uniformly, but differences from the human side of things have also to be taken into account. Much will depend upon whether it be the spiritual decline of a real Christian or simply the religious decay of a mere professor. If the former, the sequel will vary according to whether the decline be internal only or accompanied or followed by falling into open sin. So, too, there is a doctrinal departure from God as well as a practical, as was the case with the Galatians. However, whatever be the type of case this is certain, the one who lapses into a state of torpor needs to respond to that call "Now it is high time to awake out of sleep . . . let us therefore cast off the works of darkness . . ." (Rom. 13:11, 12).

II

We have sought to make clear the urgent *necessity* for recovery from a spiritual decline: we turn now to consider its *desirability*. Look at it first from the *Godward* side. Is it not inexcusable that we should so evilly requite the eternal Lover of our souls? If He who was rich for my sake became so poor that He had not where to lay His head, in order that I (a spiritual pauper) might be made rich, what is due Him from me? If He died the shameful death of the cross that you might live, is not your life to be devoted wholly to Him? If you be Christ's, you are not your own, but "bought with a price" and therefore called upon to "glorify Him in your body and in your spirit" (I Cor. 6:20). If He can be touched with the feeling of our infirmities, think you that He is unmoved if we leave our first love and divide our affections with His rivals? Do you suppose that a backslidden Christian affords Him any pleasure Surely you are aware of the fact that such a case brings no honor to Him. Then let His love constrain you to return and reform your ways, so that you may again show forth His praises and give Him delight.

Consider your case in view of *other Christians*. There is a bond uniting the saints which is closer than any natural tie: "so we, being many are one body in Christ, and every one members one of another" (Rom. 12:5), and therefore "those members should have the same care one for another" (I Cor. 12:25). So vital and intimate is that mystical union that if "one member suffer, all the members suffer with it" (v. 25). If one member of your physical body is affected, there is a reaction throughout your whole system: so it is in the mystical Body. The health or sickness of your soul exerts a very real influence, either for good or for evil, upon your brethren and sisters. For *their* sake then, it is most desirable that if in a spiritual decline you should be restored. If you are not, your example will be a stumblingblock to them, and if they have much association with you their zeal will be dampened and their spirits chilled. Surely it is not a matter of little concern whether you are a help or hindrance to your fellow-saints. "Whoso shall offend one of these little ones which believe in me, it were better for him that a millstone were hanged about his neck and he were drowned in the depth of the sea" (Matt. 18:6).

Contemplate your case in connection with *your unsaved relatives* and friends. Do you not know that one of the main obstacles in the way of many from giving a serious consideration to the gospel, is the inconsistent lives of so many who profess to believe it? Years ago we read of one who was concerned about the soul of his son, and on the eve of his departure for a foreign land, sought to press upon him the claims and excellency of Christ. He received this reply: "Father, I am sorry, but I cannot *hear* what you say for *seeing* what you do"! Is that the unuttered sentiment of your child? You may reply, I do not believe that anything in my conduct can have any influence on the eternal destiny of any soul. Then you are woefully ignorant. "Wives, be in subjection to your own husbands; that, if any obey not the Word, they also may without the Word *be won by* the conversation [behavior] of the wives" (I Peter 3:1). In saving sinners God uses a variety of means, as in prejudicing sinners Satan employs many agents; is God or Satan most likely to *use you?* Most certainly the latter, if you are in a backslidden state.

Coming lower still, let us appeal to *your own interests.* What have you gained by leaving your first love? Have you found the vanities of this world more pleasing than the feast which the gospel sets before you? Does association with empty professors and the ungodly supply more satisfaction to the heart than fellowship with the Father and His Son? No, the very opposite. Rather have you discovered that in forsaking the Fountain of living waters, you have betaken yourself to broken cisterns which hold none. The joy of salvation you once had is departed: the peace of God which passeth all understanding that formerly ruled your heart and mind through Christ Jesus, does so no longer. Today your case resembles that of "the prodigal" — feeding on husks in the far country, while the rich fare of the Father's House is no longer partaken of by you. An uneasy conscience, a restless spirit, a joyless heart is now your portion. Have you not reason to cry "O that I were as in months past, as in the days when God preserved me: when his lamp shined on my head . . . as I was in the days of my youth, when the secret of God was upon my tabernacle" (Job 29:2-4)? Then whose fault is it that you do not again have that blessed experience?

Yes, from every viewpoint, it is most desirable that a Christian be recovered from his spiritual decline. Yet it is also important that he should not conclude he *has* been recovered when such is *not* the case. Since a backslidden state is far from being agreeable, it is natural for one in it to want to be delivered from it. For that very reason it is much to be feared that many have prematurely grasped at the promise of forgiveness and said to their souls, Peace, peace, when there was no peace. As there are many ways by which a convicted sinner seeks peace for his soul, without finding it, so it is with a backslider. If he leans unto his own understanding, follows the devices of his own heart, or avails himself of the remedies advertised by religious quacks, he will rather be worsened than improved. Unless he complies with the injunctions laid down in the Word of Truth for such cases and meets the requirements therein specified, there can be no real recovery for him. Alas that this is so little realized today, and that so many who went astray and think they are returned to the Bishop of their souls are laboring under a delusion.

If there is to be a real recovery it is requisite that the right means be used, and not that which is destructive of what is desired. When trees grow old or begin to decay it is useful to dig about them and manure them, for often that will cause them to flourish again and abound in fruit. But if instead of so doing we removed them out of their soil and planted them in another, so far from that advantaging them they would wither and die. Yet there are many professing saints who suppose that the decay of grace does not arise from themselves and the evil of their hearts, but rather attribute the same to uncongenial surroundings, unfavorable circumstances, their present occasion or station in life, and persuade themselves that as soon as they be freed from those, they will return to their first love and again delight themselves in spiritual things. But that is a false notion and spiritual delusion. Let men's circumstances and stations of life be what they will, the truth is that all their departures from God proceed from an evil heart of unbelief, as is clear from Hebrews 3:13. Do not deceive and flatter yourself then with the idea that what is needed for a recovery from your spiritual decline is but a removal into more favorable and congenial circumstances.

As it is from want of watchfulness and because of the allowance of sin that all decays proceed, so a return unto unsparing mortification of our lusts, with all the duties that lead thereunto, must be the way of recovery. Yet at this point, too, we need to be much on our guard lest we substitute for the denyings of self which God has enjoined, those pharisaical or papistical inventions which are of no value. Under the name and pretence of the means and duties of mortification men have devised and enjoined a number of works, ways, and duties, which God never appointed or approved, nor will He accept; but will rather ask "who hath required *this* at your hand?" (Isa. 1:12). Self-imposed abstinences and austerities may "have indeed a show of wisdom in will worship, and humility, and neglecting of the body" (Col. 2:23), but they will not profit the soul one iota. Unless those who are weighted down with a sense of guilt conduct themselve by the light of the Gospel they will think to placate the displeasure of God by betaking themselves to an unusual course of severities which *He* has nowhere commanded. No abstinence from lawful things will deliver us from the consequences of having indulged in unlawful ones.

Again, the one who is exercised over and distressed by his spiritual decline is very liable to be wrongly counselled if he turns to his fellow-Christians for advice and help. It is to be feared that in this day there are few even among the people of God who are qualified to be of real assistance to others. In most instances their own spirituality is at such a low ebb that if they are turned to for relief, they will only be found to be "physicians of no value" (Job 13:4). And if they consulted the average preacher or pastor, the result is not likely to prove much better. Of old Jehovah complained of the unfaithful priests of Israel "they have healed also the hurt of the daughter of my people *slightly*, saying, Peace, peace, when there is no peace" (Jer. 6:14). There are not a few such today. If one who was mourning over having left his first love asked them the way of return thereto, instead of probing the conscience to ascertain the root of the "hurt," they would endeavor to quiet his fears and soothe him; instead of faithfully warning him of the seriousness of his case, they would say there was nothing to be unduly exercised over, that perfection is not attainable in this life; and instead of naming the means God has appointed, would tell him to continue attending the services regularly and contributing liberally to the cause, and all would be well. Many a wound has been skinned over without being cured.

"When Ephraim saw his sickness and Judah saw his wound, then went Ephraim to the Assyrian and sent to king Jareb: yet could *he* not heal you nor cure you of your wound" (Hos. 5:13). The historical reference is to Israel and Judah when, in great danger from the pressure of enemies, instead of humbling themselves before God and seeking His help, they betook themselves unto a neighboring nation and looked to it for protection; yet to no avail. But it has a spiritual application to those who are conscious of their spiritual decline, but who turn to the wrong quarter for deliverance. Backsliders are often aware of their wretched plight, but perceive not that sin is the cause of it and God alone can heal their backsliding (Hos. 14:4). When His chastening rod falls upon them, so far from recognizing that it is *His* mighty hand correcting them, that it is His *righteous* hand dealing with them, they imagine it is only "circumstances" which are against them, and turn to the creature to extricate them; but to no good effect. Since there has been a departure from God there must be a return to Him, and in that way He has appointed, or there can be no recovery from the evil consequences of that departure.

We turn now to consider the *possibility* of recovery. It may appear strange to some of our readers that we should deem it necessary to mention such a thing, still more so that we should discuss it in some detail. If so, surely they forget that since Satan succeeds in persuading many a convicted sinner that his case is hopeless, that he has carried his rebellion against God to such lengths as to be beyond the reach of mercy, driving him into a state of abject despair; it should not be thought strange that he will employ the same tactics with a backslidden saint — assuring him that he has sinned against such favors, privileges, and light, that his case is now hopeless? Those who have read the history of John Bunyan — and his case is far from being unique — and learned of his lying so long in the slough of despond, when the Devil made him believe he had committed the unpardonable sin, should not be surprised to learn that he is still plying the same trade and persuading one and another that he has so far departed from the Lord that his recovery is impossible.

But we do not have to go outside the Scriptures to find saints not only in a state of despondency and dejection before God, but in actual despair of again enjoying His favor. Take the case of Job. True, there were times when he could say "I know that My Redeemer liveth," and "when he hath tried me I shall come forth as gold." But his assurance was not always thus: there were also seasons when he exclaimed "mine hope hath he removed like a tree, he hath also kindled his wrath against me" (19:10, 11). True, he erred in his judgment, nevertheless such was how he felt in the dark hour of trial. Take the case of Asaph: "My sore ran in the night and ceased not: my soul refused to be comforted. I remembered God, and was troubled." Is not that an apt description of many a backslider as he calls to mind the omniscience, the holiness, the justice of God? But did he not find relief by reminding himself of God's grace and loving-kindness? No, for he went on to ask "will the Lord cast off forever? and will He be favorable no more? Is His mercy clean gone forever? Doth His promise fail for evermore? Hath God forgotten to be gracious? Hath He in anger shut up His tender mercies?" (Ps. 77:7-10). That he should speak thus was indeed his infirmity, yet it shows into what despondency a saint may fall.

Consider the case of Jeremiah. Said he "I am the man that hath seen affliction by the rod of his wrath . . . Surely against me is he turned. He hath set me in dark places. . . . He hath hedged me about, that I cannot get out: he hath made my chain heavy. Also when I cry and shout, he shutteth out my prayer. . . . He hath filled me with bitterness, he hath made me drunken with wormwood. . . . thou hast removed my soul far off from peace. And I said, My strength and my hope is perished from the Lord" (Lam. 3:1-18). Is not that the language of despair! It was not only that his hope was weak and wavering, but he felt it had "perished," and that "from before the Lord" Lower than that one cannot get. He had no expectation of deliverance; he saw no possibility of being recovered from his wretched condition. And think you my reader there are no Christians in such a sad plight today? If so, ask yourself, Why has God placed on permanent record such groanings of His people when they occupied the dungeons of despair? The time may come when such language will exactly suit *your* case, and if so, you will be very glad to hear that there *is* a possibility of deliverance, a door of hope opened in the valley of Achor.

There can be little room for doubt that the chief reason why so many professors today see no need for pointing out that *it is possible* for a backslidden Christian to be restored, is because of the defective teaching they sit under. They hold such light views of the sinfulness of sin, they perceive so faintly the spirituality and strictness of God's law, they have such a dim conception of His ineffable holiness, that their consciences are comatosed, and hence blind to their own state, and unaware of what would be involved in delivering them out of it. They have had "Once saved, always saved," "My sheep shall never perish," dinned into their ears so often, they take it for granted every backslider will be restored as a matter of course – i.e., without any deep exercises of heart on their part or compliance with the requirements which God has laid down. Yea, there are extensive circles in Christendom today where it is taught "having forgiven you all trespasses" (Col. 2:13) means "every trespass: past, present, and future," and that so far from the Christian asking God for daily forgiveness, he should rather thank Him for having already forgiven him. Of course those who swallow such deadly poison need not be informed that recovery from a relapse is possible.

But different far is it with one who lives in the fear of the Lord, whose conscience is tender, who views sin in the light of Divine holiness. When *he* is overtaken by a fault, he is cut to the quick, and should he so far decline as to leave his first love, he will find a way of recovery by no means easy; and should he continue departing from God until his case become such that he has a name to live but is dead, he may abandon hope entirely. When he seeks a return to the Lord, it will be a case of "out of the depths have I cried unto thee" (Ps. 130:1) – out of the depths of his heart, out of the depths of conviction, out of the depths of anguished contrition, out of the depths of despondency and despair. In his remarkable book on Psalm 130 J. Owen after pointing out that "gracious souls after much communion with God may be brought into inextricable depths and entanglements on the account of sin," went on to define those "depths" as "1. Loss of the wanted sense of the love of God which the soul did formerly enjoy. 2. Perplexed thoughtfulness about their great and wretched unkindness towards God. 3. A revived sense of justly deserved wrath. 4. Oppressing apprehension of temporal judgments."

But the eminent Puritan did not stop there. He went on to say, "There may be added hereunto, prevailing fears for a season of being utterly rejected by God, of being found a reprobate at the last day. Jonah seems to have concluded so: 'Then said I, I am cast out of thy sight' (3:4) – I am lost forever: God will own me no more. And Heman, 'I am counted with them that go down into the pit, free among the dead, like the slain that lie in the grave, when thou rememberest me no more: and they are cut off from thy hand' (Ps. 88:4, 5). This may reach the soul, until the sorrows of Hell encompass and lay hold upon it: until it be despaired of comfort, peace, rest; until it be a terror to itself, and be ready to choose strangling rather than life. This may befall a gracious soul on the account of sin. But yet because this fights directly against the life of faith God does not, unless it be in extraordinary cases, suffer it to lie long in this horrible pit, wherein there is no water – no refreshment. But this often falls out, that even the saints themselves are left for a season to a fearful expectation of judgment and fiery indignation, as to the prevailing apprehension of their mind."

We can bear testimony that in our extensive reading we have come across not merely a few isolated and exceptional cases of backslidden saints who had sunk into such depths of soul trouble, distress, and horror, but many such; and that in the course of our travels we have personally met more than one or two who were in such darkness and anguish of heart that they had *no hope*, and no efforts of ours could dispell their gloom. Let that serve as a solemn warning unto those who at present are enjoying the light of God's countenance: "Let him that thinketh he standeth take heed lest *he* fall" (I Cor. 10:12) — fall into a state of unwatchfulness and then into wickedness. Sin is that "abominable thing" which God hates (Jer. 44:4), whether it be found in the unregenerate or the regenerate. If we trifle with temptation then we shall be made to taste what an exceeding bitter thing it is to depart from the living God. If we enter the paths of unrighteousness we shall obtain personal proof that "the way of transgressors is hard." And the higher have been our privileges and attainments, the more painful will be the effects from a fall.

But thank God the recovery of a backslider *is possible*, no matter how heinous or long protracted it was. The cases of David, of Jonah, of Peter demonstrate that! "No man that is fallen under spiritual decays has any reason to say, there is no hope, provided he take the right way of recovery. If every step that is lost in the way to heaven should be irrecoverable, woe would be unto us: we should all assuredly perish. If there were no reparation of our breaches, no healing of our decays, no salvation but for those who are always progressive in grace; if God should mark all that is done amiss, as the Psalmist spake, 'O Lord who should stand?' Nay, if we had not recoveries every day, we should go off with a perpetual backsliding. But then, as was said, it is required that the right means of it be used" (J. Owen).

What are those right means and the very real difficulties which attend the use of them by those who have openly departed from God?

III

Its difficulty. Though reviving and restoration is needful, desirable, and possible, yet it is by no means easy. We do not mean that any problem is presented to God in connection with the recovery of one who has suffered a spiritual relapse, but that it is far from being a simple matter for a backslider to comply with His requirements in order thereto. That difficulty is at least threefold: there is a difficulty in realizing the sadness of his case, a difficulty in putting forth a real desire for recovery, and a difficulty in meeting God's stipulations. Sin has a blinding effect, and the more one falls under its power the less discernment will he possess. It is only in God's light that we can see light, and the further we depart from Him the more we engulf ourselves in darkness. It is only as the bitter effects of sin began to be tasted that the erring one becomes conscious of his sorry condition. Others may perceive it, and in loving faithfulness tell him about it, but in most instances he is quite unaware of his decline and such warnings have no weight with him. Of course, the degree of the decay of his grace will determine the measure in which the "and knowest not" of Revelation 3:17 applies to him.

But even where there be some realization that all is not well with himself it by no means follows that there is also a real anxiety to return to his first love. To some extent the conscience of such an one is comatosed and, therefore, there is little sensibility of his condition and still less horror of it. Here, too, the natural adumbrates the spiritual. Have we not met with or read of those suffering from certain forms of sickness who lacked a desire to be healed? Certainly there are not a few such in the religious world. If the reader dissents from such a statement we ask him, why then did the great Physician of souls address Himself as He did to the one by the pool of Bethseda? We are told that that man had suffered from an infirmity no less than thirty-eight years, yet the Saviour asked him "Wilt thou be made whole?" (John 5:6) — are you really desirous to be? That question was neither meaningless nor strange. The wretched are not always willing to be relieved. Some prefer to lie on a couch and be ministered to by friends than bestir themselves and perform their duties. Others become lethargic and indifferent and are, as Scripture designates them, "at ease in Zion"!

It is all too little realized among Christians that backsliding is a departing from God and a returning to the conditions they were in before conversion, and the further that departure is, the closer will become their approximation to the old manner of life. Observe the particular language used by David in his confession to God. First he said, "Before I was afflicted, I went astray" (119:67); but later, as spiritual discernment increased following upon his recovery, and as he then more clearly perceived what had been involved in his sad lapse, he declared "I have gone astray like a *lost* sheep" (v. 176) — the state of God's elect in the days of their unregeneracy (Isa. 53:6). True, the case of David was a more extreme form of backsliding than many, nevertheless it is a solemn warning to all of us of what may befall if we have left our first love, and return not promptly to it. And how clearly his experiences serve to illustrate the point we are here seeking to set before the reader. Ponder carefully what follows the account of David's grievous fall in II Samuel 11 and behold the spirit of blindness and insensibility which deliberate sinning casts upon a backslidden saint.

In view of II Samuel 12:15 it is clear that almost a whole year, possibly more, had elapsed between the time of David's fall and the Lord's sending of Nathan unto him. There is not a hint that David was broken-hearted before God during those months. The prophet addressed him in the form of a parable — intimation of his moral distance from God (Matt. 13:10-13) yet, if David's conscience had been active before God, he would have easily understood the purport of that parable. But sin had darkened his judgment, and he recognized not the application of it unto himself. In such a state of spiritual deadness was David then in, that Nathan had to interpret his parable and say "Thou art the man." Verily, he *had* "gone astray like a lost sheep," and at that time the state of his heart differed little from the unconverted. Later, when his eyes were again opened and he was deeply convicted of his sins, he perceived that he had lapsed into a condition perilously close to and scarcely distinguishable from that of the unregenerate, for he cried "*Create* in me a clean heart, O God, and *renew* a right spirit within me" (Ps. 51:10).

Does the reader now grasp more easily our meaning when we speak of the *difficulty* of being recovered from a spiritual relapse: the difficulty of one in that case becoming sensible of his woeful plight and the realization that he needs delivering from it? Sin darkens the understanding and renders the heart hard or insensible. As it is with the unregenerate sinner, so it is become — to a greater or less extent, and in extreme cases almost entirely — with the backslider. What is it that is the distinguishing mark of all who have never been born again? Not falling into gross and flagrant outward sin, for many of them are never guilty of that, but "having the understanding darkened, being alienated from the life of God through the ignorance that is in them, because of the blindness [margin, "hardness" or "insensibility"] of their heart." That is the Divine diagnosis of all who are "dead in trespasses and sins," and we have but to change "alienated from the life of God" to "severed from communion with God" and that solemn description accurately depicts the inward state of the backslider, though until God begins to recover him he will no more recognize his picture than David did when Nathan drew his.

It is much to be thankful for when a child of God becomes aware that he *is* in a spiritual decline, especially if he mourns over it. Such is rarely the case with an unregenerate professor, and never so on account of *inward* decay. A person who has always been weak and sickly knows not what it is to lack health and strength, for he never had experience of it; still less does one in the cemetery realize that he is totally devoid of life. But let one of robust constitution be laid upon a bed of sickness, and he is very definitely aware of the great change that has come over him. The reason why so many professing Christians are not troubled over any spiritual decline is because they never had any spiritual health, and therefore it would be a waste of time to treat with such about a recovery. If you should speak of their departure from God and loss of communion with Him, you would seem to them as Lot did to his sons-in-law when he expostulated with them — as one that "mocked" or made sport with them (Gen. 19:14), and would be laughed at for your pains. Never having experienced any love for Christ, it would be useless to urge them to return to the same.

It is much to be feared that is why these chapters on spiritual decline and recovery — so much needed today by many of the saints — will be almost meaningless, and certainly wearisome, to some of our readers. The real Christian will not dismiss them lightly, but rather will seek to faithfully measure himself by them, searching himself before God and being at some pains to ascertain the condition of his soul. But those who are content with a mere outward profession, will see little in them either of importance or interest. Such as perceive neither evil nor danger in their present condition, supposing that all is well with them because it is as good as it ever was, are the ones who most need to examine themselves as to whether the "root of the matter" was ever in them. And even those who *have* experienced something of "the power of godliness" but through carelessness are no longer making conscience of seeking to please the Lord in all things as they once did, are asleep in carnal security (which is hardly distinguishable from being dead in sin) if they be not exercised over their decline and anxious to be recovered from it.

The vast majority in Christendom today will acknowledge nothing as a decay *in themselves*. Rather are they like Ephraim: "Strangers have devoured his strength, and he knoweth it not," and hence it is added "they do not return unto the Lord their God, nor seek him for all this" (Hos. 7:9, 10). How is it with you, dear friend? Have *you* been able to maintain spiritual peace and joy in your soul? — for those are the inseparable fruits of a life of faith and an humble and daily walking with God. We mean not the fancies and imaginations of them, but the substance and reality: that peace which passeth all understanding and which "keeps" or "garrisons" the heart and mind; that joy which delights itself in the Lord and is "full of glory" (I Peter 1:8). Does that peace stay your mind on God under trials and tribulations, or is it found wanting in the hour of testing? Is "the joy of the Lord your strength" (Neh. 8:10), so that it moves you to perform the duties of obedience with alacrity and pleasure, or is it merely a fickle emotion which exerts no steady power for good on your life? If you once enjoyed such peace and joy, but do so no longer, then you have suffered a spiritual decline.

Spirituality of mind and the exercise of a tender conscience in the performance of spiritual duties is another mark of health, for it is in those things grace is most requisite and operative. They are the very life of the new man and the animating principle of all spiritual actions, and without which all our performances are but "dead works." Our worship of God is but an empty show a horrible mockery, if we draw nigh to Him with our lips while our hearts are far from Him. But to keep the mind in a spiritual frame in our approaches to the Lord, to bless Him with "all that is within us," to keep our grace in vigorous exercise in all holy duties, is only possible while the health of the soul be maintained. Slothfulness, formality, weariness of the flesh, the business and cares of this life, the seductions and opposition of Satan, all contend against the Christian to frustrate him at that point; yet the grace of God is sufficient if it be duly sought. If you constantly "stir up yourself to take hold of God" (Isa. 64:7), if you habitually "set your face unto the Lord God to *seek Him* by prayer and supplication" (Dan. 9:3), that is evidence of spiritual health, but if the contrary be now your experience, then you have suffered a spiritual decline.

If you realize that things are not as flourishing with you now, either inwardly or outwardly, as they were formerly, that is a hopeful sign; yet it must not be rested in. Suffer not your heart one moment to be content with your present frame, for if you do there will follow a more marked deterioration. Satan will tell you there is nothing yet for you to be worried about, that there will be time enough for that when you fall into some outward sin. But he lies, Scripture says, "to him that knoweth to do good, and doeth it not, to him it is sin" (James 4:17). You know it is good that you should return unto God and confess to Him your failures — even though those failures be more of omission than commission — but if you refuse to, that in itself is "*sin.*" To be conscious of decline is the first step toward recovery, yet not sufficient in itself. There must also be a laying of it to heart, a sensibility of the evil of it, a mourning over it, for "godly sorrow worketh repentance" (II Cor. 7: 10). Yet neither is that sufficient: godly sorrow is not repentance itself, but only a means thereto. Moaning and groaning over our complaints, spiritual or natural, may relieve our feelings, but they will effect no cure.

Sensible of our decays, exercised at heart over them, we must now comply with God's requirements for recovery if healing is to be obtained. And here too we shall experience difficulty. There are those who persuade themselves that it would be no hard matter to recover themselves from a state of backsliding, that they could easily do so if occasion required. But that is an entirely false notion.

There are many who think getting saved is one of the simplest things imaginable, but they are woefully mistaken. If nothing more were required from the sinner than an intellectual assent to the gospel no miracle of grace would be required in order to induce that. But before a stout-hearted rebel against God will throw down the weapons of his warfare, before one who is in love with sin can hate it, before one who lived only to please self will deny self, the exceeding greatness of God's power must work upon him (Eph. 1:19). And so it is in restoration. If nothing more were rquired from the backslider than a lip acknowledgement of his offenses and a return to external duties, no great difficulty would be experienced; but to meet the requirements of God for recovery is a very different matter.

Rightly did John Owen affirm "Recovery from backsliding is the hardest task in the Christian religion: one which few make either comfortable or honorable work of." Yea, it is a task entirely beyond the capabilities of any Christian. We cannot recover ourselves, and none but the great Physician can heal our backslidings. It is the operations of the Spirit of Christ which is the effectual cause of the revival under decays of grace. It is not by might nor by power, but by the Spirit of God that any wanderer is brought back. It is God who makes us sensible of our deadness, and who causes us to make application to Him "wilt thou not revive us again, that thy people may rejoice in thee" (Ps. 85:6). And when that request has been granted, each of them will own with David "*He* restoreth my soul" (Ps. 23:3). Nevertheless, in this, too, our responsibility has to be discharged, for at no point does God treat with us as though we were mere automatons. There are certain duties He sets before us in this connection, specific requirements which

He makes upon us, and until we definitely and earnestly set ourselves to the performance of the same, we have no warrant to look for deliverance.

Though the Holy Spirit alone can effect the much-to-be-desired change in the withered and barren believer, yet God has appointed certain means which are subservient to that end, and if we neglect those means then no wonder we have reason to complain and cry out "My leanness, my leanness, woe unto me! the treacherous dealers have dealt treacherously; yea, the treacherous dealers have dealt very treacherously" (Isa. 24:16), and therefore an alteration for the better cannot reasonably be expected. If we entertain hope of an improvement in our condition while we neglect the appointed means, our expectations will certainly issue in a sorrowful disappointment. Unless we be thoroughly persuaded of that, we shall remain inert. While we cherish the idea that we can do nothing, and must fatalistically wait a sovereign reviving from God, we shall go on waiting. But if we realize what God requires of us, it will serve to deepen our desires after a reviving and stimulate us unto a compliance with those things which we must do if He is to grant us showers of refreshment and a strengthening of those things in us which are ready to die. There has to be an asking, a seeking, a knocking, if the door of deliverance is to be opened to us.

It was not an Arminian, but a high Calvinist (John Brine, whose works received a most favorable reveiw in the *Gospel Standard* of Oct. 1852) who wrote to God's people two centuries ago: "Much labour and diligence are required unto this. It is not complaining of the sickly condition of our souls which will effect this cure: confession of our follies, that have brought diseases upon us, though repeated ever so often, will avail nothing towards the removal of them. If we intend the recovery of our former health and vigour, we must *act* as well as complain and groan. We must keep at a distance from those persons and those snares which have drawn us into instances of folly, which have occasioned that disorder which is the matter of our complaint. Without this we may multiply acknowledgements and expressions of concern for our past miscarriages to no purpose at all. It is very great folly to think of regaining our former strength so long as we embrace and dally with those objects through whose evil influence we are fallen into a spiritual decline. It is not our bewailing the pernicious effects of sin that will prevent its baneful influence upon us for time to come, except we are determined to *forsake* that to which is owing our melancholy disorder."

It is not nearly so simple to act on that counsel as many may imagine. Habits are not easily broken, nor objects relinquished which have obtained a powerful hold upon our affections. The natural man is wholly regulated and dominated by "the lust of the flesh, and the lust of the eyes, and the pride of life," and the only way in which their prevalency over a Christian is broken is by an unsparing *mortification* of those lusts. Just so soon as we become slack in denying self or in

governing our affections and passions, alluring objects draw us to a
dalliance with them, to the blighting of our spirituality, and recovery
is impossible until we abandon such evil charmers. But just so far as
they have obtained a hold upon us will be the difficulty of breaking
from them. Difficult because it will be contrary to all our natural inclinations and preregenerate lives. "If thy right eye offend thee, pluck it
out and cast it from thee: for it is profitable for thee that one of thy
members should perish and not thy whole body should be cast into hell"
(Matt. 5:29). Christ did not teach that the mortifying of a favorite
lust was a simple and painless matter.

As though His followers would be slow to take to heart that unpalatable injunction, the Lord Jesus went on to say, "And if thy right
hand offend thee, cut it off and cast it from thee: for it is profitable
for thee that one of thy members should perish and not thy whole body
should be cast into hell." As the "eye" is our most precious member,
so (especially to a laboring man) the "right hand" is the most useful
and valuable one. By that figurative language Christ taught us that our
dearest idol must be renounced, our bosom lust mortified. No matter
how pleasing be the object which would beguile us, it must be denied.
Such a task would prove as hard and painful as the cutting off of an
hand — they had no anesthetics in those days! But if men are willing
to have a gangrened limb amputated to save their lives, why should
we shrink from painful sacrifices unto the saving of our souls. Heaven
and Hell are involved by whether grace or our senses rule our souls:
"You must not expect to enjoy the pleasures of earth and heaven too,
and think to pass from Delilah's lap into Abraham's bosom" (T. Manton). That which is demanded of the Christian is far from being child's
play.

Again, "we must do the first works if we design a revival of our
graces. This calls for humility and diligence, to both which our proud
and slothful hearts are too much disinclined. We must be content to
begin afresh, both to learn and practice, since through carelessness and
sloth we are gone backward in knowledge and practice too. It sometimes is with the saints as with school boys, who by their negligence are
so far from improvement, that they have almost forgotten the rudiments
of a language or an art they have begun to learn; in which case it is
necessary that they must make a new beginning: this suits not with
pride, but unto it they must submit. So the Christian sometimes has
need of being taught again what are the first principles of the oracles
of God, when for the time he has been in the school of Christ his improvement ought to be such as would fit him for giving instruction to
others in these plain and easy principles. But through negligence he
has let them slip, and he must content to pass through the very same
lessons of conviction, sorrow, humiliation and repentance he learned long
since of the Holy Spirit: whatever we think of the matter, a revival
cannot be without it" (Brine). It is that humbling of our pride which
makes recovery so difficult to a backslider.

IV

Now we shall consider its conditionality, or those things on which it is suspended (a term which will hardly please some of our readers, yet it is the correct one to use in this connection; but since various writers have used the term in different ways, it is requisite that we explain the sense in which we have employed it). When we say there are certain conditions which an erring saint must fulfil before he can be restored to fellowship with God, we do not use the term in a legalistic sense or mean that there is anything meritorious in his performances. It is not that God strikes a bargain, offering to bestow certain blessings in return for things done by us, but rather that He has appointed a certain order, a *connection* between one thing and another, and that, for the maintaining of His honor, the holiness of His government, and the enforcing of our responsibility. In all His dealings with us God acts in grace, but His grace ever reigns "through righteousness," and never at the expense of it.

"He that covereth his sins shall not prosper, but whoso confesseth and forsaketh them shall have mercy" (Prov. 28:13). Now there is nothing meritorious in confessing and forsaking sins, nothing which gives title to mercy, but God requires them from us, and we have no warrant to expect mercy without them. That verse expresses the *order* of things which God has established, a *holy* order, so that Divine mercy is exercised without any connivance at sin, exercised in a way wherein we take sides with Him in the hatred of our sins. As health of body is conditioned or suspended upon the eating of suitable food or the healing of it upon partaking of certain remedies, so it is with the soul: there is a definite connection between the two things — food and strength: the one must be received in order to the other. In like manner forgiveness of sins is promised only to those who repent and believe. Whether you term repenting and believing "conditions," "means," "instruments," or "the way of" amounts to the same thing, for they simply signify they are what God requires from us before He bestows forgiveness — requires *not* as a price at our hands, but by way of congruity.

Some may ask, But has not God promised, "I *will* heal their backslidings" (Hos. 14:4)? To which we reply, Yes, yet that promise is not an absolute or unconditional one as the context plainly shows. In the verses preceding God calls upon them to "return" unto Him because they had fallen by their iniquity. He bids them "Take with you words, and turn to the Lord; say unto him, Take away all iniquity." Moreover, they pledge themselves to reformation of conduct: "neither will we say any more to the work of our hands, Ye are our gods" (vv. 1-3). Thus it is unto penitent and confessing souls, who abandon their idols, that promise is made. God does indeed "heal our backslidings" yet *not* without our concurrence, not without the humbling of ourselves before Him, not without our complying with His holy requirements. God does indispensably demand certain things of us in order to the enjoyment of certain blessings. "*If* we confess our sins, he is faithful and just to forgive us our sins and to cleanse us from all unrighteousness" (I John 1: 9). That "if" expresses the condition, or reveals the connection which God has appointed between our defilement and His removal of it.

We are therefore going to point out what are the "conditions" of recovery from a spiritual decline, or what are the "means" of restoration for a backslider, or what is the "way of" deliverance for one who is departed from God. Before turning to specific cases recorded in Scripture, let us again call attention to Proverbs 28:13. First, "he that covereth his sins shall not prosper." To "cover" our sins is a refusing to bring them out into the light by an honest confessing of them unto God; or to hide them from our fellows or refuse to acknowledge offenses to those we have wronged. While such be the case, there can be no prosperity of soul, no communion with God or His people. Second, "but whoso confesseth and forsaketh them shall have mercy." To "confess" means to freely, frankly, and penitently own them unto God, and to our fellows if our sins have been against them. To "forsake" our sins is a voluntary and deliberate act: it signifies to loathe and abandon them in our affections, to repudiate them by our wills, to refuse to dwell upon them in our minds and imaginations with any pleasure or satisfaction.

But suppose the believer *does not* promptly thus confess and forsake his sins? In such case not only will he "not prosper," not only can there now be no further spiritual growth, but peace of conscience and joy of heart will depart from him. The Holy Spirit is "grieved" and He will withhold His comforts. And suppose *that* does not bring him to his senses, then what? Let the case of David furnish answer: "When I kept silence, my bones waxed old through my roaring all the day long. For day and night thy hand was heavy upon me: my moisture is turned into the drought of summer" (Ps. 32:3, 4). The "bones" are the strength and upholders of the bodily frame, and when used figuratively the "waxing of them old" signifies that vigor and support of the soul is gone, so that it sinks into anguish and despair. Sin is a pestilential thing which saps our vitality. Though David was silent as to confession, he was not so as to sorrow. God's hand smote his conscience and afflicted his spirit so that he was made to groan under His rod. He had no rest by day or night: sin haunted him in his dreams and he awoke unrefreshed. Like one in a drought he was barren and fruitless. Not until he turned to the Lord in contrite confession was there any relief for him.

Let us turn now to an experience suffered by Abraham that illustrates our present subject, though few perhaps have considered it as a case of spiritual relapse. Following upon his full response to the Lord's call to enter the land of Canaan, we are told that "the Lord *appeared unto Abram*" (Gen. 12:7). So it is now: "He that hath my commandments and keepeth them, he that it is that loveth me: and he that loveth me shall be loved of my Father, and I will love him and *manifest myself* to him" (John 14:21). It is not to the self-willed and self-pleasing, but to the obedient one that the Lord draws near in the intimacies of His love and makes Himself a reality and satisfying portion. The "manifestation" of Christ to the soul should be a daily experience, and if it is not, then our hearts ought to be deeply exercised before Him. If there is not the regular "appearing of the Lord," it must be because we have wandered from the path of obedience.

Next we are told of the patriarch's response to the Lord's "appearing" and the precious promise He then made him: "and there he built an altar unto the Lord." The altar speaks of worship — the heart's pouring of itself forth in adoration and praise. That order is unchanging: occupation of the soul with Christ, beholding (with the eyes of faith) the King in His beauty, is what alone will bow us before Him in true worship. Next, "and he removed from thence unto a mountain" (Gen. 12:8). Spiritually speaking the "mountain" is a figure of elevation of spirit, soaring above the level in which the world lies, the affections being set upon things above. It tells of a heart detached from this scene — attracted to and absorbed by Him who has passed within the vail. Is it not written "they that wait upon the Lord shall renew their strength: they shall *mount up* with wings as eagles" (Isa. 40:31)? And how may this "mountain" experience be *maintained?* Is such a thing possible? We believe it is, and at it we should constantly aim, not being content with anything that falls short of it. The answer is revealed in what immediately follows.

"And pitched his tent, having Bethel on the west and Hai on the east." The "tent" is the symbol of the stranger, of one who has no home or abiding-place in the scene which cast out of it the Lord of glory. We never read that Abram built him any "house" in Canaan (as Lot occupied one in Sodom!); no, he was but a "sojourner" and his tent was the sign and demonstration of this character. "And *there* he builded an altar unto the Lord": from this point onwards two things characterized him, his "tent" and his "altar" — 12:8; 13:3, 4; 13:18. In each of those passages the "tent" is mentioned first, for we cannot truly and acceptably worship God on high unless we maintain our character as sojourners here below. That is why the exhortation is made, "Dearly beloved, I beseech you *as strangers and pilgrims,* abstain from fleshly lusts, which war against the soul" (I Peter 2:11) and so quench the spirit of worship. Are we conducting ourselves as those who are "partakers of the heavenly calling" (Heb. 3:1) — do our manners, our dress, our speech evidence the same to others?

Ah, dear reader, do we not find right there the explanation of *why* it is that a "mountain" experience is so little enjoyed and still less maintained by us! Is it not because we descended to the plains, came down to the level of empty professors and white-washed worldlings, set our affection upon things below, and in consequence became "conformed to this world"? If we really be Christ's, He has "delivered us [judicially] from this present evil world" (Gal. 1:4) and therefore our hearts and lives should be separated from it in a *practical* way. Our Home is on high and that fact ought to mold every detail of our lives. Of Abram and his fellow saints it is recorded they "*confessed* that they were strangers and pilgrims on the earth" (Heb. 11:13) — "confessed" it by their lives as well as lips, and it is added "*wherefore* God is not ashamed to be called their God" (v. 16). But alas, too many now are afraid to be considered "peculiar," and to escape criticism and ostracism compromise, hide their light under a bushel, come down to the level of the world.

The young Christian might well suppose that one who was in the path of obedience, who was going on whole-heartedly with God, who was a man of the "tent" and the "altar" would be quite immune from any fall. So he will be while he maintains that relationship and attitude: but it is, alas, very easy for him to relax a little and gradually depart from it. Not that such a departure is to be expected, or excused on the ground that since the flesh remains in the believer it is only to be looked for that it will not be long ere it unmistakably manifests itself. Not so: "he that saith he abideth in him, ought himself also so to walk even as he walked" (I John 2:6). Full provision has been made by God for him to do so. "Let not sin therefore reign in your mortal body, that ye should obey it in the lusts thereof" (Rom. 6:12). But Abram *did* suffer a relapse, a serious one, and as it is profitable for us to observe and take to heart the various steps which preceded Peter's open denial of Christ, so is it to ponder and turn into earnest supplication that which befell the patriarch before he "went *down* into Egypt."

First, we are told "and Abram journeyed" (v. 9), nor is it said that he had received any order from God to move his tent from the place where he was in communion with Him. That by itself would not be conclusive, but in the light of what follows it seems to indicate plainly that a spirit of *restlessness* had now seized him, and restlessness, my reader, indicates we are no longer content with our lot. The solemn thing to observe is that the startingpoint in the path of Abram's decline was that he left Bethel, and Bethel means "the house of God" — the place of fellowship with Him. All that follows is recorded as a warning of what we may expect if *we* leave "Bethel." Abram's leaving Bethel was the root of his failures, and in the sequel we are shown the bitter fruit which sprang from it. That was the place which Peter left, for he followed Christ "afar off." That was the place which the Ephesian backslider forsook: "thou hast left thy first love." The day we become lax in maintaining communion with God, the door is opened for many evils to enter the soul.

"And Abram journeyed." The Hebrew is more expressive and emphatic. Literally it reads "And Abram journeyed, in going and journeying." A restless spirit possessed him, which was a sure sign that communion with God was broken. I am bidden to "rest in the Lord" (Ps. 37:6), but I can only do so as long as I "delight myself also in the Lord" (v. 4). But, second, it is recorded of Abram: "going on still toward the south" (Gen. 12:9), and southward was *Egyptward*! Most suggestive and solemnly accurate is that line in the picture. Turning Egyptward is ever the logical outcome of leaving Bethel and becoming possessed of a restless spirit, for in the Old Testament Egypt is the outstanding symbol of *the world*. If the believer's heart be right with his

Redeemer he can say "Thou O Christ art all I want, more than all in thee I find." But if Christ no longer fully absorbs him, then some other object will be sought. No Christian gets right back into the world at a single step. Nor did Abram: he "journeyed toward the south" before he entered Egypt!

Third, "and there was a famine in the land" (v. 10). Highly significant was that! A trial of his faith, says someone, Not at all: rather a showing of the red light — God's danger-signal of what lay ahead. It was a searching call for the patriarch to pause and "consider his ways." Faith needs no trials when it is in normal and healthy exercise: it is when it has become encrusted with dross that the fire is necessary to purge it. There was no famine at *Bethel*. Of course not: there is always fulness of provision there. The analogy of Scripture is quite against a "famine" being sent for the testing of faith: see Genesis 26:1; Ruth 1:1; II Samuel 22:1, etc. — in each case the famine was a Divine judgment. Christ is the Bread of Life, and to wander from Him necessarily brings famine to the soul. It was when the restless son went into the "far country" that he "began to be in want" (Luke 15). This famine, then, was a message of providence that God was displeased with Abram. So *we* should regard unfavorable providences: they are a call from God to examine ourselves and try our ways.

"And Abram went down into Egypt to sojourn there" (v. 10), and thus it is with many of his children. Instead of being "exercised" by God's chastenings (Heb. 12:11), as they should be, they treat them as a matter of course, as part of the inevitable troubles which man is born unto; and thus "despise" them (Heb. 12:5) and derive no good from them. Alas, the average Christian instead of being *"exercised"* (in conscience and mind) under God's rod, rather does he ask, How may I most easily and quickly get from under it? If illness comes upon me, instead of turning to the Lord and asking "Show me *wherefore* thou contendest with me" (Job 10:4), they send for the doctor, which is seeking relief from Egypt. Abram had left Bethel and one who is out of communion with God cannot trust Him with his temporal affairs, but turns instead to an arm of flesh. Observe well the "Woe" which God has denounced upon those who go down into Egypt — turn to the world — for help (Isa. 30:1, 2).

We cannot now dwell upon what is recorded in Genesis 12:11-13, though it is unspeakably tragic. As soon as Abram drew near to Egypt, he began to be afraid. The dark shadows of that land fell across his soul before he actually entered it. He was sadly occupied with self. Said he to his wife, "They will kill *me* . . . say, I pray thee, that thou art my sister, that it may be well *with me*." How true it is that "the backslider in heart shall be filled with his *own* ways" (Prov. 14:14)! Fearful of his own safety, Abram asked his wife to repudiate her marriage to him. Abram was afraid to avow his *true relationship*. This is always what follows when a saint goes down into Egypt: he at once begins to equivocate. When he fellowships with the world he dare not fly his true colors, but compromises. So far from Abram being made a blessing to the Egyptians, he became a "great plague" to them (v. 17); and in the end they "sent him away." What a humiliation!

"And Abram went up out of Egypt: he, and his wife, and all that he had, and Lot with him, into the south." Did he remain in that dangerous district? No, for "he went on in his journeys *from* the south." Observe that he received no directions so to act. They were not necessary: his conscience told him what to do! "He went on in his journeys from the south, even to Bethel, unto the place where his tent had been at the *beginning* . . . unto the place of the altar, which he had made there at the *first;* and there Abram called on the name of the Lord" (13:1-4). He again turned his back upon the world: he retraced his steps; he returned to his pilgrim character and his altar. And note well, dear reader, it was "*there* Abram called on the name of the Lord." It had been a waste of time, a horrible mockery for him to have done so while he was "down in Egypt." The Holy One will not hearken to us while we are sullying His name by our carnal walk. It is "holy hands" (I Tim. 2:8), or at least penitent ones, which must be "lifted up" if we are to receive spiritual things from Him.

The case of Abram then sets before us in clear and simple language the way of recovery for a backslider. Those words "unto the place where his tent had been at the beginning" inculcate the same requirement as "teach you *again* which be the *first* principles of the oracles of God" (Heb. 5:12), and "Remember therefore from whence thou art fallen, and repent, and do the *first* works" (Rev. 2:5). Our sinful failure must be judged by us: we must condemn ourselves unsparingly for the same: we must contritely confess it to God: we must "forsake" it, resolving to have nothing further to do with those persons or things which occasioned our lapse. Yet something more than that is included in the "do the first works": there must be renewed actings of faith on Christ — typified by Abram's return to "the altar." We must come to the Saviour as we first came to Him — as sinners, as believing sinners, trusting in the merits of His sacrifice and the cleansing efficacy of His blood. We must doubt not His willingness to receive and pardon us.

It is one of the devices of Satan that, after he has succeeded in drawing a soul away from God and entangled him in the net of his corruptions, to persuade him that the prayer of faith, in *his* circumstances, would be highly presumptuous, and that it is much more modest for him to stand aloof from God and His people. Now if by "faith" were meant — as some would seem to understand — a persuading of ourselves that having trusted in the finished work of Christ all is well with us forever, that would indeed be presumptuous. But sorrow for sin and betaking ourselves unto that Fountain which has been opened for sin and for uncleanness (Zech. 13:1) is never out of season: coming to Christ in our wretchedness and acting faith upon Him to heal our loathsome diseases, both becomes us and honors Him. The greater our sin has been, the greater reason is there that we should confess it to God and seek forgiveness in the name of the Mediator. If our case be such that we feel we cannot do so as saints, we certainly ought to do so as sinners, as David did in Psalm 51 — a Psalm which has been recorded to furnish believers with instruction when *they* get into such a plight.

This is the only way in which it is possible to find rest unto our souls. As there is none other Name given under heaven among men by which we can be saved, so neither is there any other by which a backsliding saint can be restored. Whatever be the nature or the extent of our departure from God, there is no other way of return to Him but by the Mediator. Whatever be the wounds sin has inflicted upon our souls, there is no other remedy for them but the precious blood of the Lamb. If we have no heart to repent and return to God by Jesus Christ, then we are yet in our sins, and may expect to reap the fruits of them. Scripture has no counsel short of that. We have many encouragements to do so. God is of exceeding great and tender mercy, and willing to forgive all who return to Him in the name of His Son: though our sins be as scarlet, the atoning blood of Christ is able to cleanse them. There is "plenteous redemption" with Him. As Abram, David, Jonah, and Peter were restored, so may I, so may you be restored.

12

Its Evidences

I

WHAT are the principal marks of spiritual growth? what are the outstanding characteristics of the Christian's progress? To some of our readers that may appear a simple question, admitting of a ready answer. From one standpoint that is so, yet if we are to view it in its proper perspective, careful consideration is called for ere we make reply. If we bear in mind the real nature of spiritual growth and remember it is like that of a tree, downward as well as upward, inward as well as outward, we shall be preserved from mere generalizations. If, too, we take into account the three grades under which Christians are grouped, we shall be careful to distinguish between those things which, respectively, evidence growth in the "babes," in the "young men," and in the "fathers" in Christ. That which is suited to and marks the growth of a babe in Christ applies not to one who has reached a more advanced form in His school, and that which characterizes the full-grown Christian is not to be looked for in the immature one. It follows then that certain distinctions must be drawn if a definite and detailed answer is to be furnished to our opening inquiry.

But since we have already written at some length on the three grades of Christian development and have sought to describe those features which pertain more distinctively to those in the stage of the "blade," the "ear" and "the full corn in the ear," there is no need for us now to go over the same ground. If it be borne in mind that growth is a *relative* thing, we shall see that the same unit of measurement is not applicable to all cases — as the yardstick is the best means for gauging the growth of children, but the weighing-scales for registering that of adults. Then too, if we take into consideration, as we should, differences of privilege and opportunity, of teaching and training, of station and circumstances, uniform progress should not be expected. Some believers have much more to contend against than others. It is not that we would limit the grace of God, but that we should recognize and take into account the distinctions which Scripture itself draws. The relative growth of one who is severely handicapped may be much greater in reality than that of another who in more favorable circumstances makes greater progress.

The man who plants a fruit tree in a fertile valley is warranted to expect a better yield from it than one which is set in the soil of an exposed hillside. When a young Christian is favored with pious parents, or brothers and sisters who encourage him both by counsel and example, how much more may be looked for from him that another who dwells in the home of the ungodly. An unmarried woman who does not have to earn her living has much more opportunity for reading, meditation, prayer and the nurture of her spiritual life, than one who has the care of a young family. One who is privileged to sit regularly under an edifying ministry has better opportunity for Christian progress than another who is denied such a privilege. Again, the man with two talents cannot produce as much as another with five, yet if the former gain another two by them he does just as well proportionately as the one who makes his five into ten. The Lord Himself takes note of such differences: "For unto whomsoever much is given, of him shall be much required" (Luke 12:48).

Let us also point out that we are not now going to write on the marks or signs of spiritual life as such, but rather of the evidences of the *growth* of spiritual life — a much harder task. When we endeavor to examine ourselves for them, it is of great importance that we should know *what* to look for. If the Christian expects to find an improvement in the "old man," he will most certainly be disappointed: if he looks for a waning of natural pride, a lessening of the workings of unbelief, a cessation of the risings within him of rebellion against God, he will look in vain. Yet how many Christians *are* bitterly disappointed over this very thing and greatly cast down by the same. But they ought not to be, for God has nowhere promised to sublimate or spiritualize the "flesh" nor to eradicate our corruptions in this life, yet it is the Christian's duty and privilege to so walk in the spirit that he will not "fulfill the lusts of the flesh" (Gal. 5:16). Though we should be deeply humbled over our corruptions and mourn for them, yet our painful awareness of the same should not cause us to conclude we have made no spiritual growth.

An increasing realization of our native depravity, a growing discovery of how much there is within us that is opposed to God, with a corresponding despising of ourselves for the same, is one of the surest evidences that we are growing in grace. The more the light of God shines into our hearts, the more are we made aware of the filth and wickedness which indwell them. The better we became acquainted with God and learn of His ineffable purity, the more conscious do we become of our base impurity and bewail the same. That is a growing downwards or becoming less in our own esteem. And it is *that* which makes way for an increasing valuation of the atoning and cleansing blood of Christ, and a more frequent betaking of ourselves to that Fountain which has been opened for sin and for uncleanness. Thus, if Christ is becoming more precious to you, if you perceive with increasing clearness His suitability for such a vile wretch as you know yourself to be, and if that perception leads you to cast yourself more and more upon Him — as a drowning man does to a log — then that is clear proof you are growing in grace.

Growth is silent and at the time imperceptible to our senses, though later it is evident. Growth is gradual and full development is not reached in a day, nor in a year. Time must be allowed before proof can be obtained. We should not attempt to gauge our growth by our feelings, but rather by looking into the glass of God's Word and measuring ourselves by the standard which is there set before us. There may be real progress even where there is less inward comforts. Am I denying myself more now than I did formerly? Am I less enthralled by the attractions of this world than I used to be? Are the details of my daily life being more strictly regulated by the precepts of Holy Writ? Am I more resigned to the blessed will of God, assured that He knows what is best for me? Is my confidence in God growing, so that I am more and more leaving myself and my affairs in His hands? Those are some of the tests we should apply to ourselves if we would ascertain whether or no we be growing in grace.

1. Consider *the work of mortification* and seek to ascertain what proficiency you are making therein. There can be no progress in the Christian life while that work be unattended to. God does not remove indwelling sin from His people, but He does require them to make no provision unto its lusts, to resist its strivings, to deny its solicitations. His call is "mortify therefore your members which are upon the earth" (Col. 3:5), "put off concerning the former conversation the old man, which is corrupt according to the deceitful lusts" (Eph. 4:22), "abstain from fleshly lusts which war against the soul" (I Peter 2:11), "keep yourselves from idols" (I John 5:21). That is the lifelong task God has assigned us, for as long as we remain in this body the flesh will oppose from within and the world from without. If we become slack in the performance of this duty, sin and Satan will gain more and more of an advantage over us. But if we be faithful and diligent therein our efforts, by the Spirit's enablement, will not be altogether in vain.

But most of our readers, perhaps all of them, will exclaim, But this is the very matter in which I meet with most discouragement, and if I am honest it appears to me that my efforts are utterly in vain. Despite my utmost endeavors, my lusts still master me and I am repeatedly brought into captivity by sin. Though such be the case that does not mean your efforts were useless. God has nowhere promised that if you do so and so indwelling sin shall become inoperative or that your lusts shall become weaker and weaker. There is widespread misunderstanding on this subject. The word "mortify" signifies put to death, but it must be carefully borne in mind that it is used *figuratively* and not literally, for it is a physical term applied to that which is immaterial. Through no possible process can the Christian, not with the Spirit's help, render his lusts *lifeless*. They may at times appear so to his consciousness, yet it will not be long ere he is again aware that they are vigorous and active. The holiest of God's people, in all ages, have borne testimony to the power and prevalency in their corruptions, and that to their last hour.

It needs then to be carefully defined what is meant by the word "mortify." Since it does not signify "slay or extinguish indwelling sin" nor "render lifeless your lusts," what is intended? This: die unto them in your affections, your intentions, your resolutions, your efforts. We mortify sin by detesting it: "whosoever *hateth* his brother is a *murderer*" (I John 3:15) and just so far as we really hate our corruptions have we morally slain them. The Christian evidences his hatred of sin by mourning when it has gained an advantage over him. If it be his sincere intention and honest resolution to subdue every rising of his native depravity and the commission of every sin, then in the sight of Him who accepts the will for the deed, he *has* "mortified" them. Whenever the believer contritely confesses his sins to God and "forsakes" them so far as any purpose to repeat them is concerned, he *has* "mortified" them. If he truly loathes, grieves over, and acknowledges his failures to God, then he can say, "that which I do, I *allow not*" (Rom. 7:15).

"The Lord seeth not as men seeth: for man looketh on the outward appearance, but the Lord looketh on the heart" (I Sam. 16:7) needs to be borne in mind on this subject. "If a man find a betrothed damsel in the field, and the man force her and lie with her, then the man only that lay with her shall die" (Deut. 22:25). In the verses which follow we read "there is in the damsel no sin worthy of death." Not only did she not consent hereto, but we are told "she cried, and there was none to save her." Now that has a spiritual application to us. If a believer is suddenly surprised by a temptation which is to something forbidden by God and his heart agrees not thereto, but offers a resistance, which is however unavailing, though he is not guiltless therein, yet his case is very different from that of the unregenerate who found the temptation agreeable and responded heartily thereto. Note how the Spirit has recorded of Joseph of Arimathea that though he was a member of the Sanhedrin which condemned Christ to death, yet he "had *not consented* to the counsel and deed of them" (Luke 23:51)!

"What is sanctification? Sanctification is a work of God's grace, whereby they whom God hath before the foundation of the world chosen to be holy, are in time, through the powerful operation of His Spirit applying the death and resurrection of Christ unto them, renewed in their whole man after the image of God; having the seeds of repentance unto life and all other saving graces put into their hearts, and those graces so stirred up, increased and strengthened, as that they *more and more die unto sin* and rise unto newness of life" (*Westminster Catechism*). The words we have emphasized have occasioned much grief and anxiety to many, for measuring themselves by them they concluded they had never been sanctified. But it should be noted it is not there said that "*sin* is more and more dying in them," but that *they* "more and more die *unto* sin," which is a very different thing. Christians do, as pointed out above, die more and more to sin in their affections, intentions, and efforts. Yet we fail to find any warrant in Scripture for saying "the several lusts thereof are more and more weakened."

Having sought to show what the word "mortify" does not denote in its application to the Christian's conflict with sin and what it does signify let us in a few words point out wherein the believer may be said to be making progress in this essential work. He is progressing therein when he girds himself more diligently and resolutely to this task, refusing to allow seeming failure therein to cause him to give up in despair. He is making progress therein as he learns to make conscience of things which the world condemns not, being regulated by God's Word rather than public opinion or leaning to his own understanding. He is making progress therein when he obtains a clear insight of spiritual corruptions, so that he is exercised not only over worldly lusts and gross evils, but over coldness of heart, unbelief, pride, impatience, self-confidence, and thus he would cleanse himself from all filthiness of "spirit" as well as "of the flesh" (II Cor. 7:1). In short, he is growing in grace if he be maintaining a stricter and more regular watch over his heart.

2. Consider the work of *living unto God* and seek to ascertain what proficiency you are making therein. The measure and constancy of our yieldedness and devotedness to God is another criterion by which we may ascertain whether or no we are really growing in grace, for to lapse into a course of self-pleasing is a sure symptom of backsliding. Am I increasingly giving up myself to God, employing my faculties and powers in seeking to please and glorify Him? Am I endeavoring, with intensified earnestness and diligence, to act in accordance with the surrender I made of myself to Him at my conversion, and to the dedication of myself to His service at my baptism? Am I finding deeper delight therein, or is His service becoming irksome? If the latter, then that is clear proof that I have deteriorated, for there has been no change in Him nor in His claims upon me. If love be healthy then my greatest joy will be in making Him my chief Object and supreme End, but if I seek to do so only from a sense of obligation and duty, then my love has cooled.

"Be filled with the Spirit" (Eph. 5:18). Probably that means, in part at least, Let no compartment of your complex being be reserved or retained for *self*, but desire and pray that God may possess you wholly. Is that the deepest longing and endeavor of your heart? Are you finding increasing pleasure in the will and ways of the Lord? then you are following on to know Him. Are you making a more determined and continuous effort to "Walk worthy of the Lord, unto all pleasing, being fruitful in every good work, and increasing in the knowledge of God" (Col. 1:10)? then that evidences you are growing in grace. Are you less influenced than formerly by how others think and act, requiring nothing less than a "Thus saith the Lord" for your monitor? then you are becoming more rooted and grounded in the faith. Are you more watchful against those things which would break, or at least chill, your communion with God? then you are going forward in the Christian life.

To be increasingly devoted to God requires that I be increasingly occupied and absorbed with Him. To that end I need daily to study the revelation which He has made of Himself in the Scriptures, and particularly in Christ. I need also to meditate frequently upon His wondrous perfections: His amazing grace, unfathomable love, His ineffable holiness, His unchanging faithfulness, His mighty power, His infinite longsufferance. If I contemplate Him thus with the eyes of faith and love, then shall I be able to say "One thing have I desired of the Lord, that will I seek after: that I may dwell in the house of the Lord [the place of nearness and fellowship with him] all the days of my life, to behold the *beauty* of the Lord" (Ps. 27:4). The one who can do that must perforce exclaim, "Whom have I in heaven but thee, and there is none upon earth that I desire besides thee" (Ps. 73:25). That, my reader, is not a mere rhetorical utterance, but the language of one whose heart has been won by the Lord.

3. Consider *the Word of God* and seek to measure yourself by the degree in which you really *honor it*. What place do the contents of the Sacred Volume have in your affections, thoughts, and life: a higher one than formerly, or not? Is that Divine communication more valued by you today than when you were first converted? Are you more fully assured of its Divine inspiration, so that Satan himself could not make you doubt its Authorship? Are you more solemnly impressed by its authority so that at times you tremble before it? Does the Truth come with greater weight, so that your heart and conscience is more deeply impressed by it? Are more of its very words treasured up in your memory and frequently meditated upon? Are you really feeding on it: appropriating it to yourself, mixing faith therewith, and being nourished by it? Are you learning to make it your Shield on which you catch and quench the fiery darts of the wicked? Are you, like the Bereans (Acts 17:11), bringing to this infallible Scale and weighing therein all you read and hear?

Carefully bear in mind the purpose for which the Scriptures were given to us, the particular benefits they are designed to bestow. They are "profitable for doctrine," and *their* doctrine is far more than a theological treatise addressed to the intellect, or a philosophical system which furnishes an explanation of man's origin, constitution, and relation to God. It is "the doctrine which is according to *godliness*" (I Tim. 6:3), every part of which is designed to exalt God and abase man, according to Him His rightful place over us and our dependence upon and subjection to Him. It is profitable for "reproof," to acquaint us with our innumerable faults and failures and to admonish us for the same. It is "a *critic* of the thoughts and intents of the heart" (Heb. 4:12), probing into our innermost beings and condemning all within us which is impure. It is profitable for "correction," to teach us what is right and pleasing unto God; and such is its potency that the more we are regulated by it the more are our souls renovated and purified. It is profitable for "instruction in righteousness," for producing integrity of character and conduct. It is for the enlightening of our minds, the instructing of our consciences, the regulating of our wills.

Now my reader, test yourself by those considerations, fairly and impartially. Are you finding the Scriptures increasingly profitable for the doctrine which is according to godliness: if so they are producing in you a deeper and more extensive piety. Are you more and more opening your heart to their "reproof," not confining yourself to those portions which comfort, and avoiding those parts which admonish and condemn you? If so then you are cultivating closer dealings with God. Are you increasingly desirous of being "corrected" by their searching and holy teachings? If so then you diligently endeavor to promptly put right whatever they show is wrong in you. Are they really instructing you in righteousness, so that your deportment is becoming in fuller conformity to their standard? If so you are more shunned by worldlings and less esteemed by empty professors. Do you frequently examine yourself by God's Word and test your experience by its teaching? If so, you are becoming more skilled in the Word of Righteousness (Heb. 5:13) and more pleasing to its Author.

II

4. Consider your *occupation with Christ* and remember that growth in grace is commensurate with your growing in the knowledge of Him (II Peter 3:18). That knowledge is indeed a spiritual one, yet it is received via the understanding, for what is not apprehended by the mind cannot profit the heart. Nothing but an increasing familiarity and closer fellowship with Christ can nourish the soul and promote spiritual prosperity. There can be no real progress without a better acquaintance with His person, office, and work. Christianity is more than a creed, more than a system of ethics, more than a devotional program. It is a *life*: a life of faith on Christ, of communion with Him and conformity to Him (Phil. 1:21). Take Christ out of Christianity and there is nothing left. There must be constant renewed acts of faith on Christ, yet our faith is always in proportion to the spiritual knowledge we have of its object. "That I may know him" precedes "and the power of his resurrection." Christ revealed to the heart is the Object of our knowledge (II Cor. 4:6), and our spiritual knowledge of Him consists in the concepts and apprehensions of Him which are formed in our minds. That knowledge is fed, strengthened, and renewed by our spiritual and believing meditations on Christ and those being made effectual in the soul by the power of the Spirit.

The Object of our faith is a known Christ, and the better we know Him the more we shall act faith on Him. The Christian life consists essentially, in living on Christ: "the life which I now live in the flesh I live by the faith of the Son of God." The particular acts of this life of faith are beholding Christ (as He is presented in the Word), cleaving to Him, making use of Him, drawing from Him, holding free communion with Him, delighting ourselves in Him. Alas, the great majority of Christians seek to live on *themselves* and feed on their experience. Some are forever occupied with their corruptions and failures, while others are wholly taken up with their graces and attainments. But there is nothing of *Christ* in either the one or the other, and nothing of faith; rather does self absorb them and a life of sense predominates. All genuine "experience" is a knowing ourselves to be what God has described us in His Word and having such an inward realization thereof as proves to us our dire need of Christ. It consists too of such a knowledge of Him as that He is exactly suited to our case and Divinely qualified and perfectly fitted for our every lack. No matter how "deep" may be your "experience," it is worth nothing unless it turns you to the great Physician.

How often have we read in the diaries and biographies of saints, or heard them say, O what blessed enlargement of soul I was favored with, what liberty in prayer, how my heart was melted before the Lord, what joy unspeakable possessed me. But if those "mountain-top experiences" be analyzed what do they consist of? what is there of *Christ* in them? It is not spiritual views of Him which engages their attention, but the warmth of *their* affections, a being carried away with their comforts. No wonder such ecstasies are so brief and are followed by deep depression of spirits. Measure your spiritual growth rather by the extent you are learning to look away from both sinful self and religious self. Christian progress is to be gauged not by feelings but by the extent to which you live outside of yourself and live upon Christ — making fuller use of Him, prizing Him more highly, finding all your springs in Him, making Him your "all" (Col. 3:11). It is a consciousness of sin and not of our graces, the burden of our corruptions and not delighting ourselves in our enlargements, which will move us to look away from self and behold the Lamb.

5. Consider the *path of obedience* and what progress you are making therein. That which distinguishes the regenerate in a practical way from the unregenerate is that the former are "obedient children" (I Peter 2:14), whereas the latter are entirely dominated by the carnal mind, which is "enmity against God, and is not subject to the Law of God, neither indeed can be" (Rom. 8:7). The very first criterion given in the epistle which is written in order that believers may know they have eternal life is, "Hereby we know [are Divinely assured] that we know him [savingly], if we keep his commandments" (I John 2:3). Conversion is a forsaking of the path of self-will and self-pleasing (Isa. 53:6) and a complete surrender of myself to the Lordship of Christ, and the genuineness thereof is evidenced by my taking His yoke upon me and submitting to His authority. If we truly submit to His authority then we shall seek to comply with all He enjoins and not pick and choose between His precepts. Nothing less than wholehearted and impartial obedience is required from us (John 15:14). If we do not sincerely endeavor to obey in *all* things, then we do not in *any*, but merely select what is agreeable to ourselves. Then is there any such thing as *progress in* obedience? Yes.

We are improving in obedience when it becomes *more extensive.* Though the young convert has fully surrendered himself to the Lord, yet he devotes himself to some duties with more earnestness and diligence than he does to others, but as he becomes better acquainted with God's will, more of his ways are regulated thereby. As spiritual light increases he discovers that God's commandment is "exceeding broad" (119:

96), forbidding not only the overt act but all that leads to it, and inculcating (by necessary implication) the opposite grace and virtue. Growth in grace appears when my obedience is *more spiritual*. One learning to write becomes more painstaking, so that he forms his letters with greater accuracy: so as one progresses in the school of Christ he pays more attention to that word "Thou hast commanded us to keep thy precepts *diligently*" (119:4). So, too, superior aims and motives prompt him: his springs are less servile and more evangelical, his obedience proceeding from love and gratitude. That, in turn, produces another evidence of growth: obedience becomes easier and pleasanter, so that he "delights in the law of the Lord." Duty is now a joy: "O how love I thy law."

6. Consider the *privilege of prayer* and how far you are improving in that exercise. Probably not a few will exclaim, Alas, in this respect I have deteriorated, for I am neither as diligent in it nor as fervent as I used to be. But it is easy to form a wrong judgment upon the matter, measuring it by quantity instead of quality. Devout Jews and Papists spend much time on their knees, but that is simply the religion of the flesh. There is often more of the natural than the spiritual in the devotional exercises of the young convert, especially if he be of a warm and ardent temperament. It is easy for enthusiasm to carry him away when new objects and interests engage him, and for emotionalism to be mistaken for fervor of spirit. Personally we very much doubt if the Lord's people experience any true progress in their prayer life until they make the humbling discovery they know not how to *pray*, though they may have attained to considerable proficiency in framing eloquent and moving petitions as men judge. "We [Christians] *know not* what we should pray for as we ought" (Rom. 8:26): did we realize that in our spiritual childhood? The first mark of growth here is when we are moved to cry, "Lord, teach us to pray" (Luke 11:1).

As the Christian grows in grace prayer becomes more of an attitude than an act, an act of dependence upon and confidence in God. It becomes an instinct to turn to Him for help, guidance, wisdom, strength. It consists of an increasing looking to and leaning upon Him, acknowledging Him in all our ways. Thus prayer becomes more mental than vocal, more ejaculatory than studied, more frequent than prolonged. As the Christian progresses his prayers will be more spiritual: he will be more intent upon the pursuit of holiness than of knowledge, he will be more concerned about pleasing God than ascertaining whether his name be written in the Book of Life, more earnest in seeking those things which will promote the Divine glory than minister to his comfort. As he learns to know God better his confidence in Him will be deepened, so that if on the one hand he knows nothing is too hard for Him, on the other he is assured that His wisdom will withhold as well as bestow. Again, growth appears when we are as diligent in praying for the whole household of faith as for ourself or immediate family. Our heart has been enlarged when we make "supplication for all saints" (Eph. 6:18).

7. Consider the *Christian warfare* and what success you are having therein. Here again we shall certainly err and draw a wrong conclusion unless we pay close attention to the language of Holy Writ. That which we are called to engage in is "the good fight of *faith*" (I Tim. 6:12), but if we seek to gauge our progress therein by the testimony of our *senses* a false verdict will inevitably be given. The faith of God's elect has the Scriptures for its sole ground and Christ as its immediate Object. Nowhere in Scripture has Christ promised His redeemed such a victory over their corruptions in this life that they shall be slain, nor even that they will be so subdued their lusts will cease vigorously opposing, no not for a season, for there is no discharge nor furlough in this warfare. Nay, He may permit your enemies to gain such a temporary advantage that you cry "iniquities prevail against me" (Ps. 65:3), nevertheless you are to *continue resisting*, assured by the Word of promise you shall yet be an overcomer. Satan's grand aim is to drive you to *despair* because of the prevalency of your corruptions, but Christ has prayed for thee that thy faith fail not, and proof His prayer is being answered is that you weep over your failures and do not become a total apostate.

The trouble is that we want to mix something with faith — our feelings, our "experiences," or the fruits of faith. Faith is to look to Christ and triumph in Him alone. It is to be engaged with Him and His word at all times no matter what we encounter. If we endeavor to ascertain the outcome of this fight by the evidence of our senses — what we see and feel within — instead of judging it by faith, then our present experience will be that of Peter's "when he saw the wind boisterous" while walking on the sea toward Christ, or we will conclude "I shall now perish" (I Sam. 27:1). Did not Paul find that when he would do good evil was present within him, yea, that while he delighted in the law of God after the inward man, he *saw* another law in his members warring against the law of his mind and bringing him into captivity, so that he cried "O wretched man that I am." *That* was his "experience," and the evidence of sense. Ah, but he did not, as so many do, stop there. "Who shall deliver me?" "I thank God through Jesus Christ" (Rom. 7) he answered. *That* was the language of *faith*! Is it yours? Your success in this fight is to be determined by whether — despite all failures — you are continuing therein and whether you confidently look forward to the final issue — that you *will* triumph through Christ.

If we received a letter from a native of Greenland's icy mountains asking us to give him as accurate and vivid a word picture as possible of an English apple-tree and its fruit, we would not single out for our description one that had been artificially raised in a hothouse, nor would we select one which grew in poor and rocky ground on some desolate hillside; rather would we take one that was to be found in average soil in a typical orchard. It is quite true the others would be apple trees and might bear fruit, yet if we confined our word picture unto the portraying of either of them, the Greenlander would not obtain a fair concept of the ordinary apple tree. It is equally unfair and misleading to take the peculiar experiences of any particular Christian and hold them up as the standard by which all others should measure themselves. There are many kinds of apples, differing in size, color and flavor. And though Christians have certain fundamental things in common, yet no two of them are alike in all respects. Variety marks all the works of God. Above we have referred to seven different phases of the Christian life by which we may test our progress. In what follows we mention some of the characteristics which pertain more or less — for in germ form they are found in all — to a state of Christian *maturity*.

Prudence. There is a well-known adage — though often ignored by adults — that "we cannot put old heads on young shoulders." That is true spiritually as well as naturally: we live and learn, though some learn more readily than others — usually it is because they receive *their* instruction from the Scriptures while others are informed only by painful experience. The Word says "Put not your trust in princes, nor in the son of man, in whom there is no help" (146:3), and if we heed that injunction we are spared many a bitter disappointment; whereas if we take people at their word and count on their help, we shall frequently find that we leaned upon a broken reed. In many other ways the young convert's zeal becomes tempered by knowledge and he conducts himself more prudently. As he becomes more experienced he learns to act with greater caution and circumspection, and to "walk in wisdom toward them that are without" (Col. 4:5), as he also discovers the chilling effects which frothy professors have upon him, so that he is more particular in selecting his associates. He learns too his own peculiar weaknesses and in which direction he needs most to watch and pray against temptations.

Sobriety. This can be attained only in the school of Christ. It is true that in certain dispositions there is much less to oppose this virtue, yet its full development can only be under the operations of Divine grace, as Titus 2:11, 12 plainly shows. We would define Christian sobriety as the regulation of our appetites and affections in their pursuit and use of all things — we can be righteous "over much" (Eccles. 7: 16). It is the governing of our inward and outward man by the rules of moderation and temperance. It is the keeping of our desires within bounds so that we are preserved from excesses in practice. It is a frame or temper of the mind which is the opposite of excitedness. It is a being "temperate in *all* things" (I Cor. 9:25), and that includes our opinions as well as conduct. It is a holy seriousness, calmness, gravity, balance, which prevents one becoming an extremist. It is that self-control which keeps us from being unduly cast down by sorrows or elated by joys. It causes us to hold the things of this life with a light hand, so that neither the pleasures nor the cares of the world unduly affect the heart.

Stability. There is a spiritual childishness as well as a natural one, wherein the young convert acts more from impulse than principle, is carried away by his fancies, and easily influenced by those around him. To be "tossed to and fro and carried about with every wind of doctrine" (Eph. 4:14) is one of the characteristics of spiritual immaturity, and when we waver in faith and are of a doubtful mind then we halt and falter in our duties. Even that love which is shed abroad in the hearts of the renewed needs to be controlled and guided, as appears from that petition of the apostle's "I pray that your love may abound yet more and more in knowledge and in all judgment" (Phil. 1:9). As the Christian grows in grace he becomes "rooted and built up in Christ and established in the faith" (Col. 2:7). As he grows in the knowledge of the Lord it can be said of him "He shall not be afraid of evil tidings: his heart is fixed, trusting in the Lord" (Ps. 112:7). He may be shaken, but will not be shattered by bad news, for having learned to rely upon God, he knows no change of circumstances can do more than lightly affect him. No matter what may befall him, he will remain calm, confident in his Refuge: since his heart be anchored in God his comforts do not ebb and flow with the creature.

Patience. Here we must distinguish between that natural placidity which marks some temperaments and that spiritual grace which is wrought in the Christian by God. We must also remember that spiritual patience has both a passive and an active side to it. Passively, it is a quiet and contented resignation under suffering (Luke 21:19), being the opposite of acting "as a wild bull in a net" (Isa. 51:20). Its language is "The cup which my Father hath given me, shall I not drink it?" (John 18:11). Actively, it is a persevering in duty (Heb. 12:1), being the opposite of "turning back in the day of battle" (Ps. 78:9). Its language is "be not weary in well doing" (II Thess. 2:13). Patience enables the believer to meekly bear whatever the Lord is pleased to lay upon him. It causes the believer to quietly await God's hour of relief or deliverance. It prompts the believer to continue performing his duty in spite of all opposition and discouragement. Now since it is tribulation (Rom. 5:3) and the trying of our faith (James 1:3) which "worketh patience," much of it is not to be looked for in the spiritually inexperienced and immature. We are improving in patience when more spiritual considerations prompt us thereto.

Humility. Evangelical humility is a realization of my ignorance, incompetency and vileness, with an answerable frame of heart. As the young believer applies himself diligently to the reading of God's Word and acquires more familiarity with its contents, as he becomes better instructed in the faith, he is very apt to be puffed up with his knowledge. But as he studies the Word more deeply, he perceives how much there is therein which transcends his understanding, and as he learns to distinguish between an intellectual information of spiritual things and an experimental and transforming knowledge of them, he cries "that which I see not, teach thou me" and "teach me thy statues." As he grows in grace he makes an increasing discovery of his ignorance and realizes "he knows nothing yet as he ought to know" (I Cor. 8:2). As the Spirit enlarges his desires, he thirsts more and more for holiness, and the more he is conformed to the image of Christ the more will he groan because of his sensible unlikeness to Him. The young Christian attempts to perform many duties in his own strength, but later on discovers that apart from Christ he can do nothing. The father in Christ is self-emptied and self-abased and marvels increasingly at the longsufferance of God toward him.

Forbearance. A spirit of bigotry, partisanship and intolerance is a mark of narrowmindedness and of spiritual immaturity. On first entering the school of Christ most of us expected to find little difference between members of the same family, but more extensive acquaintance with them taught us better, for we found their minds varied as much as their countenances, their temperaments more than their local accents of speech, and that amid general agreement there were wide divergencies of opinions and sentiments in many things. While all God's people are taught of Him, yet they know but "in part" and the "part" one knows may not be the part which another knows. All the saints are indwelt by the Holy Spirit, yet He does not operate uniformly in them nor bestow identical gifts (I Cor. 12:8-11). Thus opportunity is afforded us to "forbear one another in love" (Eph. 4:2) and not make a man an offender for a word or despise those who differ from me. Growth in grace is evidenced by a spirit of clemency and toleration, granting to others the same right of private judgment and liberty as I claim for myself. The mature Christian, generally, will subscribe to that axiom "In essentials unity, in non-essentials liberty, in all things charity."

Contentment. As a spiritual virtue this is to have our desires limited by a present enjoyment, or to find a sufficiency in and be satisfied with my immediate portion. It is the opposite of murmurings, distracted cares, covetous desires. To murmur is to quarrel with the dispensations of Providence: to have distracted cares is to distrust God for the future: to have covetous desires is to be dissatisfied with what God has assigned me. God knows what is best for our good, and the more that be realized the more thankful shall we be for the allotments of His love and wisdom — pleased with what pleases Him. Contentment is a mark of weanedness from the world and of delighting ourselves in the Lord. The apostle declared "I have learned in whatsoever state I am, therewith to be content" (Phil. 4:11), and as Matthew Henry said, that lesson was learned "not at the feet of Gamaliel, but of Christ." Nor was it something he acquired there all in a moment. By nature we are restless, impatient, envious of the condition of others: but submission to the Divine will and confidence in God's goodness produces peace of mind and rest of heart. It is the mature Christian who can say "Thou hast put gladness in my heart, more than in the time their corn and their wine increased" (Ps. 4:7).

INDEX

Of Scripture

195

Of Authors